FLUID CITY

D0225138

TRANSFORMING MELBOURNE'S URBAN WATERFRONT

KIM DOVEY is Professor of Architecture and Urban Design at the University of Melbourne. He has published, lectured and broadcast widely on issues of meaning, place and ideology in architecture and urban design. Previous work includes *Framing Places: Mediating Power in Built Form* (1999).

For Betty and Eric

FLUID CITY

Transforming
Melbourne's
Urban
Waterfront

Kim Dovey

with
Leonie Sandercock,
Quentin Stevens,
Ian Woodcock
and
Stephen Wood

A UNSW PRESS BOOK

© Kim Dovey 2005
First published 2005

This book is copyright. Apart from any fair dealing for the purpose
of private study, research, criticism or review, as permitted under the
Copyright Act, no part may be reproduced by any process without
written permission. Inquiries should be addressed to the publisher.

Simultaneously published in

Australia and New Zealand by
University of New South Wales Press Ltd
University of New South Wales
Sydney NSW 2052
AUSTRALIA
www.unswpress.com.au

National Library of Australia
Cataloguing-in-Publication entry:

 Fluid city: transforming Melbourne's
 urban waterfront.

 Bibliography.
 Includes index.
 ISBN 0 86840 669 4.

 1. Docks – Remodeling for other use –
 Victoria – Melbourne. 2. Waterfronts –
 Victoria – Melbourne – Planning. 3.
 Urban renewal – Victoria – Melbourne.

 711.4099451

Page design Dana Lundmark
Cover design Di Quick
Cover photo Cover photo by Ian
Woodcock: Stitched and reversed panorama
of the Melbourne waterfront.
Printer Everbest, China

The rest of the world by
Routledge
2 Park Square, Milton Park, Abingdon
Oxfordshire, OX14 4RN

Routledge
270 Madison Avenue, New York, NY
10016

*Routledge is an imprint of the
Taylor & Francis Group*

British Library
Cataloguing in Publication Data
A catalogue record for this book is avail-
able from the British Library

Library of Congress
Cataloging in Publication Data
A catalog record for this book
has been requested

ISBN 0-415-35923-6

CONTENTS

PREFACE AND ACKNOWLEDGMENTS

This book has its roots in over a decade of responding to waterfront projects in Melbourne, living the double life of an academic trying to make sense of practice and trying to make theory practical. In teaching architecture and urban design, I have long felt the peculiar fluidity of identity that is the lot of those who are stranded between disciplines. I enjoy this 'between' condition, which is where I think the cutting edge of ideas and new approaches to practice are found—they are not called 'disciplines' for nothing. This is a book that is intended to slip between disciplines and also between theory and practice.

Melbourne is an edgy city in several senses: a city on the edge of a self-centred global 'empire'; a city uncertain of itself and therefore productively 'on edge'. It is also a highly civil city with a generous and vital network of public space. A large part of this critique stems from the desire to see how such qualities can survive and thrive in the increasingly fluid economy of global markets. While a good deal of what follows is critical of the design and planning outcomes, it is not written to target individuals who were doing their best to take the opportunities or to shape an urban future. There is no ideal urban or architectural ideology from which this critique springs; the city that submits to the most comprehensively rational decision-making, or the finest ideas of a single designer, will end up comprehensively dull. If there is a central task for urban design it is to construct and sustain urban diversity; good urbanism has many forms, but they are all open to difference.

Originally, this book was to be co-authored with Leonie Sandercock, who was then teaching in the urban planning program at the University of Melbourne, and is now at the University of British Columbia. This architect-planner collaboration (then called 'The Seductive City') was to embody an interdisciplinary tension in the authorial voice, a tension ultimately stretched by both distance and difference. I remain indebted to Leonie for much of the conceptual thinking behind the book and for her intellectual insights and friendship. Ian Woodcock and Stephen Wood, the 'woodies', have been a formidable team of research assistants and interlocutors, many of their insights have slipped in unacknowledged and I am deeply grateful. The book has turned out to have a somewhat fluid authorship as Ian and Stephen (along with Quentin Stevens) have become co-authors. Thanks for various reasons are also due to Rob Adams, David Beynon, Iain Borden, David Brand, Catherin Bull, Teresa Crowley, Kess Dovey, Philip Goad, Nigel Flannigan, Ruth Fincher, Karen Franck, John Friedmann, Sandra Gifford, Trevor Hogan, Jim Holdsworth, Sandra Kaji-O'Grady, Ross King, Sue McGlynn, James McGregor, Paul Mees, Greg Missingham, Julia Nevarez, Kevin O'Connor, Darko Radović, Jane Rendell, Julia Robinson, Kate Shaw, Evan Walker, Paul Walker, Steven Whitford and David Yencken. There are many students, too numerous to list, who bring their experiences, desires and designs; it is a great privilege to be paid to learn from those whose imagination and hope for a better city has not been closed down. Finally, the deepest thanks of all to Sandy, Kess and Simon with whom I most share this great city.

The initial database for this project was produced with a grant (shared by Leonie Sandercock) from the Australian Research Council in 2000, followed by smaller research grants from the Faculty of Architecture, Building and Planning at the University of Melbourne. Fragments of the book have been adapted and rewritten from earlier critiques as follows: On Riverscapes: Dovey, K. 'Icon or Eyesore' *The Age*, October 17, 1998; Dovey, K. 'New Civic Square', *The Age*, August 26, 1997; Dovey, K. 'Selling the Corporate State – by Design', *The Age*, May 28, 1997; Dovey, K. 'An Icon of Excess and Sign of the Times', *The Age*, March 17, 1997; Dovey, K. 'The Design is Just a Beginning', *Landscape Australia*, 4, 1997, p.328; Dovey, K. 'Fast Cars, Slow Cities',

Arena Magazine, 28, April–May, 1997, pp.32–7; Dovey, K. 'The Square Dilemma', *The Age*, April 12, 1996; Dovey, K. 'Time's Up for the Towers', *Herald-Sun*, January 15, 1994; Dovey, K. 'Should Southbank Look Like This … or This?' *The Age*, November 12, 1993; Dovey, K. 'Simulation City', *Arena Magazine*, August, 1993, pp.21–3; Dovey, K. 'Southbank/Southgate/Surrogate', *Architect*, January, 1993, pp.6–7; Sandercock, L. & Dovey, K. 'Pleasure, Politics and the Public Interest: Melbourne's Waterfront Revitalization', *Journal of the American Planning Association*, 68 (2), 2002, pp.151–64. On Dockscapes: Dovey, K. 'Would the Grollo Tower be Good for Melbourne?' *Herald Sun*, June 26, 1998; Dovey, K. 'Why Bigger is not Necessarily Better', *The Age*, October 1, 1997, p.15; Dovey, K. 'Sale of the Century', in Long, C. (ed.), *Docklands Forum*, People's Committee for Melbourne, 1997; Dovey, K. 'Trouble on the Waterfront', *The Age*, September 18, 1996, p.17; Dovey, K. 'Tall Towers and Short-Sighted Cities', *Tirra Lirra*, Winter,1996, pp.2–3; Dovey, K. 'Melbourne 'Docklands and the Sense of Place', in: *Picking Winners: Melbourne's Urban Development Game*, Social Justice Coalition, Carlton, 1991, pp.33–45; Dovey, K. & Sandercock, L. 'Hype and Hope', *City*, 6 (1), 2002, 83–101.

All unattributed photographs and maps are by Kim Dovey. The author has made all efforts to contact copyright holders of materials used in this volume and would be grateful to hear from any he has been unable to contact.

INTRODUCTION

> ... it is pointless trying to decide whether Zenobia is to be classified among happy cities or among the unhappy. It makes no sense to divide cities into these two species but into another two: those that through the years and changes continue to give their form to desires, and those in which desires either erase the city or are erased by it.
>
> Italo Calvino[1]

The best of cities have always been a curious mix of economic engine and seductive surface; places of work and play; producing wealth and desire in abundance. In the late twentieth century, under an accelerating globalisation of markets and cultures, many cities have been fundamentally transformed. Adapting to changing economic realities and competing for a more significant role in the world economy, they have reinvented themselves to attract new flows of capital investment. During this period the formal imagery of cities has become more central to urban development; the 'spectacle' of the city with its seductive surfaces and urban iconography has been seen as a key to prosperity. This transformation of urban imagery has often focused on waterfront sites with wonderful opportunities to reclaim disused waterfront land and create new forms of public amenity.

This book traces the transformation of the urban waterfront of Melbourne. As the financial and industrial centre of Australia, in the late nineteenth century Melbourne developed a new world exuberance evident in its architecture, streetscapes, parks and public monuments. Labelled 'marvellous Melbourne', by the 1880s it was one of the great Victorian-era cities with a vibrant street life thronging the footpaths and arcades of the central city grid laid out less than 50 years earlier. Yet the twentieth century saw an increasingly staid city and by 1980 Melbourne was suffering from a declining industrial and economic base, a somewhat dour image and uncertainty about its future. The city in the 1980s was de-industrialising, caught in an identity crisis, unsure of its future and envious of Sydney's global image and growing prominence. A key strategy in addressing these issues was the revitalisation of the waterfront – the Yarra River, Melbourne Docklands and Port Phillip Bay. The river had long been severed from the city by railway lines and subject to sustained industrial use and public denigration. The docklands, once the busiest port in the southern hemisphere, had become a disused and unseen backwater within a kilometre of the central city. The bay frontage several kilometres away was seen as under-utilised and underdeveloped. This re-facing of the city to the water was a key urban strategy of the 1980s and 1990s, and a catalyst for economic transformation.

Fluid City is fundamentally about a city becoming 'unsettled'. We generally approach cities as 'settlements', as sites or places where forms and identities have become stabilised. While I have a good deal of respect for settled notions of place identity, the focus here is on understanding urban change as a confluence of flows of different forces, both global and local. Both the title and the chapter structure are inspired by Appadurai's ideas about the various global flows that he terms 'scapes': the 'ethnoscapes' (flows of tourists, refugees and immigrants), 'mediascapes' (flows of information and images), 'technoscapes' (flows of technology), 'finanscapes' (flows of capital) and 'ideoscapes' (flows of ideas, values and ideologies).[2] This is linked to Castells' notion that what are seen as stabilised and localised experiences of 'place' become dissolved in the 'space of flows' of global capital.[3] Bauman uses the phrase 'liquid modernity' to refer to the deregulated flows of consumer capitalism replacing the settled territories of industrial cities.[4] The work is also inspired in part by Deleuzian ideas of a world based in 'flows of desire'[5] – desires for profit, power and place; the desire for waterfront living; the desire to face the city to the water and to face this waterfront city to the world.

The idea of fluidity is here used in several senses. A city turning its face to the waterfront is also facing up to increased fluidity in terms of flows of global capital, design imagery and planning process. In the 1980s and 1990s many perceived certainties of urban development were melting. The inertia of the agricultural, mining and manufacturing industries was giving way to the flexibilities of the information industries and economies. The experiences of 'place' in the city became increasingly produced by the flows of global capital. The image of the city became increasingly important in strategies to capture these flows; conservative barriers to *avant garde* architecture melted and the waterfront became a frontier where new forces for change were thrown into sharp relief. This frontier mentality also produced flexibility in urban planning as traditional practices of urban regulation and rational action were dissolved. Everywhere boundaries were eroded – between architecture and planning, culture and commerce; design and politics; between public and private interests. Political practices became ever more insinuated into forms of architecture and urban design. Such a period of rapid transformation is exciting, offering possibilities for urban innovation – new visions of the city in the form of urban design, public art and architecture that reconstruct the cognitive map of the city. There are also enormous possibilities for urban infrastructure redevelopment, which service public transport, community life and public amenity. However, there is simultaneously the potential for significant damage to the city – the erosion of local diversity; commodification of place identity; the erosion of public space through privatisation, and its tranquilisation through new forms of exclusion and purification.

One of the key changes of this era is what we might call an 'ungrounding' of urban development processes. Urban transformation is traditionally grounded in both local site conditions and local communities of interest. Site conditions embody the material 'ground' of the city, together with its histories, territories and experiences of 'place'; the taken-for-granted status quo. One dimension of the fluid city is a realisation that the concept of 'place' is itself inherently fluid; while it is reified as a stable ground of everyday life, it is also formed from a confluence of flows – of water, geology, histories, events, memories, colonies, industries and designs. Urban development is necessarily a place-making activity in the sense that urban experience is transformed – new places are created and old ones disappear, for better or worse. The ungrounding comes from a realisation of the fluidities of place; places are not a stable ground that are simply subject to flows of ideas, people, information and money; the experience of place is produced by such flows.

The transformation of public space is also grounded in local communities of interest; social constructions of the 'public interest' are proclaimed, explicitly or implicitly, as the basis for urban planning and design decisions. Yet, any notion of the 'public interest' is also a confluence of flows – of opinions, desires, votes, tactics, strategies, visions and decisions. The illusion of a stable 'public' with a stable 'interest' is constructed rather than found, and the concept of the 'public interest' has been widely critiqued as a cover for the dominance of certain interests and the marginalisation of others.[6] There are those who would eschew or abandon such a concept but I am not among them. To abandon the concept of 'public interests' is to abandon the concept of 'public space' because the sharing of space between citizens necessarily implies a shared interest in its possible transformation.

Many of the forces of urban transformation on the Melbourne waterfront are forces for the erosion of public space as projects become 'design driven' by public/private partnerships under entrepreneurial modes of urban governance. Public interests become redefined for the new entrepreneurial city as 'place myths' are constructed through advertising. New desires are produced to construct political legitimacy. The tension between private and public interests becomes a key issue. Public interests do not exist in some pre-formed state, but are largely created (or limited) by the imagination of urban visions that shape such interests by simulating alternate futures and desires for them; by catching (or limiting) the public imagination. A key question here is the scope of opportunity that has been lost or gained by pursuing one course of development rather than another. A rich urban imagination and understanding are prerequisites to informed debate; democratic planning may be necessary but it will never be sufficient. Waterfront planning and design is a form of wealth creation with a key task to ensure that such wealth is both created and shared. And the vast majority of those who will share it have not yet been born; urban design and planning decisions have very long term consequences.

As will become apparent, the success of these new waterfronts is mixed. Yet by the turn of the millennium economic indicators showed a significant turnaround in Melbourne's metropolitan economy – jobs and investment were up, unemployment was down, out-migration was reversed. One cannot attribute these to urban design, but they did occur in parallel and there has been a significant shift in the self-image of the city, which is not unrelated. This is the story of a city becoming transformed by flows of desire and capital, which cannot be unhinged from the critique of public interests. Such a critique, however, cannot presume a static position outside these flows of desire because such flows are the ground from which 'interests' and 'publics' emerge. The book is thus written with a deliberate ambivalence towards the fluid conditions of urban development; there are values in both 'going with the flow' and in resisting its place-destructive tendencies.

Fluid City is written with the intent to bridge significant gaps between different discourses about the city and to challenge singular ways of viewing it. The book is written for a multiplicity of audiences: architects and planners, theory and practice, professional and lay, global and local. It will inevitably fall uneasily between stools, particularly between the disciplines of architecture and urban planning. Uneasily, because most such studies remain locked within the disciplinary paradigms of architecture (with a focus on design imagery) or urban planning (with a focus on the regulatory and decision-making context). Bridging this gap is rendered imperative by transformations of the city that are at once urban in scope yet design-driven. The fluidity of the city is both a condition and an ideology. This is a condition reflected in the flows of desire for urban waterfronts, in the flows of global capital, and in the flexibility of urban planning regulation. It is an ideology reflected in the state slogan '*on the move*' and in the architectural images of dynamism and fluidity.

Fluid City is not a book of urban design theory, yet it cannot be ignorant of theory any more than theory can be of practice. In many professional fields there are self-contained bodies of theory that drive practice without the need for clients to understand them. One learns to trust the calculations of the engineer, the prognosis of the doctor and the strategies of the lawyer. This is not possible in architecture, urban design and planning, which are fundamentally social and aesthetic practices, driven by more contentious values and interests. Indeed, as Deutsche and others have suggested, it is the contentious nature of urban design that makes urban space 'public'.[7] Without a theory base, public debate on urban design will be reduced to 'opinion' about whatever visions of the future city are released to the public. The task for urban design is to render ideas accessible to public debate. Some of the best urban design theory is quite arcane, insulated from public debate by a language that never leaves the universities. Writing is a practice not unlike urban design itself, it must communicate on a number of levels and with a multiplicity of audiences – in this case both academic and general. Theoretical excursions are largely limited to chapter 1 and then the co-authored chapters 4, 6 and 9 (each of which is linked to the co-author's doctoral work). The risk of diluting the theory to suit an audience who may not be interested is matched by the risk of losing readers in the quest for academic respectability; the aim here is to produce a text that flows between the two, and as the adage goes: 'there is nothing so practical as a good theory'.

The book is organised into three parts: Riverscapes, Dockscapes and Bayscapes. The first chapter outlines the context in global and theoretical terms. It begins with some of the forces that frame waterfront regeneration in the global context: competition between cities, the revaluing of local places for global consumption and the focus on urban iconography to signify city identity. The final part of chapter 1 briefly outlines a series of theoretical contexts to be deployed in the interpretation of current urban transformations – framed as flows of people, practices, meanings and desires.

'Riverscapes' (chapters 2–6) is an account of the transformation of the Yarra River in less than two decades from the butt of jokes to a seductive and largely vibrant landscape; from an industrial sewer to a site of spectacle, which has become central to the new place-marketing of the city. This section describes the vision of the new Labor government in 1982 for the transformation of the urban river, which was to be both public-sector led and design-driven, and critically examines the implementation of this vision. This riverscape has transformed the iconography and mental map of the city for both residents and visitors alike with a series of commercial, retail, residential and public projects, including a shopping mall, casino, exhibition centre, convention centre, aquarium, public plaza and riverside park – laced together with waterfront promenades. Riverscapes concludes with a critique of Federation Square and the quest to produce a fundamentally new urban space for a multiplicitous 'public'.

'Dockscapes' (chapters 7–11) relates the story of Melbourne Docklands, 200 hectares of land and water nudging the western edge of the central city. This is a redundant port typical of many that have been targeted for redevelopment since the 1980s. But the planning and design process has not been typical. During the 1990s the site was put out for tender in large precincts with design and development control largely privatised. This is a story of urban development which was at once market-driven and design-driven, an experiment in just how fluid waterfront developments can get. Dockscapes remains a story in process with many lessons for large-scale redevelopment.

'Bayscapes' (chapter 12) is an account of the four-kilometre stretch of beachfront lining Port Phillip Bay from Port Melbourne to St Kilda. The former working-class dockers town of Port

Melbourne and the diverse and bohemian beachfront city of St Kilda have both been subject to powerful development forces during the 1980s and 1990s due to the enormous amenity of their waterfront locations. The issues here are those of balancing heritage, urban character and amenity against the values of new development and investment in a highly politicised urban design process. This chapter opens up the nebulous concept of 'urban character', the creation and protection of which both drives and inhibits urban transformation.

While the book is written in a narrative sequence, I recognise that this is often not how books are read; many of the theoretical issues that lace through it are best explored using the index. The final chapter, 'Loose Ends', will unravel these threads and explore some contradictions that run through these narratives of waterfront transformation. This will entail a return to the question of public interests and the mediation of flows of desire. The fluid city offers both opportunities and challenges. The opportunities are those of opening up the city to the water, to new forms of place identity and urban 'becoming'. The challenge is to understand, to manage and to regulate the city in a manner that mediates flows of capital and desire without paralysing them; it is to find ways to reconcile the many desires that create the city with public interests upon which any urban development process must be legitimated.

CHAPTER ONE

FLOWS

WATERFRONTS

The regeneration of urban waterfronts is one of the key urban design and planning stories of the late twentieth century. No longer required to serve as working ports or industrial sewers, waterfronts have become places of urban transformation with potential to attract investment and reverse patterns of decline. The waterfront has also been a primary scene of experimentation in architecture, planning and urban governance. These transformations are played out in a globalising world with increasing tensions between global capital and local place identity – tensions that are mediated by city and state governments with strong imperatives to attract investment and construct images of progress. The urban waterfront has become a new frontier of the city with opportunities for significant aesthetic, economic, social and environmental benefits; it is also the new battleground over conflict between public and private interests.

Most waterfront land that becomes available for redevelopment is disused industrial land related to former port uses. Ports are fundamentally places of flow, portals that mediate local/global flows. The harbour or dock connecting the city/state to the world shares this function with the 'port' connecting my computer to the World Wide Web. Ports were generally the first sites of global colonisation, funnelling flows of people, products, capital and ideas. They traditionally developed a close and intimate relationship with the city and its labour force, often involving districts of working-class housing within walking distance. Developments in transport technology throughout the twentieth century have seen port activities moved progressively to smaller and deeper sites without the need for contiguity with the central city. The result is often large tracts of derelict public waterfront in close proximity to the older city; what Hoyle has called the 'abandoned doorstep' becomes the opportunity for an urban facelift.[1] While such places are no longer geared to the flow of goods, they are increasingly geared to the flows of capital and ideas of an information economy.

The shift from an economy dominated by manufacturing to one focused on information industries has a range of effects. The increased flexibility of global capital in the late twentieth century has transferred manufacturing activity to cities with cheaper labour. Formerly wealthy manufacturing cities are often faced with a loss of jobs, an outflow of population and a declining tax base. There is also often a loss of collective self-esteem and business confidence. The city can become studded with abandoned sites that become both symbols of decline and opportunities for regeneration. The future of the city becomes dependent on attracting new industries, investment and jobs. The 'new economy' is driven by technology and information industries such as leisure, tourism, banking, finance and science; it is dominated by what Reich calls 'symbolic analysts': those whose job it is to manipulate numbers, words and images in the knowledge industries.[2] The increased flexibility of capital investment brings a focus on capturing these flows of footloose capital for purposes of job-creation and economic regeneration.

There is now a substantial literature on the global trend towards waterfront regeneration.[3] The primary global models were developed in the 1970s and 1980s in North American cities such as Baltimore, Boston, Seattle and New York with global dissemination from the 1980s. A rich variety of schemes incorporates project types such as markets, maritime heritage districts, shopping malls, theme parks, housing, commerce, hotels, convention and exhibition centres, sport stadia and museums. Many such waterfront projects are part of a wider move to what Hannigan calls the 'urban entertainment district' formed from a collage of mix and match components.[4] He invents neologisms such as 'shoppertainment', 'eatertainment' and 'edutainment' to describe these new functional hybrids. Not all waterfront developments are formula driven and there is considerable scope for visionary architecture, urban design and planning. The best example is probably Bilbao in northern Spain where a waterfront strategy (incorporating the Guggenheim art museum) is geared to broader infrastructure development. The museum (by architect Frank Gehry) is a thoroughly seductive and masterful piece of design that serves to transform the image of the city.

There are, however, dangers and contradictions to be faced by cities engaging in strategies to attract global capital for waterfront regeneration. The increased flexibility of capital flows enables developers to play off one city against another. Cities desperate for jobs and investment compete to create the conditions attractive to global investment, a form of global 'discount war'. Key incentives can include public subsidies through tax shelters, infrastructure provision and low land prices.[5] Others include a weakening or removal of planning restrictions and a willingness to 'streamline' democratic processes. Transformations in the planning process that take decision-making out of the public domain, also often render it opaque through 'commercial-in-confidence' secrecy agreements. This protects both the government and the project from public critique; the level of public subsidy can be hidden making assessment of public interests very difficult. The absence of public policy discourse creates a vacuum that is generally filled by marketing visions of the project, which have no legal relation to the contract. A key danger here is that such incentives and subsidies can simply siphon local investment from one part of the city to another with a tax loss to the public purse and a windfall profit for local investors.[6] The major hedge against such siphoning is to ensure that waterfront land is effectively reserved for mega-projects on large precincts, with subsidies restricted to new investment. The result is to close out smaller projects and reduce diversity. All of this places the state in an unenviable position – seemingly unable to attract investment without substantial subsidies coupled with a loss of public control and democratic process. With the state unable to afford infrastructure costs, the temptation is to cede control to private capital in return for infrastructure funding. Yet the project then becomes driven by private interests and over a shorter time span, subject to the unpredictable cycles of boom and recession in local and global markets.

In this context, state control of infrastructure and urban design guidelines are seen by many as the 'dead hand' of bureaucratic regulation that will neither meet the global market for footloose capital nor satisfy the demand for new urban imagery.[7] It is as if the 'hidden hand' of the market will service public interests better than the 'dead hand' of the state. New modes of entrepreneurial governance emerge in the form of public–private partnerships. The city becomes increasingly governed by coalitions of public and private interests; 'authorities' with a clear autonomy from elected government blurring the boundary between public and private sectors.[8] This slippage enables governance without electoral obligation – the legitimation of authority is granted on the basis that autonomy is necessary to wealth generation. This is an elite form of governance which presumes that entrepreneurship is the preserve of private industry. It also tends to be focused on instant large-scale projects with short-term profits. Some of the contradictions of waterfront developments are seen in case studies such as Baltimore's Harbour Place, which is widely touted as a success story. Yet as Harvey points out, this was a public–private partnership with substantial public subsidies for hotels, convention centres and stadia; and its broader effects have been to exacerbate disparities of wealth and power: 'The private–public partnership means that the public takes the risks and the private takes the profits. The citizenry wait for benefits that never materialize.'[9]

In this global market, intercity competition focuses attention on the urban imagery that identifies the city and differentiates it from other cities. Such imagery includes the iconography of architecture and landscape, as well as the more subtle dimensions of heritage and culture. The 'image of the city' originally explored by Lynch[10] as a form of urban cognition takes on a new and crucial economic role as a form of discourse and branding. In this new market, urban iconography is not simply found but is constructed, both on the ground and as a form of discourse. One of the first effects of this focus on the image of the city is that the market seeks to exploit local authenticities of place – the 'local colour' or 'difference' embodied in heritage, architecture, urbanism and culture. This quest to exploit the uniqueness of the local faces the contradiction that the market also tends to destroy that which it seeks to preserve. Highly valued places have a 'monopoly' on that amenity, yet as such places are incorporated into marketing and branding, 'place myths' are constructed. Local experiences of place become global commodities; differences are ironed out and the monopoly is weakened. The market pursuit of the authenticities of place remains reliant on local distinctions, and a part of what is attractive about the local is the vibrant 'buzz' of a diverse urban community. The paradox, as Harvey points out, is that capital cannot afford to eliminate forces which may be antagonistic to redevelopment.[11] The goose that lays the golden egg cannot be turned into a battery hen.

Many waterfront projects are focused on a wholesale reconstruction of the urban image with spectacles of artistic, social and economic dynamism. There is a special synergy about waterfront projects that turns large tracts of highly visible public land into the opportunity for a new urban iconography; such projects can revitalise the waterfront, attract investment, build local political capital and serve as effective advertising for further investment.[12] Both of these trends, towards the exploitation of the unique and the transformation of the derelict, often come together in waterfront projects. What they have in common is the focus on place mythology and marketing – urban identity is reconstructed as it is commodified. The rise of 'brand marketing', which focuses on the packaging of an ever-expanding range of products, fits the move to place marketing well – the city becomes the brand name as its iconic images become logos. This process places a premium on attracting the kinds of urban development that will in turn help to transform the imagery of the city as a brand.

The shift from manufacturing to an information economy since the 1970s has fundamentally changed the relation of image to content in architecture and design. Brand marketing has led to a substantial rise in the symbolic component of commodities – the 'symbolic capital'. The economic development of cities has come to depend more strongly on aesthetic production, a shift that has transformed the relationships between the architecture and planning disciplines. While planning can be effective in protecting existing places, the production of new forms of place imagery turns the focus on to urban design and architecture. We see a new alliance of high style and *avant garde* architectural production with broader development processes. Architecture has become more integrated into the constructions of place and place marketing – the production of imagery (both fictional and real projects) begins to play a key role in the advertising and legitimation of projects to both clients and community.[13] Advertising imagery for both the waterfront and the city becomes crucial to this process, and one effect here is the partial replacement of urban plans by urban design and marketing visions.[14] The discursive construction of the city and its future has become a key dimension of urban transformation and discourse analysis in turn becomes crucial to its interpretation.

The global trend to waterfront developments is also part of what has long been called the 'disneyfication' of the city as a thematic, scripted and branded form of place-making.[15] These are projects where as Goodwin puts it: 'images and myths are relentlessly packaged and presented until they become "hyperreal"... the distinction between the "real" and the "representation" is effaced'.[16] There is also a blurring between private and public space, between culture and commerce. The liminal spaces of the shopping mall and housing enclave, where public meanings are merged with private control, migrate to the waterfront, blurring the line between public and private interests. Thus waterfront projects are often highly choreographed and packaged urban lifestyles that construct new forms of social and cultural identity.

In the information economy, urban development also becomes characterised by the pursuit of what Mitchell calls 'smart places' with high levels of IT infrastructure producing global 'electronic propinquity': 'investment, jobs and economic power seem certain to migrate to those neighbourhoods, cities, regions and nations that can quickly put the infrastructure in place ...'.[17] Paradoxically, a key attraction of 'smart places' is the liberation from the inertia of place: 'Commerce isn't impeded by distance. Community doesn't have to depend on propinquity.'[18] Yet the attractions remain local – not just the IT infrastructure, but also the local networks of globally connected managers and the buzz of creativity and authenticity.[19] This is a city of 'live/work' spaces, '24-hour neighbourhoods' and electronically mediated meetings – one can conduct global business while enjoying the local colour. Others see the emergence of 'smart places' in a more critical light. For Dear, as planning becomes less integrated cities polarise into an information rich 'cyburbia' contrasted with an information poor 'cyberia'. The city develops as '... a non-contiguous collage of parcelized, consumption-oriented landscapes devoid of conventional centers yet wired into electronic propinquity ... a partitioned gaming board subject to perverse laws and peculiarly discrete, disjointed urban outcomes.'[20] Likewise, Graham and Marvin suggest that the new networked infrastructures lead to a 'splintering urbanism' that is internationally integrated yet locally fragmented, privileging certain places and users while by-passing others.[21]

Hannigan suggests that the proliferation of entertainment

districts in North America is based on a social contradiction: a voracious middle-class appetite for the consumption of authentic place experience is coupled with a deeply rooted reluctance to take risks.[22] Put another way this is a desire to experience 'diversity' without risking contact with genuine 'difference'. The quest for experience leads to themed environments, spectacle, festivity, public art and major 'events'. The avoidance of risk leads to the enclosure and sanitisation of such experience, together with the exclusion of lower social classes. Urban waterfronts then often meet a market as 'protected playgrounds for middle-class consumers'.[23] The middle-class penchant for predictability and safety, long evident in the suburbs, is directed at the inner city and its new waterfronts. The desire for diversity means that techniques of exclusion become more sophisticated than the gated enclave; they include distance, parking prices, lack of public transport and aesthetic codes. Gender and racial equity may be celebrated while the exclusions of social class are repressed.[24] The illusion is created of a cosmopolitan society of difference, while entrenching and increasing the spatial divisions between privilege and poverty.

SPATIAL PRACTICES

While this is not primarily a theory book, its critiques are driven by a further range of ideas and modes of analysis that can help in understanding the stories to follow. The desire here is not to reduce the city to theory, but rather to use theory to help elucidate urban transformations. At the risk of alienating some readers I want to sketch some theoretical frameworks for understanding these transformations.

The first of these has its roots in the seminal work of Jane Jacobs and Christopher Alexander in the 1960s, with a focus on urban spatial structure. Both Jacobs and Alexander engaged in critiques of modernist planning ideologies which sought to stamp a rational hierarchical order on the city – a place for everything and everything in its place.[25] These approaches were different, but united in the celebration of the diverse flows of urban life and in a quest to understand underlying principles of urban vitality – perhaps best encapsulated in Alexander's dictum: 'a city is not a tree'. His insight was to show how the vitality of urban life can be killed by hierarchical 'tree-like' thinking where the synergies of urban life are eradicated. Urban life is sustained by horizontal connections between different practices, by rhizomatic rather than tree-like structures. For Jacobs the conditions for urban diversity were found in the mixing of functional zones rather than their separation; in the synergies between functions that sustain economic vitality and the vitality of public street life. These conditions were also found in the permeable or 'ringy' structure of urban spatial networks; in a relatively small grainsize of urban fabric; and in the relatively high urban densities necessary to sustain dense pedestrian networks and 'pools of use'. The work on linking urban spatial structure to social structure and urban economics has been taken further in Hillier and Hanson's work on 'spatial syntax analysis' and urban 'movement economies'.[26] Flows of pedestrian life are heavily mediated by the urban spatial structure.

These principles are now generally understood in urban design practice, they have been deployed and adapted to some degree in the waterfront formulae outlined earlier. One of the key phenomena of the late twentieth century, however, has been the production of pseudo-diversity within privatised quasi-public space. The shopping mall has been the incubator for such internally permeable developments with high pedestrian densities and a formularised diversity of functions. These are inversions of urban life that purify and kill genuine urban places under the illusion of creating them.[27] Many such developments have the spatial structure of a closed network – locally permeable but globally enclosed like a walled city. As the scale of private urban development projects becomes larger, the critique of urban spatial structure and of 'tree-like' thinking becomes more relevant than ever.

One of the key values of urban public space is that, like the old town square, it carries the potential for the high-density random social encounter of the 'crowd'. Sennett has long argued that such an encounter with difference is the key quality of urbanity; the density and diversity of public space has a civilising function that produces tolerance of difference, and enables the formation of new identities.[28] For Canetti, the dense crowd has an inherent and liberating value of dissolving the fear of being touched by others. Within the dense crowd there is equality: 'Distinctions are thrown off and all feel *equal* ... It is for the sake of this blessed moment, when none is greatest or better than another, that people become a crowd'.[29] Canetti distinguishes between the 'open' and fluid crowds that absorb everyone, and 'closed' crowds where boundaries, entrances and fees are deployed to stabilise the crowd. In much current urban development the liberating effect of the open crowd – its density, festivity and carnival – is commodified through a carefully designed urban spatial structure. 'Open' crowds are converted into 'closed' crowds.

Critiques of urban spatial structure require a different approach from the traditional views of either the planner or the architect. It requires what Allen suggests is a shift in design thinking from a focus on the formal qualities of the 'object' to a focus on 'field' relations.[30] A 'field' in this sense consists of contingent relations, forces, trajectories and patterns of movement such as those that govern a 'crowd' or 'flock' of birds. The lessons here parallel those of Alexander and Jacobs; 'permeable boundaries, flexible internal relationships, multiple pathways and fluid hierarchies' are seen as responding to a higher level of complexity of urban contexts.[31] An understanding of spatial practices entails a capacity to understand the ways flows of everyday life are mediated by urban spatial structure.

The work of Lefebvre is also crucial for understanding the production of urban space and the experience of place within it as a result of struggles between the appropriation of space for profit and for play. For Lefebvre, many of the pleasures of the city are linked to different forms of spatial practice and experience that are possible in marginal and interstitial spaces such as the beach and waterfront which, to some degree, escape the instrumentalisation of the market.[32] His famous call for the 'right to the city' is not only about rights of access, but about rights to play and appropriation; it is about the capacity to generate new forms of meaning and identity through everyday action. Such appropriations are linked to practices of liberation, but these are not so much liberating places as they are 'moments' of possible transformation. At the same time Lefebvre is interested in the ways space can construct illusions of freedom, forms of control operating under the guise of innocence and transparency.[33] For de Certeau, like Lefebvre, the meanings of place are continuously constructed and reconstructed through action in everyday life: 'Like words, places are articulated by a thousand usages'.[34] Places are the warehouses of memory, always haunted with a myriad of possibilities for meaning and behaviour. He celebrates the possibilities of resistance through everyday practices in public space. In opposition to the ways in which 'space' becomes 'place' through the construction of territory and identity, he celebrates the manner in which 'place' becomes 'space' as territories and identities are transgressed – urban space becomes fluid through the practices of everyday life. For de Certeau walking in the city, negotiating the field of pedestrian networks, is a rhizomatic activity in stark opposition to the tree-like conception within which the city is often conceived.

MEANINGS

The spatial network or field is a material condition, rather than a discursive or symbolic practice. However, spatial structure has a key linkage to such issues in that it frames and mediates access to certain forms of place experience.[35] The critique of such projects can benefit from social theories as a context to the ways urban design is deployed to produce 'place myths' and 'symbolic capital'. The work of Barthes has long been useful for the semiotic insight that images and signs tell stories and construct narrative myths.[36] He uses the term 'myth', because signs evoke a way of seeing or making sense of the world, they tell us a story. Politics operates through the illusion of being apolitical – myth is 'depoliticised speech', it transforms history into nature. Architecture and urban design construct and stabilise certain visions of the world, making the world credible and legible. Meanings are 'cooked' to produce 'truth effects'. This is not to simply reduce architecture or urban design to a didactic function; indeed, the irreducibility of meaning to literal interpretation is a key to its potency. Such an approach relies upon discourse analysis, one of the most crucial and misunderstood of critical research methods.[37] It is important to note that the purpose of discourse analysis here is not to uncover or decode hidden meanings that somehow reveal an underlying reality; rather, it is to show the production of mythology, to enter what Barthes calls the 'kitchen of meaning'. Waterfronts are highly visible parts of the city and major sites for the production of new design imagery. Design images tell stories about who we are, where we have come from and where we are going; they establish what matters.

The work of Bourdieu gives an insight into the ways that the resources we broadly refer to as 'capital' extend from the economic domain into 'social capital' and 'symbolic capital'.[38] For Bourdieu social capital is a resource that inheres in social relations or networks of family, friends, school, church and neighbourhood, often based in class membership like the 'old school tie'. Social capital is collective rather than individual; if you leave the group you lose the capital. While Bourdieu depicts social capital primarily in terms of the power of dominant groups, the concept (in a rather different sense) also has a popular currency as a positive resource base of all community networks.[39] Trust, solidarity, community and class are all forms of social capital while fear, alienation and isolation indicate its absence. Social capital is embedded in the built environment where it is sustained and reproduced by architectural programs as spatially structured patterns of social encounter. Buildings and neighbourhoods both ground and structure social networks, enabling and constraining the development of social capital whether in housing enclaves, waterfront precincts, sporting venues and public space. A large portion of the public wealth created through urban design and planning is embodied in the ways places and spatial relations sustain social capital.

'Symbolic capital' is more problematic to define and there is considerable slippage in Bourdieu's use of it. Symbolic capital is the value of distinction, recognition or honour that accrues to those with 'class' and 'taste'.[40] But symbolic capital circulates through 'fields' of cultural production and aesthetic discourse, rather than simply accumulating in individuals. Symbolic capital is not something one possesses so much as something that infuses the field. A key part of the definition of symbolic capital is that it is 'denied capital'; it is not seen as a resource. It is seen as a universal quality that establishes the distinction of people, places and things, rather than a function of the discursive field. Its potency lies in this masking effect; the fluidity of the definition of symbolic capital is not coincidental. The production of symbolic capital is a kind of 'alchemy' through which social division becomes a naturalised distinction.[41] Unlike social capital, of which more or less may be produced, symbolic capital is a fixed resource, a zero/sum game. There is only so much distinction and prestige to be distributed. If everyone gets 'distinctive' architecture, if every city is distinctive, no one wins the symbolic capital.

The production of symbolic capital is the architect's key market niche and the *avant garde* has a key role to play in overturning and reinvigorating codes of aesthetic taste. For Bourdieu the *avant garde* fulfils a key role of keeping the images within a field from becoming stale; it changes and enlivens the field without disturbing its foundations. Radically new imagery that upsets the prevailing order is highly valuable as symbolic capital so long as it is adequately framed for contemplation and consumption. The relative autonomy of the *avant garde*, its symbolic opposition to the mainstream, is structurally necessary to its role as the primary source of new symbolic capital. The apparent autonomy of the *avant garde* is geared to its structural role in keeping the field supplied with a stream of new images.

Symbolic capital is not reducible to economic capital, although it can be 'cashed' under certain conditions. Symbolic capital flows not only through buildings, but also through their representations, publicity (coffee table books and magazines) and the name of the signature architect. For Bourdieu, symbolic capital is embedded in culture as one form of 'cultural capital', which in turn is a resource based in social distinction. Symbolic capital is not as fluid as finance, but it is in some ways more slippery and less stable. From such a view aesthetic codes operate to camouflage practices of power because they are seen as autonomous. To view architecture and urban design as symbolic capital is not to reduce architecture to economics, nor to extinguish the ideal of aesthetic autonomy; without creative innovation and the relative autonomy of the *avant garde* the field would become stale and production would cease. The production of symbolic capital is crucial to the development of monopoly rent on the waterfront, and to global place marketing.

DESIRES

From the philosophy of Gilles Deleuze I want to pick up some ideas about the production and flow of desire.[42] The Deleuzian world is a difficult one to grasp; indeed, grasping it is not recommended, launching oneself would seem to be the approved metaphor. This is a world fuelled by 'flows of desire', where 'lines of flight' take precedence over points of order or stability, where 'being' gives way to processes of 'becoming'. What we call buildings and cities, identities and institutions, what gets congealed as symbolic capital, are effects of these flows of desire. Deleuze (with Guattari) has been at the forefront of the development of an immanent ontology of 'becoming'. From a Deleuzian perspective the city is an immanent flow of desires. Space is not the stable framework within which things exist or events happen so much as the connections of desire between them. The world is not a collection of subjects who have desires, rather desires construct subjects. From such a view urban development is based in desires for waterfront property, views, amenity, distinction, profit, investment, privilege, power and identity. This is not, however, a humanist conception; there is no pre-given subject who desires, rather identities are constructed through flows of desire. A key to the Deleuzian perspective is that desire does not stem from a 'lack' or 'need', rather it is the immanent productive force of life itself; without desire there is no city. Flows of desire are the life force of the fluid city.

    Deleuze and Guattari make a distinction between what they call 'striated' and 'smooth' space.[43] The term 'striated' captures the etymological links to the Latin word *stringere*: 'to draw tight', linked to 'strict' and 'stringent'. This is contrasted with the 'smooth', which they intend to be read, not as homogeneous, but rather without boundaries or joints. Smoothness implies a slipperiness and movement where one slides seamlessly from one site (place, meaning, image) to another. These are not different types of space so much as spatial properties. Striated space is where identity has become stabilised, as opposed to the smooth space of 'becoming'. Striated space is identified with the sedentary, with territorial roots; smooth space is identified with movement, the space of the nomad, the refugee or the migrant. Smooth space is a field of vectors or lines of flight upon which we ride or slide, like surfing on the crest of turbulence. Striation is identified with socially controlled identities and strictly bounded territories where such identities are stabilised. Smooth space is linked to 'deterritorialisation', the movement through which stabilised territories, identities and meanings are escaped.

The smooth and the striated are not types of space or place so much as conceptual tools for thinking about space. Every real place is a mixture of the two in a reciprocal relation where they are constantly 'enfolded' into each other: 'Nothing is ever done with: smooth space allows itself to be striated, and striated space reimparts a smooth space ... all progress is made by and in striated space, but all becoming occurs in smooth space.'[44] 'Folding' is a key term for Deleuze, a liminal condition associated with 'becoming'. It is not a 'crease' or boundary, rather it involves a focus away from things, elements or points of stability and on to the movements and 'foldings' between them. This focus on the 'between' is also a way to rethink binary and dialectic oppositions as an enfolding of each other; for our purposes here this entails the enfolding of public with private, of architecture with urban planning and urbanism with politics.

For Deleuze, concepts such as 'smooth space', 'flows of desire' and 'deterritorialisation' are intellectual tools; the test is whether they are useful in enabling new ways of thinking and understanding the city. In this regard there is an important point of connection to the urban design theories of Jacobs, Alexander and Hillier in this opposition to tree-like thinking and spatial conceptions. Striated space is structured like a tree, hierarchically organised and deeply rooted with a vertical stem. Smooth space is identified with the 'rhizome' – a largely underground and horizontally migrating form of life that thrives within the interstices of a larger order. A great deal of urban life in terms of both spatial practices and representational practices can be understood as rhizomatic, particularly those that produce a genuine diversity and difference.[45] Analysis of urban spatial structure can be rethought in terms of rhizomatic networks. A labyrinth is a multiplicity of spatial folds where the twists and turns of lanes and alleys disorients and produces a mix of desire/danger.[46] The effect of the maze is to 'amaze'; the 'folds' of the 'labyrinth' are its 'labia' where a dominant spatial order 'folds' into a fluid space of slippage and danger. The labyrinth is multi-lipped, it is an edge condition where one loses the controlling tree-like gaze over spatial order.

There is a certain optimism in Deleuzian thought for the politics of desire, privileging movement over stasis, the 'line of flight' over stable points of order, 'smooth' over 'striated' space. This is one reason why Deleuze has been followed to a considerable degree within the architectural *avant garde*.[47] Liberation is identified with 'deterritorialisation', the movement through which stabilised territories, identities and meanings are escaped. Deterritorialisation creates space for a 'reterritorialisation' as new boundaries, forms and identities are inscribed. One of the key dilemmas which Deleuzian thinking introduces to urban design is that flows of desire are often implicated and insinuated into flows of capital. Capitalism legitimates new flows of desire. As Colebrook puts it: 'Capitalism is a surplus of flows; anything is allowable and permissible if it can be translated into a capital flow...'.[48] In capitalism, flows of desire become grounded in flows of capital, the laws of the marketplace become the laws of the land. Markets, which enable the exchange of values, become misrecognised as the source of such values. The ways in which capital legitimates the flows of desire loosens the authority of the state. This is one way of understanding the weakening of planning controls in the 1980s and 1990s. The massive flows of capital in deregulated global markets are forms of deterritorialisation and many Deleuzians see a liberatory potential in the deterritorialising tendencies of capital. The optimism here lies in a faith that the reterritorialisation will not be worse than the existing city. A key question for a Deleuzian approach to urban development focuses on the inevitability of reterritorialisation: how does one judge the new waterfront against other possibilities when there is no transcendent ideal on which to ground such judgement? There is an important connection here with the long theorised phenomenon of 'creative destruction', the 'perpetual struggle in which capital builds a physical landscape appropriate to its own condition at a particular moment in time, only to have to destroy it ... at a subsequent point in time ...'.[49] The task of urban design and urban critique is to understand the ways in which certain interests and desires are swept aside in the deterritorialisation process and others are produced and channelled through the reterritorialisation.

WATER

When promoting the prospective development of Melbourne Docklands in 1989, the Premier of the day, John Cain, was selling the need to turn the 'face' of the city to the water and was quoted as follows:

> ... in psychological terms, water, in its soft, lapping, lake-like condition, symbolizes the mother – that to which most of us want to return. For those who don't want to, water, in its torrential or stormy aspect, also symbolizes the father. So whichever way you look at it, this development is going to be a very significant re-bonding experience. It will reunite Melburnians with their eternal mother – and on rough days with their father.[50]

This was a rather creative piece of speechwriting for a rather dour Premier, but it hints at the kind of meanings that are widely associated with bodies of water. The human fascination with water has long been a subject of reflection and speculation, both at a philosophical level and in architecture, landscape and urban theory. The idea of urban waterfronts as places of pleasure is extremely widespread and seems rooted in more than some rational conception of 'amenity'. While it is easy to dismiss the kind of essentialising comments quoted above, the attractions of water and the productions of desire on the waterfront have not and will not be fully explained as arbitrary social constructions.

In Western traditions of philosophy and mythology, water has a complex set of associations: life, mystery, play, danger, youth, cleansing and regeneration. Water has long had a spiritual dimension linked to the dissolution of identity and regeneration; the fluidity of water symbolises potentiality as a source of life, of being and identity.[51] It is this sense in which water can be seen as a source of life, fertility and healing; a fount of youth. Yet such symbolism also incorporates a darker side of mystery and danger. In Greek mythology, nymphs as the divinities of water were both feared and worshipped as sources of madness and joy. Water was also the source of masculine monsters – the untamed god Poseidon and the many-headed Hydra as figures of chaos and danger. In psychoanalytic theory, water is symbolic of the unconscious and of the unformed potentiality of the human spirit. For Freud, the unconscious is largely synonymous with the id, for which he uses the fluid metaphor of a 'great reservoir of libido', a body of cathartic energy wherein the 'pleasure principle' reigns.[52] This 'reservoir' represents both the source of libidinous energy and its containment. From this view aesthetic pleasure is a form of transference from the reservoir of libidinous energy on to an aesthetic object of desire.[53] From such a view, waterfront developments can be seen in terms of a channelling of flows of libidinous desire that are immanent in the 'body' of water. For Deleuze and Guattari, water is one of the models used to describe the opposition between the 'smooth' space of 'becoming' as contrasted with the static striated spaces of stabilised identity: 'the sea is smooth space par excellence ... the archetype of all smooth spaces'.[54]

The urban waterfront can also be understood in terms of the spatial dialectic of land and water. The waterfront is a boundary, an edge condition between the stable striations of the city and the smooth flows of the water. It is a spatial 'between' condition that mediates a series of dialectic oppositions – order/chaos; being/becoming; place/space, culture/nature, closed/open, striated/smooth; solid/void. It is the mediation of these oppositions, which lends the waterfront a good deal of its experiential potency, the occupation of the 'between' zone. The waterfront is an edge of the city and it has a certain edginess; it is a 'front' or 'frontier', a 'face' or 'mask' of the city that constructs urban character and identity.

Urban waterfronts often represent a margin to the predominant urban spaces of political and commercial power. And they often represent a form of liberation from the city and its forms of spatial and social containment. 'Underneath the pavement – the beach' was the catchcry of the Situationist movement in Paris in the 1960s, as they tore up the paving as part of a quest for a more liberated urban space.[55] This was a metaphoric beach, a place of bodily pleasure on the margins of social control, where codes of dress and behaviour are relaxed. In his study of Tokyo in the Edo period, Jinnai describes a waterfront of ludic spaces contrasting with the dominant urban spaces of political, social and economic control. Linked to the Japanese ideal of the 'floating world', urban places near and over the water were places of liberation: 'sanctuaries from the obligations of city life'.[56] Urban waterfronts were constituted as a ludic fantasy world of theatres, tea-houses, brothels and wandering entertainment. This was an urban life that flowed across the boundaries between earth and water, where the rigidities of social order and identity melt. This description of ludic Japanese waterfronts has its parallels in many Western cities. From Barcelona and Bilbao to Brighton and Blackpool, on to Baltimore and Boston, the lure of the waterfront is that of the place of pleasure. What follows is the Melbourne story from Southbank to St Kilda.

PART A

RIVERSCAPES

CHAPTER TWO

RIVERSCAPES I – OVERVIEW

Kim Dovey and Leonie Sandercock

MELBOURNE

Melbourne is widely known as Australia's second city and occasionally receives the accolade of the world's 'most livable' city. The weather, mild and sunny by global standards, is the butt of jokes from other Australians. Melburnians are often marked by their admiration of the weather and the often spectacular skyscape – 'four seasons in one day' as the Crowded House song puts it. The character of Melbourne stems from its urbanity rather than its landscape, which is generally flat and, with the exception of the bay, unremarkable. The city is located on the Yarra River, several kilometres inland from Port Philip Bay, an inlet of about fifty kilometres diameter that is entered from the southern ocean through a narrow channel. Prior to European appropriation this landscape was inhabited by a variety of Aboriginal groups collectively known as the Kulin nation. While the details of this invasion and displacement are only marginally relevant to this work, the erasure of Aboriginal rights and the repression associated with the description of this 'settlement' need to be acknowledged. The memory of this era has haunted much of the subsequent occupation of the site. Melbourne was first settled by Europeans in the 1830s under the aegis of British law on the legal basis that the land was uninhabited: the doctrine of *terra nullius*, which was overturned in 1992 by the Australian High Court. While such a judgement does not re-establish any Aboriginal rights to the city, it has served to shake the ground of belief in sovereignty and ownership, as it raises questions about rights and responsibilities towards the landscape.

The site of the city centre was established by the limits to navigation of the Yarra River, where a rocky outcrop formed some shallow falls. A natural pool below the falls provided a turning basin for ships, with fresh water available above the falls. The name 'Yarra Yarra' was thought to be the Aboriginal name of the river later found to translate loosely as 'flowing flowing' or 'waterfall'. In the mid-1830s a broad grid of streets was laid out on the northern bank of the river (Figure 2.1). This was a grand scheme for a city that was initially to be governed as a sub-colony from Sydney. It was designed entirely without spatial hierarchy – there were no privileged streets or directions, no sites set aside for monuments or institutions.

The grid can be understood as a conjunction of several ideologies. Primary among them was the imperative for a rational ordering of a strange space, establishing an idealised European urban space coupled with a distancing of the strange Aboriginal landscape. The streets were conceived as civic space quite unlike the military encampments and penal colonies established as the basis of most Australian cities. The naming of the streets reflected the politics of the day, immortalising a range of kings, queens, politicians, governors and explorers. The grid also had a major function to package land for sale and speculation. Many of the blocks were first bought, sight unseen, by investors from Sydney who swiftly proceeded to subdivide and resell at substantial profit. This speculative subdivision process eventually led to an intricate and highly permeable structure of north/south lanes and arcades that have contributed to the very rich and diverse urban fabric of the central city.

The gold rush of the 1850s brought a sudden urbanisation of Melbourne as the population quadrupled in three years to 80,000. While the gold did not last forever, much of the population and the wealth remained, sustained by wool, finance and manufacturing. The 1880s saw a major boom fuelled by massive British investment – an era known as 'Marvellous Melbourne', when Melbourne became Australia's largest city and financial capital.[1] The city grid filled out to become one of the world's finest Victorian-era cities with a rich street life and an exuberant architecture strongly contained within a 40-metre height limit.[2] The generous network

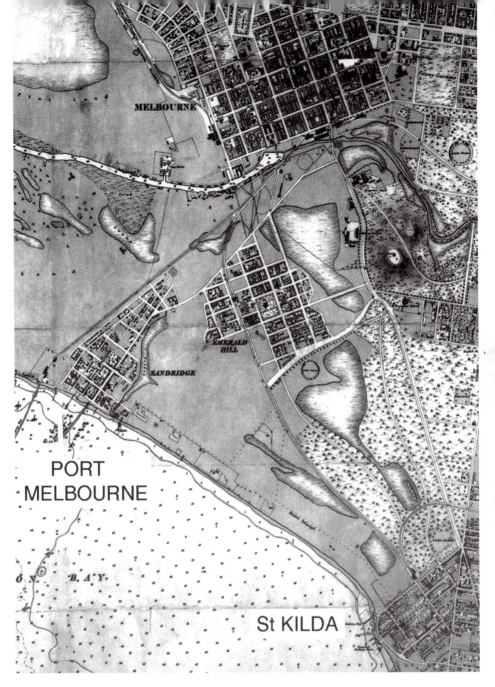

Figure 2.1
Detail, map of Melbourne, 1864
(*LaTrobe Picture Collection/State Library of Victoria*)

of public space was supplemented both by the intricate network of lanes and arcades within the grid and the ring of parkland to the east and north. The city was urbane and staid with a gritty underside – home to both the wealthiest bourgeois class and the most powerful working class in the country. When independence came to Australia in 1901 with the Federation of the Australian colonies, Melbourne was the largest and grandest city in the new nation and hosted the national parliament until it moved to Canberra in 1927.

The turn of the century also saw the construction of extensive railways and tramways into the suburban hinterland. A stable economy and rising car ownership from the mid-century led to continuous suburban growth, fulfilling the 'Great Australian Dream' of home ownership. By the 1970s Melbourne had expanded into a carpet of low-density suburbs with a population of almost three million. From 1970 to 1990 the economy entered a global phase of economic restructuring and de-industrialisation, losing jobs in manufacturing while gaining in the tertiary sector. When the Australian economy was largely deregulated during the 1980s the impact of global markets accelerated. While Melbourne had traditionally been the home of the nation's major financial and industrial corporations, new players were increasingly locating in Sydney. As the major gateway for international air traffic and a growing share of emerging information industries, Sydney was consolidating a higher position in the emerging hierarchy of 'world cities'.[3]

One of the effects of this Sydney/Melbourne rivalry is what might be called landmark envy. Sydney's distinctive image of the harbour, Opera House and bridge contrasts with the Melbourne image of trams, parks, streetscapes and monuments. The city's leaders have intermittently diagnosed some form of identity crisis. When a competition was held in the late 1970s to design a major Melbourne landmark, the prize was distributed among a large number of winners and none were built. This result was consistent with Melbourne's rather multiplicitous character; an acquired taste that resists conflation into iconic imagery. The tourist images of trams, streetscapes, parks, laneways and monuments are important to this character, but so are the rich and distinctive artistic cultures evident in food, film-making, theatre, comedy and music. The discourse and practice of architecture and urbanism in Melbourne is the best developed in the country with robust debate and a rich and fertile mix of formal approaches.[4]

In 1982 a progressive Labor government won power in Victoria and replaced a tired conservative regime. With the exception of some serious damage from high-rise buildings in the 1960s, the image of the city had changed very little in a long period. Based on a realisation that this image was crucial to attracting global investment, the river, the bay and later the docklands became the focus of an urban facelift. The Labor government (led by Premiers John Cain and Joan Kirner) remained in power from 1982–92; replaced by the Liberal government (led by Premier Jeffrey Kennett) until 1999 when the pendulum swung back to Labor (led by Steve Bracks). The waterfront transformations over these two decades are the subject of this book.

SOUTHBANK VISION

The riverscape referred to here is the one-kilometre stretch of river forming the southern edge of the downtown grid. Here the eighty-metre wide river, opening into the turning circle below the falls, was lined on the city side with wharves that became the front door to the city from the 1840s onwards. Customs House nearby was the first public building, regulating the flows of trade between the colony and the empire. Two blocks north of the river and up the hill, Collins Street became the financial centre of the city. The river was first bridged in 1845 and connected to the bay along St Kilda Road – a ceremonial entry for visitors who disembarked at St Kilda pier and paraded along St Kilda Road over the bridge and into the city. Thus was established the major north–south civic axis intersecting the grid and the river; locating Princes Bridge as the primary urban entrance. The city was connected to Port Melbourne (then called Sandridge) in 1854 with the Sandridge railway, which sliced across the river at a very oblique angle just above the falls and established the corner of Flinders and Swanston Streets as the central railway station and major node of the city. As new capital flowed in the 1880s these two bridges were replaced by those that remain today.

The era of the waterfront city declined at the end of the nineteenth century when the wharves moved downstream and the development of the railways severed the city from the river. By the mid-twentieth century most traces of the waterfront history, except the Customs House building (now an Immigration Museum), had been erased. The railway viaducts and a collection of car parks and shoddy buildings underneath them had sealed the city from the river visually and functionally. The commercial and social vitality of the waterfront was gone. The northern riverbank became a thin, overgrown and largely unwalkable strip between the rail lines and the water. With the exception of a small portion of the river to the south east of the grid that was swathed in park-land, the riverscape was treated with disdain.

The marshy ground to the south of the river was subject to occasional flooding and utilised primarily for temporary functions, most notably the tent city that sprouted during the gold rush of the 1850s. The south bank became a conceptual 'other' to the city, uncontained by the rational grid and ungrounded in the Euro-centric vision of civic space established by the grid. The river became the division between the stabilised territory and rigid geometry of the colony and the largely unclaimed and unstable ground of south bank. In the 1870s, when the boom era known as 'marvellous Melbourne' was just taking off, this area on the southern side of the river adjacent to Princes Bridge was first used for circus tents and temporary fun parks. In the early twentieth century it became a more permanent circus site and a large entertainment precinct developed with skating rinks, dance hall, water-chute, open-air theatre, tea house and toboggan run. The opposite sides of the river were thus conceptually opposed – the fluid versus solid ground, leisure versus work, and temporary versus permanent. One crossed the water from the strongly grounded and orderly civic spaces of the grid to a fluid landscape of pleasure.

By the 1950s this landscape was being replaced by industrial uses and car-parking space. In 1964 the National Gallery of Victoria was built on the site of a former fun park, followed by the Arts Centre theatre complex on the adjacent site bordering the river. The precinct, designed by architect Roy Grounds and completed in 1984, is formed of three separate buildings – all fully publicly funded. The arts precinct turned its back on the industrial riverscape, utilising the waterfront as a stage door for the Concert Hall. The landscape of pleasure became more permanent and exclusive as it turned its face away from the river and towards the civic axis of St Kilda Road. The more proletarian and visceral fringe activities of the marshy site were replaced by the more cerebral arts on high stable ground.

This urban riverscape, lined with railways and factories, had become a zone of shame reinforced by its brownish water and its history as an industrial sewer. It was crossed by four road bridges, plus the bulky and disused Sandridge railway bridge. In 1980 the editor of *The Age* newspaper (Michael Davie) mounted a campaign to 'Save the Yarra' through a series of articles designed to open debate and generate ideas. When the Labor government came to power in 1982 a well-known architect, Evan Walker, was named as Minister for Planning and Environment, with David

Yencken, an innovative housing developer and urbanist, as Head of Department. They began a strategy to develop this stretch of the Yarra as an urban river – an allusion was made to the Seine in Paris based on the similar width of the two rivers.

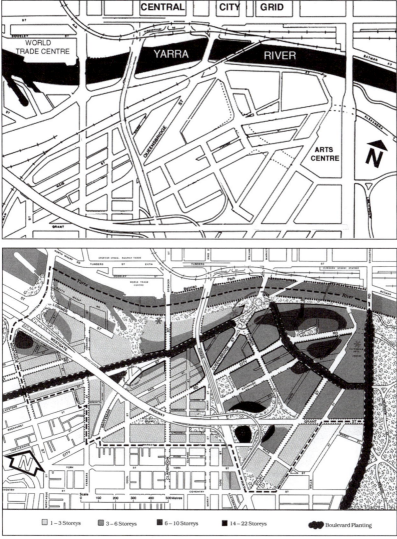

Figure 2.2
Southbank area – existing infrastructure (top)
and proposed framework (bottom) 1985
(Southbank: A Development Strategy,
Ministry for Planning, 1986.)

The Southbank vision involved several key policy and design principles. First, this river precinct should be complementary to downtown, rather than competitive with it; it should build upon the attractions of the Arts Centre with a cultural and entertainment focus on the waterfront to attract both locals and tourists. Second, it should be mixed functionally (retail, commercial and residential), socially (both luxury and social housing) and formally (low and high-rise). Third, the precinct should be designed to create a lively public waterfront with full public access. Finally, the government would, where possible, amalgamate and re-parcel land packages, build public infrastructure, and set guidelines for development, but it would not act as the developer. As a model of urban redevelopment this was not unlike the many public/private partnerships that emerged globally in the 1980s.

The planning strategy incorporated a string of potential projects along more than a kilometre of river plus a hundred hectares of hinterland to the south. Deploying the idea of a 'magnet' from the shopping mall typology; the Southbank promenade was to be 'anchored' at its western end by a new building for the Melbourne Museum, and would thus extend from the Arts Centre to the museum. These two civic anchors on the south bank were to be mirrored on the north bank by a Trade and Convention Centre opposite the Museum, and by the existing train station opposite the Arts Centre. Southbank was to be developed in two major stages from the east to the west. A new pedestrian bridge would improve access from the city and train station. Public infrastructure would include a generous promenade along the south bank. Another pathway was to follow the north bank, but the adjacent railway and lack of sun gave it much less urban design potential. Substantial government land holdings along the river enabled significant public-sector leverage over development. The hinterland of about 1000 hectares to the south, much of it industrial land, was targeted for residential, arts and commercial redevelopment (Figure 2.2 bottom).

This strategy was long term, in recognition that it might take the private sector some time to see the potential. It included the development of two major new boulevards to provide access from the south. The first of these was Southbank Boulevard, formed from a collection of acquired private properties, and designed to form a major new connection from the gallery and St Kilda Road and parkland to the centre of the new south bank and on into the city. The other boulevard was to be established along the alignment of the old Sandridge Railway, designed to reinforce this remnant of history and to connect the city to the bay visually and functionally (Figure 2.2 bottom).

From its inception the Southbank strategy was also driven by the desire to attract global investment. It was conceived as a project of state significance and in the early phases a struggle for control between state and local government (then the City of South Melbourne) delayed the project for two years. The first phase of public infrastructure took shape in the mid-1980s in the form of Southbank Boulevard, creating a string of new development sites lining the boulevard that were then sold back into the private sector at considerable profit to the public purse. This drew criticism from the private sector who argued that the Planning Minister had a conflict of interest in operating as both developer and regulator.

Largely as a result of the Southbank experience, the Office of Major Projects was formed in 1987 to deal with large-scale redevelopments of state as well as local significance. It enabled the state to develop large sites in public ownership, while maintaining a distance between the state's entrepreneurial and regulatory functions. The tensions being mediated here were not only between local and state interests, but also between public and private interests. Clearly, the government was engaged in a major wealth creation activity and the private sector wanted more of the action. While the Office of Major Projects was partly set up to separate the two functions, it had other uses. It enabled the state to separate the urban development process from the constraints of democratic governance, to negotiate flexibly and confidentially with private developers, and to by-pass the public planning process in doing so.

By 1992, in spite of conflicts with particular developers over site-specific issues, and handicapped by economic recession after 1989, the eastern section of the river's revival was well under way. Two large private-sector projects, Riverside Quay and SouthGate, were completed. The former was a rather mediocre outcome, but when the SouthGate project was opened in 1992 the river burst into life, transforming the iconography and mental map of the city for visitors and residents alike (Figure 2.3). While this was in many ways a formulaic waterfront shopping precinct, coupled with a hotel and some corporate towers, the key to its success was that the development provided an active, sunny waterfront with a brand new panorama of the city skyline across the river. By 1993, this had become the most visited tourist destination in the city, transforming the image and the meaning of the central city for both insiders and outsiders. The river became a part of a new urban spectacle with the water as stage and the city skyline as backdrop.

Just as the first projects came to fruition in 1992, Labor government stocks fell into decline as a result of global recession, financial mismanagement and the swing of the pendulum after a decade in power. The completion of the first phase of Southbank now stands as the most visible achievement of that government. The new Melbourne Museum was under construction at the western end of the urban river precinct, but no new housing had emerged on the river. Plans for the second major precinct, which would extend the promenade to the museum, had not progressed.

ON THE MOVE

In late 1992 the Labor government was soundly defeated at the polls. The Liberal–National Coalition led by Premier Jeff Kennett promised to get the state 'on the move' – the new slogan for the state of Victoria reflecting a somewhat Thatcherite agenda that would dominate the rest of the decade. Drastic measures were deemed necessary to restore the flagging economy, and any criticism was labelled 'un-Victorian'. The new Minister of Planning, Robert Maclellan, announced that 'red tape' would be cut and planning laws would be changed to speed up important projects. This marked the beginning of an era in which planning was redefined as an obstacle to development, and planners were derided as obstructionist. The restructured role of planning was signalled by a change of name from the 'Department of Planning and Environment' to the 'Department of Infrastructure'. Planning as a regulatory framework became more flexible and the word 'planning' was replaced in the Department's documents with 'facilitation' and 'coordination'. The desire to enhance the symbolic capital of the city through new flagship projects produced a heightened interest in its image and iconography (Kennett's background was in advertising). The government amended planning law, streamlining the planning approval process and introducing secrecy provisions similar to those in corporate law, which restricted the disclosure of information.

Barely six months after taking office, the Kennett government launched *Agenda 21*, a list of major civic projects for Melbourne, a number of which were to affect the river precinct. A new Exhibition Centre would replace the Melbourne Museum already under construction on the south bank, which in turn would be relocated north of downtown. A casino (initially conceived by

Figure 2.3
Riverscape from Princes Bridge
1983 (top) – 1999 (bottom)

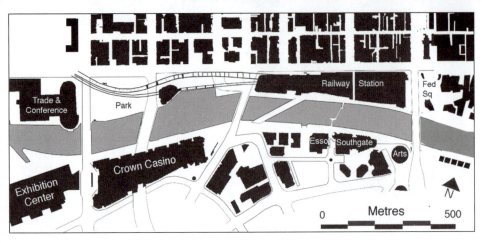

Figure 2.4
Riverscape map 2000

the former government) was to occupy the entire remaining section of Southbank – a half kilometre of river frontage previously designated for residential and retail use (Figure 2.4). The boulevard planned for the Sandridge railway alignment was quietly abandoned and the Casino constructed across it. This was the end of the civic vision of a waterfront anchored by the museum and arts centre and strongly connected to the bay. The new projects were intended to revitalise the city economy, by enhancing its ability to attract 'footloose' capital and tourism. Public debate on these projects was stifled by new and strict 'commercial confidentiality' agreements; notions of the 'public interest' were simply proclaimed and advertised rather than constructed through debate. The *Agenda 21* document was peppered with the language of 'place-marketing', which in turn rested on the place-making of 'flagship projects', seen as essential in a world of intercity economic competition.

In 1993, as part of a local government 'restructuring', local government democracy was suspended for three years.[5] During this period a manifesto for the emerging entrepreneurial city was released entitled *Creating Prosperity*. While the glossy presentation and promotional hyperbole were new, the message was broadly similar: repositioning the city in the national and international economy, with a focus on the river as a landscape designed to capture both the flows of desire and of global capital:

> The Yarra River corridor will be opened up to become the heart of City life. Globally attractive cultural, entertainment, commercial, exhibition and sporting facilities will

develop along the river banks … International companies will be encouraged to view the City as the best headquarters location in Australia … Organisers of international conventions, festivals, exhibitions and trade shows will think first of Melbourne when planning such events.[6]

Melbourne was again being re-imagined and re-imaged to take its place in the global economy. But the tactics and visions of the new government were different. *Creating Prosperity* was prepared without input from community groups and consultation was seen as an obstruction. While the image of the successful part of the south bank was promoted as evidence of the 'city on the river', the vision for the western precinct of the river was to be even more spectacular. The economic and political motives were not very different from what they had been under the former government. Both regimes were eager to attract new investment in the built environment and to demonstrate a certain 'flexibility' in doing so. One crucial difference lay in the method of financing projects. The new government fast-tracked the casino project, enlarged its size, granted it a monopoly and waterfront development rights for a license fee of $250 million and projected annual taxes of $50 million. This was the pot of gold that would fund both the new Exhibition Centre (on the Museum site) and the part of the new Museum (on a new site). The Melbourne Exhibition Centre opened in 1996 and was followed a year later by the Casino across the street. The Casino lined nearly half a kilometre of waterfront with a row of pillars exploding a series of huge fireballs on the hour. The riverscape in front of the Casino was widened to re-establish the original ship turning circle, cleaned up and eventually lined with public artworks and an aquarium.

The political credibility of this government was buoyed by the contrast between the new city of desire, and the more sedate, conservative past. When alarm bells rang about the social damage of gambling, and about state reliance on such a tax base, many people would point to the seductive riverscape and say: 'You have to admit, they get things done!' The new urban spectacle became a legitimating image in a newly seductive city. Yet for all the apparent success in getting Melbourne 'on the move' the Liberal government was narrowly defeated in elections in late 1999. The backlash came primarily from voters in suburban and regional Victoria – those out of sight of the new urban spectacle who felt abandoned by the privileging of the central city over suburbs and regions, of image over infrastructure, of global over local, and private over public.

The specific precincts and projects that comprise this urban waterfront will be explored in more detail in chapter 3. There are also three further threads of this riverscape narrative that will be articulated through following chapters. Chapter 4, 'Appropriations', explores everyday life on the south bank promenade where the contradictions of public/private space and the new urban spectacle come into play. What may appear to be a largely privatised and depoliticised space has also become a new focus of urban politics. Chapter 5, 'Urban Living', explores housing developments in the south bank hinterland, an infusion of life and capital that came much later than intended and in far greater doses. Initially resisted by developers, once the waterfront came alive, the housing followed: initially mid-market and low rise in the early 1990s, becoming up-market and high-rise from the mid-1990s as social housing agendas completely vanished. This residential resurgence has helped to turn around a century of suburban dominance in the residential property market. However, by the time this housing investment came on line, planning and urban design controls for the south bank hinterland area had been largely abandoned.

Chapter six, 'Federation', will critique the final thread of riverscape development along the northern bank of the river east of Princes Bridge encompassing Federation Square and the new Birrarung Marr park. These publicly funded and controlled projects comprise the largest additions to public space in Melbourne for many generations. Federation Square was conceived to reconnect the city grid to the river, bridging the railway lines and creating a genuinely new public space as a focus for politics, arts and civic life. In design and public interest terms, these final projects are perhaps the finest of the riverscape projects. Yet without the significant turnaround in state finances linked to the earlier projects, would these projects even exist? The riverscape projects are all the product of contradictions; an industrial landscape becomes a complex post-industrial landscape of profit and pleasure where public and private interests, global and local forces, intersect in a complex and contradictory manner. The following chapters will trace these projects in greater detail.

RIVERSCAPES II – PRECINCTS AND PROJECTS

EASTERN PRECINCT

The first phase of the Southbank redevelopment comprised a 500-metre stretch of river frontage adjacent to the Arts Centre, where about eight hectares of land was consolidated out of a number of smaller sites during the mid-1980s and put to tender in two large development parcels. The urban design framework was to enforce a four-storey urban wall set back 15 metres from the water with a public promenade, stepping up to the south. The new development was to be a mix of residential, commercial and retail uses with a minimum of 20 per cent residential use (Figure 3.1). To ensure an active edge on the river a minimum of 50 per cent of the ground floor on the waterfront was to be retail. This phase began with the design and construction of public promenades on both sides of the river, connected by a new pedestrian bridge (Figure 3.2). The pedestrian bridge was designed to generate direct access to both the city and railway station on the north, connecting to Southbank at the junction of the two new development sites. This was a smart move that added considerable value to each of these sites. The cost of the bridge and promenade was partially funded by each of the developers.

Bridge and Promenade

Both the bridge and public promenade were constructed in advance of the private development and completed in 1989. The pedestrian bridge was a fine piece of urban design (by Cocks Carmichael Whitford), conceived with a small island and a pier breaking the journey across the river into three parts. From the bridge one can descend on to a tiny sliver-shaped island with allusions to a rowing shell or a fragment of the south bank. The island is close to the water, below flood level with a sense of the sublime. The bridge decking above is lightweight with gaps through which the river is seen; as one of the architects put it: 'We think of it as a way of slowing people down so that they experience the river more as they go through ... You really feel you're on the water, you're at risk ... As kids we love to run out over water, over planks on a little stream. This is a vast plank, an adventure'.[1] The island contains a large wall that temporarily blocks the view of the city as one crosses the bridge, diverting attention to the river, playing with the dialectics of city and river, of nature and culture.

The promenade that lines this eastern precinct of Southbank (by architects Denton Corker Marshall) is a robust bluestone water's edge which provides paths on two levels – a lower level to give access to the water and an upper level for the main development protected from floods. This is also a fine design that provides generous public spaces on both levels. However, the design was compromised to some degree by being subject to the whims of the developers for the first of the private projects known as Riverside Quay, which formed the western section of this precinct.[2]

Riverside Quay

Riverside Quay was initially conceived as a cluster of buildings organised around a cul-de-sac canal cutting about 100 metres into the site to produce additional water frontage (Figure 3.1). We see here the seeds of a problem that will become all too common: after having ignored the riverfront for nearly a century, the first impulse was to try to manufacture more of it. This plan, based on global formulae for canal developments, was later reduced to a water feature and finally abandoned. The mindset of the development industry was that precinct sizes must be large enough to control the urban design and then draw that waterfront amenity back into the site. The opportunity that was missed here was to slice the site into a larger number of parcels and to form a stronger urban wall; this would in turn reinforce the river's edge with a greater diversity of architectural expression. While the developers had

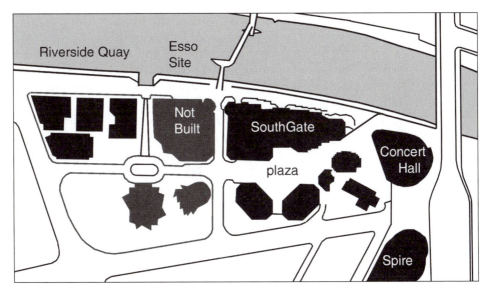

Figure 3.1
Eastern precinct proposal, 1985
(*Based on an illustration in* Architect, *January, 1993*)

Figure 3.2
Pedestrian bridge
(*Architects: Cocks Carmichael Whitford*)

(reluctantly) contributed to the cost of the pedestrian bridge and promenade, which quite clearly added value to their site, the canal concept was driven by the imperative to add value to the rear of the site. The legacy of this aborted plan is a large gap in the lower promenade that now houses a rather mediocre artwork and collects litter.

The canal concept was abandoned largely because it relied on the redevelopment of the whole precinct, the size of which was too large for the available investment. The precinct size was based on market analysis, but the real market turned out to be geared to smaller lots. The result was that the site consolidation undertaken by the state facilitated a new private subdivision as the land was re-parcelled to be sold for later projects.

The first cluster of three buildings on this site were completed in 1989 and the results were not good in either urban or architectural terms. These rather dark and icy glass boxes lining the riverfront promenade were described by Dimity Reed as 'designer funeral parlours' (Figure 3.3).[3] The canal formula was replaced by the office park; corporate space was advertised with the image of a managing director in swimming gear about to take advantage of the cheaper office space by crossing the river. The development strategy was reduced to an unimaginative attempt to siphon office development from the central city. The urban controls that required active ground floor frontages were also clearly not working; many ground floor tenancies became showrooms or remained vacant for years and some cafes that did appear were closed on weekends. A part of the problem here lay in the fact that the Sandridge rail bridge sliced across the river at an oblique angle right in front of this site, obscuring views across the river at ground level.

SouthGate

The SouthGate proposal on the eastern precinct of this first phase of Southbank was finalised in 1987 after four years of negotiation.[4] The proposal was for a mixed-use development with a retail waterfront, two office towers of twenty-five and eighteen storeys, some housing and a hotel. This development also seemed to stutter along in the early years. Within a year of the agreement the developers wanted to renegotiate the deal, cancel the hotel, increase the height of the towers and reduce the residential component. There was no clause in the agreement requiring completion of the project and by 1988 it was being labelled, 'one of the government's greatest planning embarrassments'.[5] The deal was renegotiated

Figure 3.3
Riverside Quay and Sandridge Bridge

with height limits increased to twenty-nine storeys and residential requirements eased. Here we see a strategy whereby the political and financial fluidity of the development process was used to generate flexibility in the planning process – lock in the political commitment then renegotiate under the threat of collapse. The media were eager participants in this process since stories about the inflexibility or ineptness of government have a ready market. The government in this case held reasonably firm; the substantial public infrastructure had already massively increased the value of the land.[6]

The SouthGate complex opened in September 1992, as part of the Melbourne Arts Festival, with a display that included the figure of a phoenix in the sky representing the new riverscape rising from the ashes of the old. A temporary artwork adorned the pedestrian bridge, 'Running Girl' by Robin Best was a flashing neon sculpture of a female jogger running across the arc of the pedestrian bridge. This was a fine piece of work bringing together elements of local tradition and changing values. It alluded to Melbourne's premier heritage advertising sign for 'skipping girl' vinegar, along with the idea of yuppies jogging across the river. It captured the dynamism of the new development with allusions to

Muybridge photographs and Duchamp's fractured gaze of the 'nude descending a staircase'. The work was designed to run from Southbank to the city, but was reversed at the instigation of SouthGate management: all movement was to flow towards the new waterfront.

SouthGate was greeted with popular acclaim coupled with a mixed critical reception. Norman Day described the building as: 'A banal palette of dung brown stone and funeral windows'.[7] The building indeed had more than a whiff of the suburban mall coupled with a fetish for replicating Melbourne's bluestone traditions. However, to some degree this critique missed the point; this was not so much a building to look at as a place to inhabit and from which to view the city and riverscape. My own line at the time was that the best place to see SouthGate was from the cafes looking north.[8] This was the most dramatic new public place created in Melbourne in a long time. The potency came not from the architecture, but from the way in which it transformed the image of the city and river. It had long been Planning Minister Walker's view that while good architecture cannot be legislated, good urban design can ameliorate the effects of mediocre architecture, and this was powerful evidence. The north-facing bank trapped the winter sunshine as the river became a stage with the city skyline as backdrop. The high design standards of the public promenade and pedestrian bridge helped to redeem the architecture and the public and private contributions meshed reasonably well. Within a few years SouthGate had become a major new focus for the city, identified in one government document as the 100 per cent location with the highest restaurant rental value in the city. Opened on the eve of the demise of the Labor government, the Southbank precinct was certainly their most important urban design achievement. Its most significant long-term value lay in the way it changed the public imagination. If this was possible in ten years, then what else could be possible?

Such a positive view, however, must be tempered by the realisation that much more was possible. With all its obvious benefits for the city, SouthGate can be construed as an up-market shopping mall with added restaurants. Like the shop frontages inside a mall, the facade is arbitrarily stepped to generate an impression of variety and vitality. And as in a shopping mall, the mix of tenancies is tightly controlled by centre management. A clue to the commercial strategy lies in the name – the design is conceived as a 'gateway' via the galleria to the private shopping mall behind. The strategy was to use the river as a people generator, an 'adjacent

Figure 3.4
SouthGate project 1992
(*Architects: Buchan Group*)

attraction'. Once through the 'gate' we have shops, a hotel and hectares of towering office space surrounding a slickly designed and windblown corporate plaza (since redeveloped). The city did not need another wind-swept plaza and the corporate fetish for the tower typology should never have been permitted in this precinct. The height limits had initially been established to avoid overpowering the adjacent Arts Centre spire, a primary public symbol and icon of the city that appears widely on postcards and television broadcasts. Its prominence has been seriously diminished by the towers, which are corporate flagships for IBM and the local Murdoch newspaper, the *Herald Sun*. In the end the problem was partially addressed in the 1990s when the spire was reconstructed and raised with public funds. The damage, however, was largely caused by the decision to allow the corporate tower building type to leap the river. The towers were clearly a key economic driver enabling the deal to be sealed, but the subsequent economic success suggests that development could have been achieved without them.

There is also a serious lack of functional integration between SouthGate and the Arts Centre. The synergies between the two precincts were always a key part of the strategy, yet here the public and private interests were in conflict. The public interest called for a continuous public promenade from the waterfront to St Kilda Road and the Arts Centre, yet the developers wanted this connection filtered through the shopping mall to stimulate impulse consumption. The rather convoluted compromise is that the Concert Hall terrace connects directly to the mall while the public connection is threaded through a large dark and often empty undercroft. Such critiques are never simple, however, and this undercroft with its buskers and Sunday markets will be redeemed somewhat in the following chapter. The lost opportunity here was to step up from the river to bridge the busy City Road, opening the river to flows of pedestrians, adding value to the land to the south and connecting directly to the Arts Centre.

Southgate was also engaged in the production of new forms of subjectivity and identity. In the early years of its life a network of speakers continuously broadcast an artificial soundscape of birds, people and running water. The speakers were camouflaged within both the SouthGate building and the design of the public promenade such that it was often impossible to distinguish the real people, birds and water from the virtual. 'Applause' would cause heads to turn, seeking a view of the spectacle; finding only other gazes seeking the fictional 'event'. The many small camouflaged speakers were mixed with security cameras with a reverse function – transmitting real events back to centre management. One day I saw a film being shot near the main stairs of the galleria – a 'director' with an 'accent' in an 'argument' with a glamorous 'star'. The 'film shoot' was, of course, the performance, the signifier that marked this as a site of exotic consumption. Street theatre was reframed as everyday life that in turn becomes theatre. Inside the mall people lined up to enter a Virtual Reality machine, but it was hard to determine where the entrance lay. While the enjoyment of this spectacle may be genuine, it has an insidious quality to it. The new surrogate city offers a manufactured encounter with diversity and difference. The waterfront spectacle is tightly controlled by SouthGate management who treat the public promenade as private property. On at least one occasion management attempted to prevent photography on the public waterfront, saying: 'We don't want SouthGate to appear in anything that's not in our best interests'.[9] SouthGate is an excursion into an ambiguous liminal zone between private and public, where commerce is disguised as culture. Like the shopping mall it attempts a marriage of convenience between the public interest and private control.

In overall terms, however, the SouthGate project must be deemed a success – if I spend more words on criticism than on praise, it is because the benefits are clear and the problems demand elaboration. The enjoyment of the urban river as a place is rendered problematic by the fusions of commerce/culture and surrogate/real. This was the first example in Melbourne of this kind of overdetermined and thoroughly saturated form of urban spectacle in public space. Its character has changed over the decade since its completion, the soundscape and the choreographed street theatre have faded and the place becomes more authentic with time.

Esso

The completion of the SouthGate and Riverside Quay projects left a gap of about 100 metres in the river frontage between the two projects, intended as the second phase of Riverside Quay. However, when the cul-de-sac canal was abandoned the remaining riverside site was sold to the Exxon corporation who proceeded to develop it as a corporate flagship building for the local Esso brand. Esso's primary interest was in the visibility of the site and the corporation immediately began negotiating to have the 'active edge' requirements watered down. In 1991 Esso was informed by a senior planning officer that although its proposal did not comply with this law, it could be reinterpreted: 'Interest to the public may not necessarily mean access by the public. A creative design solution is called for ...'.[10] Here the 'public interest' was being redefined in terms of the capacity to 'interest' the 'public' in a spectacle that one views without access or engagement. An 'active edge' was being redefined as one which people walk past rather than a space of social activity. Design 'creativity' was to be deployed as the means to overcome urban design controls. Encapsulated in a few words here we can see a broader reduction of 'place' to 'text', and the new alliance of aesthetics and politics. This advice indicates a growing alignment between state bureaucracy and development interests. While no agreement was reached with Esso before the change of government in 1992, the winds of change were in the air.

When the new government took power in late 1992, promising a new flexibility in planning matters, this site was a highly visible chance to demonstrate the new regime. The Esso project was approved in 1993 as a fourteen-storey office tower with a large 'greenhouse/atrium' occupying most of the river frontage, floodlit at night and housing 'endangered species'. It was fronted by a corporate landscape designed with native grasses and sealed off from public access by a water feature that operated as a 'moat'. There was no public access to the river frontage of the building, its greenhouse or landscaping. This was the 'creative solution' called for: 'interest to the public' rather than 'access by the public'. It was a travesty of the larger Southbank vision that turned this key piece of riverfront into a billboard site with 100 per cent office use and 0 per cent active frontage. The design must be understood as a form of advertising discourse. The Exxon Valdez oil spill three years earlier caused massive damage, not only to the Alaskan environment but also to the Exxon/Esso corporate image. Here on Southbank the damage continued as, desperate for some 'green' credentials, the building became advertising for the new green corporate image. The building was to be pure spectacle, but it could not function as spectacle without the passing flow of pedestrians; in this sense the project is parasitic upon the larger urban strategy and the significant public investment that made it possible. This project is so bad it is almost redeemed by its transparent awfulness: the permanent security guards required to keep people out, the unused native garden and greenhouse, and the silver and black aesthetic that some would liken to an oil stain on the river.[11]

Sandridge Bridge

The Sandridge rail bridge has long been a derelict horizontal shaft of steel covered with advertising and blocking views across the river for about 200 metres in front of Riverside Quay (Figure 3.3). Although not a pretty site, the bridge is a remnant of the first rail line from the city to the bay with high heritage value; it was classified by the National Trust in 1985 just as Riverside Quay was being designed. The highly oblique angle at which the bridge crosses the river is the source of both its primary heritage value and the damage caused by the blockage of the view. The trajectory of the bridge is the only remnant of this primary line of communication between Port Melbourne and the city grid, a line of sight later blocked by Crown Casino. The oblique angle is also the source of considerable aesthetic value – a disjunctive urban element with the potential to enliven the river because it is of a different spatial order. The bridge is a fine example of the ways in which the dialectics of history produce certain clashes of spatial order: the rigid straightness of the railway against the fluid order of the landscape. The spectacle of rowing shells slicing through the narrow and oblique rows of columns has long been one of the delights of this riverscape.

There have been a number of moves to demolish the bridge and many ideas for redeveloping it: a giant Ferris wheel, shops, apartments, helipad, sculpture garden, tramway, artworks, cafes, walk-through aviary and transport museum. The best suggestion has been to demolish the bulky superstructure leaving only the neo-classical steel columns capped with a new lightweight deck. This would serve as a pedestrian link and produce substantial new public space above the water for a multiplicity of public activities, events and temporary structures. The current plan is close to this, but tragically leaves the bulky superstructure in place. There is little about the superstructure that is beautiful; it has not been covered in advertising for nothing. The bridge is the most important piece of urban heritage on the river, but it is the memory of the alignment of the city to the port that needs to be preserved rather than the obstructive urban object. The larger tragedy of the bridge is that the failure to rethink its role from the beginning has contributed to the failure of the Riverside Quay project and inhibited development of the north bank. Public investment at this stage simply adds a windfall capital gain to the Riverside Quay project. The redevelopment of the bridge is now linked to the development of Queensbridge Square, a rather late attempt to integrate the eastern and western precincts that remain under construction.

WESTERN PRECINCT

Redevelopment of the riverscape west of the city grid began in the late 1970s with the construction of the publicly funded World Trade Centre on the north bank (Figure 2.4). This is but one of many such projects spawned globally at that time in the desire to attract global capital. It was an economic, architectural and urban design failure from the start, closing public access to the river and figuring prominently on every list of Melbourne's 'white elephants' and ugliest buildings. It was extended in the mid-1980s to encompass the World Congress Centre and attached hotel. This was marginally better architecture, but even worse in urban design terms since the twelve-storey hotel projects right over the river alignment and casts the river into shade. There had long been a small pier projecting into the river at this point that was used by developers as the excuse to claim construction rights above the water. The driving force was clearly the desire for a river view from the hotel rooms, reflected in the hotel name (at that time) 'Eden *on* Yarra'. The effect, of course, is that the public view of the river is now dominated by the hotel, a classic case of private desires destroying public ones.

Across the river to the south had long been a somewhat derelict and low-key mix of industrial and maritime uses. This included the dock of the Polly Woodside – an antique sailing vessel that had become a tourist and recreation site. In 1988 it was first announced that the Melbourne Museum would be moved from the central city to this site. The appointment of Daryl Jackson as architect was the subject of some criticism since he was the former architectural partner of Minister Walker. There was also criticism over the issue of displacing the museum from the central city grid.[12] There was a case for keeping the Museum in the central city, but there were also good reasons for the new site: to anchor the western precinct of the riverscape and to add size and flexibility to the museum. With the public purse in a very poor state, only the first stage of funding was in place when construction began. By the time of the change of government in late 1992, the building was a four-storey structure with $24 million already spent (Figure 3.5 top). Within six months the decision was made to abandon construction in favour of an exhibition centre and move the museum to a site in Carlton, also outside the city grid. This decision was the first indication of a major turnaround in the riverscape strategy. The new strategy was to link with the trade and congress centre across the river and create a zone of global finance; a synergy that would extend to the Casino under construction next door. Thus the museum as a major people-attractor was replaced by exhibitions; culture by commerce. These projects were to bring together three clusters of facilities: first, the convention halls, auditoria and hotel of the convention centre; second, the exhibition halls, auditoria and meeting facilities of the exhibition centre; and finally, the riverfront restaurants, ball-rooms, hotels and entertainment facilities of the casino complex. This constellation of facilities was also linked into a larger network of new global events and facilities, including the new and adjacent CityLink freeway to the airport and the Formula 1 race-track at Albert Park about two kilometres to the south.

Exhibition Centre

The Melbourne Exhibition Centre, completed in 1996 to a design by Denton Corker Marshall, is an extruded 'shed' with a curvi-linear roof nearly half a kilometre long. The size was designed to outstrip the capacity of regional competitors for global exhibitions (especially Sydney's Darling Harbour) – the exhibition hall is the largest in the Asia Pacific. The four-storey concrete structure of the partially completed museum was adapted and swallowed to become the entry and conference facility of the centre; supplemented with a large diagonal blade that projects across the river towards the city (Figures 3.5 bottom, 3.6). This is a fine design that immediately captured the spirit of the times and the public imagination; it received an award from the Institute of Architects for the best new building in Australia in 1996.[13] The building was also seen from the beginning as a political symbol, decorated with posters of the Premier and given the popular name of 'Jeff's Shed'.

The entry canopy operates as a potent political image, a salute to a new order. As a government brochure put it at the time the blade symbolises 'the forward looking stance of a government that means business',[14] reflecting the state slogan: 'on the move'. Like a plane taking off, like rising profits, like a 'can-do' government, this is the dynamic assertive image of a city *'on the move'*. The blade suggests some powerful antecedents, including the revolutionary traditions of Russian constructivism and Italian futurism. Italy of the 1930s shared both a state slogan (*Italy On the Move*) and an architecture that doubles as state propaganda.[15] Denton Corker Marshall received a number of commissions from this government that John Denton has described as a 'benevolent dictatorship'.[16] The potency of the work stems from the skilful exploitation of the 'can-do' spirit of the mid-1990s, fuelled by a widespread desire for change and an aestheticisation of politics. The Exhibition Centre was produced in an era of democratic submission to authoritarian order. The blade signifies and celebrates this 'line of flight', this new 'becoming' of the corporate state, as it legitimates and stabilises it. According to architectural office gossip the Exhibition Centre blade was originally designed to slant in two directions, a 'salute' with a certain 'slippage'. But this less stable image, perhaps more 'bolshevic' than 'futurist', was 'straightened out' by the client Minister. The blade also gains some of its aesthetic impact from the dialectic image it produces in conjunction with the former museum structure. The new building effectively signifies the turn of political history – the new authority consuming the old; commerce consuming culture; the global consuming the local. The image is a form of symbolic capital that condensed the new forces for change into a logo or brand image for the city. The museum was removed from this site in part because it was initiated by the previous government and could not be used to legitimate the new one. But the museum was also displaced because it has less spin-off value for a new constellation of global projects – exhibition centre, convention centre and casino, all designed to attract the global 'high-rollers'.

Figure 3.5
Museum (1992 top) becomes Exhibition Centre (1996 bottom)
(*Architects: Daryl Jackson associates and Denton Corker Marshall*)

The World Congress Centre and Melbourne Exhibition Centre are now advertised to the global market as a single complex – the Melbourne Exhibition and Convention Centre, 'a spectacular location on both sides of Melbourne's Yarra River ... where Australia meets the world'.[17] Connecting them is a new foot-bridge; funded by the state in 1998 this bridge makes an interesting contrast with the first pedestrian bridge almost a decade earlier. Unlike the first, it does not generate pedestrian permeability; it is directly alongside the Spencer Street bridge with its existing footpaths. The primary idea was to provide a weather protected and symbolically valorised connection from convention to exhibition centre. It also has the effect of separating the new bridge from the old, framed as a new global space for the global flows of people, money and ideas. The design, by Peter Elliott, is a fine piece of work with a roof canopy formed from cantilevered steel spikes and glass sheet (Figure 3.6). It turns away from the rather dour existing bridge and provides a choice of two new pathways for windy and calm weather separated by a glass wall. In contrast to the earlier pedestrian bridge, which exposed its users to the river and the city, this is a bridge designed to protect its users from the elements. It has an exquisite formal quality but it is less urban; it is the product of a different set of forces – global rather than local, economic rather than social.

Figure 3.6
Exhibition Centre and Pedestrian Bridge
(*Bridge architect: Peter Eliott*)

CROWN CASINO

The first proposal for a casino on the south bank of the river was put to the long-serving Liberal government in 1979 by a major hotel chain. This vision, in the form of a giant glass pyramid on the riverbank, was strongly supported by the Liberal Tourism Minister of the time, a young Jeffrey Kennett. Gambling in Victoria had long been under tight control, casinos were prohibited and the proposal was rejected. In 1982 the new Labor Government held an inquiry on the issue and concluded that the dangers of corruption and social damage were too great. However, it was clear that the state was losing tourism, jobs and investment to other states because of this stance. In 1989, with the state economy in decline, the decision was reversed and a major casino was proposed. Many sites were touted but none was chosen; the Yarra bank area of Southbank was planned for mixed use and was not on the list. While the casino project had bipartisan political support, the new government after 1992 had few qualms about the social impact – the Casino was to be the lynchpin of economic recovery. The choice of site was a key to this strategy and the Yarra bank site on the western half of the riverscape was chosen. This was not an easy site for such a large project: split into two by the King Street bridge and flyover, confined to the south by the proposed boulevard (see Figures 2.2 and 2.4). In order to make the site large enough for the Casino, the boulevard plan was abandoned to create a single precinct of 5.5 hectares and 450 metres of waterfront. Tenders were called in 1993 and the shortlist was reduced to two: Pacific and Crown.[18] Final bids were prepared under tight secrecy with bidders threatened with disqualification if they leaked information. The confidentiality applied to both the financial details and the urban design; no project with such a scale or impact on the city had ever been approved without public debate and there was substantial public outcry.[19] The Premier's answer was that this was an issue of 'probity' – the tender process was conducted by the Casino Authority with all planning and urban design issues for the project to be judged by an expert Design Panel.[20]

Crown Casino was announced as the winning bid in September 1993. The proposal was for $800 million of total investment; a casino of 200 tables coupled with a 25-storey hotel; ancillary features such as rooftop gardens, showroom, ballroom, glass enclosed Ferris wheel and roller coaster; a cluster of cinemas; and an 'Australian Experience' theme park (Figure 3.7 top).

The Design Panel strongly affirmed the superiority of the Crown design; however, there was little public debate since the losing vision was not released and there were no detailed plans of the proposal. This bidding process later erupted into a scandal when it became apparent that some information did leak.[21] Two days after final bids were submitted, the decision was delayed and bidders were given two weeks to revise their bids. A sub-committee of Cabinet had been provided information on the competing bids and it is widely believed that the Crown consortium (with strong connections to the Liberal Party) raised its bid during this period to match that of Pacific. The Labor Prime Minister (Keating) used parliamentary privilege to suggest that the process was corrupt; however, a later inquiry found insufficient evidence. The implication of this for design was that once Crown matched the Pacific/Leighton bid in financial terms, the decision was then deferred to the Design Panel and made on design criteria.

The architects for the Crown project comprised three firms in collaboration.[22] The major urban design problem facing the architects was that of how to make a 5.5 hectare building housing an entirely internal casino appear like something better than a blank box. The answer was to line the riverfront with restaurants, cafes and shops with grand casino entries to the west and east (down-market and up-market respectively). Almost the entire southern edge on Whiteman Street was reduced to service frontage. The building also became highly impermeable and blocked off all through access from the south, compromising future hinterland development. However, the design did have its champions. Dimity Reed suggested that it: 'might just do for Melbourne what the Opera House did for Sydney ... In this project we have an outstanding piece of urban design and placemaking ...'.[23] She suggested that the rooftop gardens would be a marvellous addition to Melbourne's public space and that the project would be highly permeable: '... people will be able to walk through the project at any number of points and go straight to the river'. This turned out to be complete nonsense, but it was difficult to dispute since no detailed plans were available. The losing design by the Pacific Leighton consortium was not released to the public at the time but is now available (Figure 3.7 bottom).[24] Given that the final design of the Casino does not resemble either of the bids, it is perhaps a moot point to debate their merits. However, the alternative was a more permeable structure that did not block the full length of the river and left more opportunities for hinterland development.

Figure 3.7
Crown Casino tender designs 1993: Crown (top) and Pacific/Leighton (bottom)
(*Sources: Crown – Agenda 21 (1) December 1993 (Vic. Gov. publication);*
Pacific/Leighton – Courtesy Cox Sanderson Ness. Architects: Daryl Jackson
Assoc., Bates Smart & Perrott Lyon Mathiesson; Pacific/Leighton – Cox
Sanderson Ness)

The difficulties for the architects were unprecedented and profound. All architects working on the project were required to relocate to the Crown headquarters building adjacent to the site where all drawings were held and all architects signed confidentiality agreements. Many were disturbed that such a major urban development should be so secret and the proposals often leaked. However, the design changed so much and so regularly that leaks were rarely accurate for more than a month. There was constant interference from Crown CEO, Lloyd Williams, who insisted on bringing in additional architects and interior designers with new ideas to be incorporated during construction.[25] When the Exhibition Centre building was completed across the street in 1996 he was said to have been worried that it would upstage the western end of the Casino that was already under construction. This facade was then partially demolished and redesigned.

The program for the building continually expanded throughout construction as the design that had won the tender became almost unrecognisable. Within six months of the tender came a proposal to add twelve storeys to the hotel tower. This was sent to the Design Panel of the Casino Authority, who initially rejected it on environment and planning grounds. In June 1994 Crown submitted new plans with more entertainment, car park, tennis courts and an artificial beach – the Ferris wheel and much of the roof garden was scrapped.[26] Approval was given for this scheme, yet within six months yet another design was approved with a thirty-eight-storey hotel. The development was now 50 per cent larger than the original bid and Crown began buying up all the property it could to the south of the site to cope with the ever-expanding complex. In October 1995 the size of the gaming floor was almost doubled, making it the second-largest casino in the world. The project gained approval for an additional car park, training facilities and a second hotel across Whiteman Street to the south. In July 1996 an 1800-seat theatre was added; the number of cinemas was doubled; and the retail, cafe and nightclub space was vastly expanded. By the time of its final completion in March 1997 the casino complex had expanded from 200 000 to 500 000 square metres; from 3000 to 5400 parking spaces; and from twenty-five to forty-three storeys. The site expanded from 5.5 to over 8 hectares and the cost increased from $800 million to $2 billion. All of this meant that the urban design grounds upon which the tender decision had been made were entirely obsolete. Many of the changes were sent back to the Design Panel for approval, but such advice was kept secret and it remains unclear to what degree the final design was approved by the Panel or the Minister. Paradoxically, the Casino was later faced with penalties when the second hotel and theatre were not built as agreed. In a sense there could be no public debate until the Casino was complete because the plans remained fluid throughout construction.

Most of this expansion was fuelled by the economic success of the temporary casino, which had opened in June 1994 (in the disused World Trade Centre building). Since this casino did not have a global market, it became clear that the local market had been underestimated, as crowds flocked from the poorer parts of the city to try their luck. Alarm bells rang in the broader community – this was no longer just a casino with ancillary functions, but an entire urban precinct that threatened the vitality and viability of other parts of the city. It was clear that the Casino was siphoning spending and investment from one part of the city to another. Research showed that low-income people were the most frequent visitors to the Casino. Abandoned children were occasionally rescued from the car park and there was rising evidence of gambling-related crime, domestic violence, poverty and suicide.[27] It seemed to many that the state had entered into partnership with the Casino as a revenue source to such a degree as to compromise responsibility for the public interest.

One of the most tragic urban aspects of the project is the degree to which it is oriented to private rather than public transport. The building sits on a vast raft of underground car park supplemented by a five-storey high parking structure to the south. The King Street bridge and flyover was utilised as an opportunity to catch the passing traffic with lanes in each direction turned into car park entries. A large car park entrance appeared in the centre of Southbank Boulevard and it became apparent that public land underneath Queensbridge Square had become a private car park. The Casino entrance is less than 500 metres from the Flinders Street Station and the Sandridge Bridge in direct alignment could have made a fine pedestrian connection. The lost opportunity here was to use the Casino to leverage private funds for the redevelopment of both the bridge and Queensbridge Square. Instead, the Casino was conceived as car-based, to be entered via the vast car park, filtered through the shopping mall.

The Casino opened in May 1997 in a building quite unlike the approved design (Figure 3.8). The opening party was a night of nights for the movers and shakers of the new Melbourne as they alighted from their limousines to enter the black marble foyer. The spirit of excess was marvellously mocked by actor Rachel Griffith

Figure 3.8
Crown Casino as completed, 1999

who arrived topless and was hustled away by security. There was a broad consensus that the Casino was a bit crass, a view that even extended to the Planning Minister: 'It's a casino ... and I think one should make allowances. It's not a good-taste zone, and I am not the Minister for Good Taste.' With a passion for stirring and a confused sense of history he added: 'Mussolini would have loved it'.[28] Architectural critics agreed that this was a poor result and even Dimity Reed, who had proclaimed the original design 'an outstanding piece of urban design and placemaking', now saw it as: 'just dead ordinary ... with every bit of 80s and 90s cliches tacked on to it'.[29] Neville Quarry saw it reflecting a rather fundamental immorality: '... if you think a brothel is immoral, it doesn't matter what its exterior packaging looks like'.[30] The cartoonist Michael Leunig put this morality argument succinctly:

> Bass Strait would be an ideal location for the casino; as deep as possible. A mature and healthy society does not ... entertain such crass and exclusive visions regarding the use of riverside land ... We've considerably abandoned ourselves to aesthetic, moral and economic rationalism and this will produce, I believe, a horrible city. The moral functioning of a society will determine its aesthetic form.[31]

There is, however, a critique which suggests that the designers took the building too seriously; that the architects have tried to temper the forces of excess, the flows of desire, the proliferation of imagery and superficial meaning. Architect Ian MacDougall suggested: 'It's not kitsch enough'.[32] Indeed, it would have been interesting to see an approach to the architecture that exposes and exploits rather than covers the crassness of its operations; this of course was the Griffith approach.

The Casino effected a transformation in urban discourse that was more than just a building on the waterfront. As part of the alliance between Crown and the state, direction signs to the Casino appeared on street signs at strategically located intersections and arteries around the city. The Casino was incorporated into the class of public destinations framed as public interest information. The larger city was thereby lined with these regular reminders to gamble and framed to make it clear that this was endorsed by the state. This discursive linkage of public and private interest was also apparent in the Crown logo – a figure of a 'crown' formed out of a series of white dots spraying upwards and outwards. At the micro-scale the image of splayed dots were like 'splayed' cards or the dots of the rolling dice. The image of the 'splash' evoked the idea of 'splashing out', an unleashing of energy in joyful climax in the free flow of desire – a new becoming. However, the logo also draws on associations with royalty, tradition, sovereignty and power in ways that help to stabilise this flow of desire and ground it in the state. The Crown logo joined the unleashing of desire to the legitimacy of state power, but the advertising also sought to ground its legitimacy in the local and the everyday – as one of the slogans put it, the Casino was 'as Melbourne as the MCG'. The Melbourne Cricket Ground has a long history as the site of the 1956 Olympic Games, international cricket and Australian football; it is the nation's premier sporting arena. With regular crowds of 90 000 people and a vibrant sense of place, the MCG is one of those rare and authentic public places where everyday desires are, within limit, unleashed. As the Casino's advertising director put it, the approach was 'to capture the "spirit of the MCG" and package it ...'.[33] The Casino was to be the 'biggest game in town' and one advertisement shows the stadium with its massive circular crowd morphing into a roulette wheel and then into the exploding crown logo.

At an urban design level, the row of exploding gas fireballs along the river echo the logo design, turning the waterfront into a giant billboard (Figure 3.9). The precedent set on Southbank by

Figure 3.9
Crown Casino publicity
(*Courtesy of Crown Entertainment Centre*)

the Esso building, using the public waterfront for its billboard
potential, was here taken to a new level. Thus the Casino formed
a representational package, a discursive formation that successfully captured the public imagination and generated a powerful
illusion that the Casino was in the public interest. Television
advertisements produced for the opening showed carnivalesque
figures leaping out of the Casino and dancing among the fireballs
along the waterfront. John Carroll wrote an interesting account of
this advertising and its constructions of desire in the city:

In his court jester costume, topped by signature red cap
with flapping tails and bells, he evokes all of circus clown,
Shakespearean fool, naughty sprite and devil. His face is a
mask, a wicked grin playful with deceit. He dances his
seductive temptation, open in his presentation, as if
saying: you know I am neither good nor nice. I am the end
of innocence. Follow me, throw off your drab everyday
self, take a risk. I offer adventure, transport into a different
world, one of excitement, energy, fancy dress, a new self
for a while – as in a masked ball. Be tempted, live your
life, for what have you to lose. Dare to follow me.[34]

This was the lure. Melburnians were offered a very different kind
of city – a city of carnival, risk and abandon, where old identities
could be discarded along with the planning codes and public
debate. The Casino was a place of escape – its five hectares of
gaming tables and machines were housed in a spaceless and timeless world – a dream world where the winning never stopped until
you ran out of money. And it is not surprising that this dream
appealed most to those whose everyday lives were already infused
with the desire for escape.

By 1998 the Casino license and taxes had funded over half a
billion dollars of major projects with more to follow. The Casino
and its tax base provided a kick-start for the new Exhibition
Centre and Melbourne Museum, as well as renovations to the
State Library, National Gallery and other highly visible projects.
These projects have all provided ongoing benefits to the economy,
the construction industry and the cultural life of the city. However,
it remains problematic to determine just where the public interest
lies since the kick-start was provided largely by a siphoning of
investment from the poorer parts of the city to the centre.

CHAPTER FOUR

APPROPRIATIONS

Kim Dovey and Quentin Stevens

The range of projects outlined in earlier chapters is linked by the kilometre-long stretch of Southbank promenade extending from the Arts Centre to the Exhibition Centre. This promenade has been designed as a postmodern riverscape of urban spectacle, where a spontaneous and playful urban life is simulated, choreographed and passively consumed. The transformation has succeeded in attracting high densities of people. Both the SouthGate and Crown Casino projects were launched with a spirit of festivity and carnival. They each created a waterfront lined with scheduled entertainment venues and saturated with choreographed street theatre, public artworks and illusory soundscapes, intended to attract a well-heeled clientele and to frame leisure within a context of consumption. The riverscape has been designed as a contrived form of permanent carnival, filled with representations of excess and release. Yet the practice of liberation is largely reduced to a spectacle that stimulates the senses of a passive body. The urban design serves an instrumental function: feeding the Dionysian desires that the city awakens, and channelling them into consumption and carefully managed forms of play. Yet this riverscape is in reality much more complex and interesting than such a view would suggest. These commodifications of place experience also have their paradoxes: they create conditions for spontaneous, unexpected and resistant activities. This chapter will explore this landscape of desire through a series of dialectic tensions and movements, where new forms of genuine urban life emerge in the form of play and politics. The new spectacle of global waterfront projects is at once superficial and ersatz, yet also becomes the site of authentic local practices. Southbank's success in stimulating desires also gives rise to the genuine abandon of the carnival. And, to the extent that the riverscape is a rule-bound interdictory landscape, it also produces a dialectic tension between authority and resistance. The urban riverscape is rendered more authentic by the ways in which the spontaneity of play and politics cuts through the pre-packaged spectacle.

WALKING THE WATERFRONT

To describe the everyday life of Southbank we will take a walk from east to west, which is roughly the order in which the riverbank was developed. We begin on Princes Bridge, adjacent to the Concert Hall, the building that provides the best evidence of the utter disdain with which the river was treated just 20 years ago. On the waterfront side of the hall are a loading bay and stage door facing on to a large, dark undercroft hard up against the river's edge. The task for the designers of the adjoining SouthGate project was to generate a pedestrian link between the busy arts precinct on St Kilda Road, with its four major theatres and art gallery, and the vitality of the new riverbank below. As outlined in the previous chapter, the primary connection was created with commercial imperatives in mind – to direct pedestrian traffic through the shopping mall. However, despite the attempted manipulation, the undercroft remains the most direct route between the arts precinct and the riverbank promenade.

Figure 4.1
Busking in the undercroft

This undercroft is a gloomy and cavernous space that opens to the river on one side through a row of low arches. It is quite literally a 'backstage' area housing the stage door and loading dock. At first glance it seems like a major missed opportunity and a possible crime trap. Yet the passage through this clumsy interstitial zone is generally more interesting than the terrace above (Figure 4.1). The undercroft has a dark and slightly menacing atmosphere, which lends it a touch of the sublime. It has a very long reverberation time, which attracts buskers (street performers), many of whom are talented music students from the nearby Victorian College of the Arts. A space of transition, it catches the passing leisure traffic moving between parkland, food and theatre. As one of the few large public spaces of the city that is protected from rain and summer heat, it is used on Sundays for a busy craft market. However, it was the initial failure of this building to address the river that allows such new opportunities to emerge. The undercroft provides relief from the staged and choreographed street life of the Arts Centre and SouthGate surrounding it, forming a crack in the riverscape spectacle.

As our walk proceeds from the undercroft towards SouthGate, the public space folds into the pseudo-public, and the gap available for temporary appropriations closes. Here we enter a zone of choreographed spectacle lined with public dining as outlined earlier. This is a voyeuristic zone that frames the seeing-and-being-seen activities of eating, shopping and promenading. While this is legally public space, it is fully controlled by SouthGate management; street theatre is staged on Sundays and busking is prohibited. The promenade here is on two levels with the less-trafficked lower level allowing for boat access and flooding; and the staged spectacle loosens as one approaches the water. The additional privacy of the lower level creates a zone for somewhat marginal activities flowing over from the throng above: teenagers kissing, smoking, playing and wrestling (Figure 4.2).

Figure 4.2
SouthGate promenade and undercroft

The pedestrian bridge nearby has been through several cycles of use during the first decade of its existence. The boat-shaped artificial island surrounding the base of one of the bridge's supports is both physically isolated and visually exposed. It has been subject to a good deal of graffiti over the years and its single tree has not exactly thrived. It has gained a more vibrant life as the home of the city's smallest cafe. This is the place where urban life comes closest to the water, and like the undercroft, it has a touch of risk about it. The bridge above is a site for a good deal of playful behaviour, from the harmless and incidental to the very risky. The flat upper surface of its structural steel arch frames the possibility that one might walk up and over it. This transgression was first suggested when the 'Running Girl' sculpture was mounted on the arch for the opening of SouthGate; the traces of use, frequently painted over, suggest it has been attempted many times. This exceedingly dangerous undertaking has now been made more difficult, with barriers at either end.

Esso Headquarters is located where the pedestrian bridge intersects with the Southbank promenade. It blots out this stretch of riverscape with a deadly dull security-controlled building, entirely bereft of public functions. Here, as in the undercroft, we see the paradox that poor quality urban design can nurture distinctive forms of urban life. The creation of a blank frontage at such a busy intersection of pathways renders the space in front of the Esso building useful and available for performances (Figure 4.3). A low flight of steps leading up to the blank facade provides an ideal stage that is continuously occupied on weekends by street performers, often pulling a larger crowd than that in front of SouthGate. Here there are no distractions, no compulsion to consume and the promenade has not been narrowed by alfresco dining. By refusing to contribute an active edge, Esso has relinquished control over the promenade; beyond the private guards defending the building there appears little control of the spectacle as this waterfront vacuum is filled with fire-eating, juggling, comedy and climbing through tennis racquets – anything that can pull a crowd. Gold and silver painted 'statues' line the walkway, which pavement artists cover with chalk. Performers and their audiences often block much of the promenade. Passers-by are confronted by the action; drawn in to see what's going on. Some get into the act, helping jugglers mount unicycles, tossing them knives and flaming torches. In the absence of carefully regulated zones and roles, the safe, pre-packaged routine gives way to unplanned, active and risky involvement.

Figure 4.3
Filling the Esso vacuum

Figure 4.4
'Flushing' at Queensbridge
Square, 1998

Over recent years, however, this 'smooth' space has become subject to stricter control as busking licences are required and the space has been mapped into a series of 'pavement art', 'circle act' and 'musical act' sites. While the zone is strictly policed ('real' buskers never stray into SouthGate), the locations of the specific 'act' sites are relatively fluid. This Southbank precinct is regarded as up-market – only buskers with a six-month track record of successful busking elsewhere in the city can be awarded permits for Southbank. Busking permits can be revoked if there are complaints from either the public or adjacent traders.[1] The pavement art has become a form of symbolic capital with its own spin-offs; local charities set up stalls nearby and the pavement art sites are occasionally appropriated for corporate logos.

This busking zone terminates at Queensbridge Square, a rather derelict open space between the eastern and western precincts (at the time of this study). In 1998 this became the site of a temporary sculpture by Israeli artist Avraham Eilat – a series of white ceramic toilet pedestals stacked vertically to form a glistening white column (Figure 4.4). This surreal and beautiful work, with allusions to Brancusi's 'endless column' and Duchamp's 'urinal' based on themes of 'flushing, fluidity and transformation', was wonderfully juxtaposed with the glistening casino across the street.[2] It was unfortunately removed after the exhibition period, yet it was this leftover crack in the larger plan, the unfinished quality and lack of amenity, which created the opportunity in the first place. Located near the pedestrian crossing it seemed precariously balanced, but was frequently climbed.

Beyond the Queensbridge intersection stretches 500 metres of riverbank promenade in front of the Casino and entertainment centre, the largest stretch of quasi-public space in the city. One side is lined by almost continuous restaurants and shops, with the row of towers, cascading water and exploding fireballs on the riverside. The landscape design here is a high-quality mix of concrete and grass, with steps and ramps to the water, generous seating and many changes of level. This is a landscape designed to encourage leisure and playful behaviour. One of the features is a fountain set flush into the pavement, which squirts upward unexpectedly at people walking across. These small fluid eruptions also reflect the form of the exploding fireballs and casino logo. While this is a somewhat formulaic design element, reproduced from such tourist attractions as CityWalk in Los Angeles, the wetness is real, and so is the delight experienced by those who engage with it. A crowd often gathers to observe the spectacle of the dancing jets. The combination of the fountain's unpredictability and the expectant audience also encourages un-programmed action: people often step out on to the stage and engage with the water. The otherwise passive consumers become actors as strangers encounter each other in informal games framed around the jumping jets. The fountain is not without its instrumental functions, framing the Casino as a place of fun and representing the games of chance inside. The carefully orchestrated risks of engagement with this landscape of play are an illustration to potential gamblers that taking chances can be both fun and safe.

While busking in front of the Casino is prohibited, the passing crowd and the surfeit of un-programmed open spaces adjoining the promenade here inevitably give rise to a variety of performances. On one rather featureless plaza, teenage cyclists undertake tricks directly in the line of sight of strolling customers. The Casino management has responded by plugging this gap with planters, which block the cyclists' run, and new sculptures, which recapture the tourist gaze for more profitable forms of escapism. Skateboarding is another unintended consequence of the sophisticated landscape treatment (Figure 4.5). The promenade's many ledges and edges lend themselves to the exploration of a wide range of skating moves. Anti-skating lugs have been fixed to many edges; this in turn heightens the challenge for the skaters, who then have to jump and weave to avoid the lugs. Attempts to deter skaters appear not only to have failed, but to have heightened the fun.

Figure 4.5
Skating the Casino waterfront

THREE DIALECTICS

These brief descriptions cut across the notion that the meanings and spatial practices of this riverscape are in any way fixed or singular. These practices can be framed as a series of dialectic movements within which the complex realities of urban life cut through this ersatz landscape of desire and consumption. These dialectics can be phrased as paradoxes: failure brings success; carnival cannot be contained; and control brings resistance.

Failure Brings Success

The first is that this urban spectacle is neither integrated nor totalising; there are cracks in the spatial field. This interpretation is linked to the work of de Certeau, who argues that the production of urban spectacle and an over-determined choreography of urban life produces a city with the qualities of a 'sieve', in that the attempt to contain meaning and action consistently 'leaks' through the cracks.[3] From such a view the global 'strategies' of dominant power can be infiltrated by the 'tactics' of difference. Both the semantic field and the functional layout of the riverscape have gaps and margins, where new meanings and practices can insert themselves. The transgressive and the truly unexpected remain possible. Setback requirements have produced a generous waterfront zone of publicly accessible, yet privately controlled space that is at times under-used – other uses and users fill the void. The Arts Centre undercroft and the Esso building both provide special kinds of public amenity that arise, paradoxically, from the very absence of a conscious design intent. In the case of the Esso building, perhaps the worst piece of formal urban design on the waterfront, the pursuit of one kind of spectacle (the billboard building) creates a vacuum that is then filled by another. The reduction of space to text renders it available for new forms of practice. The Casino's ongoing efforts to mend gaps in the spectacular facade show that the struggle between careful scenography and free public play continues to evolve.

In this context, poor quality urban design and dormant, under-programmed spaces have their role in framing authentic experiences of fantasy and release. They allow space for more marginal practices and identities to flourish. Primary attractions such as the Arts Centre and the Casino draw the necessary crowds of leisure-seekers along the path that leads past these unexpected distractions. A seamless landscape of spectacular consumption would lack much of the diversity and vitality that we find here. It would be easy to conclude that a bit of bad design may be a good thing, yet urban spaces such as the undercroft and the Esso building are regularly produced in other locations where they have no positive effects. The positive effect of poor urban design is a dialectic phenomenon that operates in reaction to an over-determined landscape.

Poor urban design seems to have a certain value in over-determined landscapes because it produces a certain 'looseness' and in the context of the 'tight' choreography of the spectacle new forms of urban life become possible. Pockets of emptiness in a landscape full of predetermined meanings and behaviours contribute to urban diversity. It is useful here to reflect upon the principles of urban diversity outlined by Jacobs four decades ago, particularly the need for the urban fabric to develop in a somewhat piecemeal manner at a relatively small grain size.[4] This ensures a mix of building age and type, a mix of rental rates and the integration of marginal (low-rent) activities. Here, in a quite different context, we see a parallel principle operating. In this regard there is a significant distinction between the eastern and western zones of the riverscape. While the Casino is essentially one large project framing a controlled diversity, the eastern zone has developed as four separate riverfront sites with two of them forming gaps in the spectacle as outlined above. The relatively smaller grain size appears to enable this dialectic to operate in a manner that it does not along the Casino riverscape. Jacobs also noted that small-scale secondary activities can best be sustained by a mix of primary uses to maintain a flow of people through a district at different times. In the case of Southbank, the variety of primary leisure attractions stretching from the Arts Centre to the Casino help sustain the many more fleeting and marginal forms of play that spring up in the cracks between them.

Containing Carnival

The second dialectic is that in its attempts to create the spectacle of the carnival, the waterfront can stimulate a genuine sense of excess that spills over into spontaneous behaviour. The riverscape creates a place and a time set apart from serious, everyday urban society; it creates the illusion of a space where rules are relaxed. Based on contradictory desires for fantasy and authenticity, this is a place where one comes close to large flows of water and explosions of fire, but in a safe context. Thus we get what Featherstone calls 'ordered disorder' – a packaged experience of urban diversity, to be consumed without risk of contact with genuine difference.[5] The paradox, as Hannigan has argued, is that the desire for authentic experience is combined with the desire to avoid risk.[6] As outlined earlier, the Casino is marketed as permanent carnival;

and carnival traditionally operates as a social safety valve for letting off steam.[7] For Lefebvre, carnivals and festivals 'tighten social links and at the same time give rein to all desires which have been pent up by collective discipline and the necessities of everyday work'.[8] The spectacle stimulates desires it cannot contain, leading to unbridled and spontaneous forms of escapism. People find ways to transcend its limits, explore, and create new identities. The eruptions of the fountain in front of the Casino encourage a diversity of games and social encounters that can be difficult to control. Skating off ledges and climbing on the arch of the pedestrian bridge are risky engagements with the place, stimulated in part by the contradictory ways such transgressive behaviour both cuts through the audience expectation yet meets the market for spontaneity and authenticity of experience.

These more transgressive, socially unacceptable and active forms of teenage escapism are often hidden from the view of the general public. Turning aside from the spectacle, they are not a display for strangers, so much as a part of the identity formation of teenagers, seeking to explore and extend their bodily potential, through direct engagements with each other and the material landscape. The riskiness of activities like wrestling is heightened by proximity to the water's edge. Rather than mediating social relations through purchasable commodities and pre-packaged fantasies that fix and reaffirm identities, the unexpected, risky and sensual potentials of this landscape actually help to stimulate and unpack authentic forms of bodily experience of place and social encounters that can lead to the construction of new identities. The Southbank landscape packages certain forms of identity which are framed and mediated by the urban design and its spectacle.

This postmodern riverscape, with its mix of uses and blurring of boundaries, results from a strategy to first produce the fluid city and then keep it contained within the imperatives of consumption. It both incorporates and violates the Jacobs and Alexander lessons – 'tree-like' thinking must be first abandoned to generate desire, then reincorporated to capture it. The riverscape can also be interpreted through Deleuze and Guattari's distinction between smooth and striated space.[9] The highly 'striated' spaces of the Casino and the upper promenade become 'smoother' as one approaches the water, the quintessentially 'smooth' space which stimulates the flows of desire that the spectacle seeks to capture. The multiplicity of activities along this waterfront show how difficult this can be. The rhizomatic busking activities along the 'loose' space in front of the Esso building have become more striated, mapped and regulated over time, limited to experienced buskers on specific sites. The dialectic between the Esso and SouthGate busking zones is interesting in this regard. While the Esso vacuum becomes increasingly regulated and fixed to specific sites, SouthGate employs a company called 'Explosive Media' to produce fluid 'events' that weave throughout its zone on Sundays. The individual buskers in the public zone then have to compete with a well-funded spectacle with far looser spatial constraints.

Control Brings Resistance

Pile has suggested that the politics of public space can be construed as a form of 'dance', a reciprocity between authority and resistance that is our final dialectic.[10] Playful uses of the physical terrain such as skating are not only dangerous, they challenge behavioural conventions. They thrive on confrontations with the spectacular scenography and with passive ways of consuming it. The raised steel lugs installed along the stone and concrete edges in the hope of deterring skating actually operate to stimulate the desire. Their locations can be read as a map of the frontiers of struggle between different modes of appreciating a seductive surface. The attempt to control desire encourages the invention of new forms of practice that slide over, weave between and sometimes damage the lugs. In some cases, skaters merely move to other parts of the landscape as a spatial 'dance' ensues between the nomadic and rhizomatic practices of the skaters, and the proliferating lugs that both follow and attract them. Attempts to hinder teenage transgression show how the dialectical struggle between authority and resistance constantly reworks the cracks in the spectacle. Yet such additions to the landscape, and the crowds they draw, continue to stimulate the desire for real transgression. The three dialectics continue to unfold through each other.

Each of the three dialectics outlined shows tensions behind the facade of a postmodern leisure landscape. These dialectics also suggest different ways in which the spectacularised urban space of the waterfront serves to propagate real social life. Authentic experience feeds off the very attempts to purify and rationalise social experience in place. Spectacular landscapes such as Southbank tend to organise social relations and social practices, by mediating them through a predetermined, generic and predictable palette of images, perceptions and opportunities for action. They tend to distance citizens from the diversity of the city, and to produce forms of passivity. Yet, as outlined above, the urban spectacle can also generate new forms of genuine urbanity, stimulating desires and resistances that break out of the contrived spectacle and produce the real excitement of urban life. The point here is not to privilege the 'real' over simulation, rather it is to confound this opposition – the authentic emerges from the dialectics of social life. There is a constant movement between masking and revealing. Urban life is paradoxical because it is always social and meaning is always under construction. The task is to resurrect the idea of the authentic from its essentialist stereotypes; it is to assert the authority of action in everyday life, to see the pedestrian as an author of urban meaning.

LOCAL/GLOBAL POLITICS

For one week in September 2000, the entire riverscape precinct became engaged in a major inversion of use and meaning when it served as the host site of a major World Economic Forum (WEF) congress, the Davos group dedicated to the development of free trade agreements. Attracting global events of this kind was precisely the goal of the later waterfront strategy, drawing together global decision-makers and raising the profile of the city through a celebration of the triumphs of international commerce. Demonstrations against the forum were organised by an Internet-based coalition of environmental and social groups, encouraged by the success of the Seattle and Washington demonstrations in broadening the agenda of the WEF and the World Trade Organization. Expecting trouble, the Crown authorities sealed the entire complex with a concrete and steel barricade, forming a seventeen-hectare fortress encompassing the river and surrounding streets. For three days the Casino compound was cordoned off by more than 2000 police on the inside and encircled by tens of thousands of demonstrators outside, the largest political activity seen in Australia since the Vietnam War. This leisure landscape briefly became a space of genuine public engagement (Figures 4.6, 4.7). Its manufactured atmosphere of playful abandon gave way to real social agendas, real conflict and violence.

Figure 4.6
The Casino as fortress – September 2000
(*Courtesy of* The Age, *16 September 2000*)

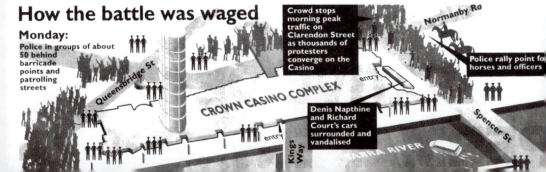

How the battle was waged

Monday:
Police in groups of about 50 behind barricade points and patrolling streets

Crowd stops morning peak traffic on Clarendon Street as thousands of protesters converge on the Casino

Normanby Rd

Police rally point for horses and officers

Queensbridge St

CROWN CASINO COMPLEX

entry

Denis Napthine and Richard Court's cars surrounded and vandalised

Kings Way

entry

Spencer St

YARRA RIVER

The waterfront spectacle was turned inside-out: the Casino and riverfront promenade became a serious operation of helicopters, boats and police, while an informal public carnival enveloped the perimeter barricade – a promenade of music, costumes and banners. The carnival of 'clowns, ten-foot puppets and twenty-foot dragons' became an ironic echo of the Casino advertising.[11] An instant 'tent city' emerged on Queensbridge Plaza as temporary accommodation. The Casino's postmodern landscape of packaged festivity was temporarily replaced by a festival of protest. These informal festivities contested the Casino's monopoly on the framing of leisure. In its attempt to provide a global stage for the WEF congress, the Casino was effectively closed down and up-staged.

This carnival of protest was punctuated by occasional outbursts of violence as the new Labor Premier (adopting the tactics, if not the style of his predecessor) ordered police to force access for delegates to the conference. The compound fence inscribed a temporary boundary between local and global space, as VIPs such as Bill Gates and the Australian Prime Minister were forced to enter and leave by helicopter and police launch. The image of the Casino juxtaposed with graffiti covered barricades, the carnival of demonstrators and rows of police in riot gear produced powerful imagery that the mass media could not resist because of its capital value as media image. The casino complex became a symbol of the wealth and intransigence of a globalised, privatised economy under siege.

Figure 4.7
Casino cordon, September 2000

While global demonstrations against the WEF focused primarily on the Casino, they also spread up and down the Southbank promenade. Across the street to the west, the Exhibition Centre with its dynamic global imagery was draped in banners calling for 'global justice'. To the east, the entire Southbank promenade was covered with graffiti, with its global icons in particular being targeted: Esso/Exxon, Sheraton and IBM. Partly as a result of the violence, the struggle for media time was won by the demonstrators. The Casino became a global spectacle of a very different kind to that envisioned in the place-marketing strategy as 'protesters tactically transformed Crown Casino into a place from which they could contest corporate capital's domination of global space'.[12] The abstract and flexible flows of global capital became temporarily grounded and territorialised in the Casino compound, where they were confronted by local conditions and local sentiments. This event thus exemplifies the ways that seemingly totalising and opaque mega-projects can become opportunities for new forms of transparency and agency. Global projects can attract global politics, creating a new contestation over both the use of public space and the meanings of the new urban imagery.

One of the most troubling challenges facing urban designers and planners today is that the economic and cultural forces of globalisation so often lead to a proliferation of formularised place-making – the sense that if you've seen one waterfront, you've seen them all. Attempts to ameliorate the juggernaut of placelessness with authentic local heritage and artworks can often result in the appropriation of local authenticity and its reproduction for a global market. Yet in some of the observations outlined here, we see a surprising paradox: a formulaic, spectacular, economically instrumental space gains new and authentic uses and meanings despite or even because of globalisation. Everyday urban life continues to evolve in response to the excesses of global spectacle. We are in no way suggesting that formulaic global mega-projects are somehow redeemed by the semantic and functional inversions that occur. In some ways these lessons are old ones: that the city is not a 'tree' (Alexander); that the real vitality of urban life lies in its diversity, its marginal activities, its tensions and its creativity (Jacobs). These earlier lessons from Alexander and Jacobs need to be brought to bear on a new generation of themed, packaged, spectacular environments which attempt to circumscribe the spontaneity, excitement, risk and discord that make urban life truly vital and authentic. And there are also other theoretical tools and critical ideas that can be usefully deployed in the new and emerging contexts of the fluid city.

CHAPTER FIVE

URBAN LIVING

HINTERLAND STRATEGY

The Southbank strategy was always aimed at a mix of housing with retail and commercial development extending into the hinterland area to the south of the river. The 1986 plan set the rough boundaries of this area and the various urban design and planning controls to guide development (Figure 2.2 bottom).[1] This hinterland area was an industrial zone in decline; primarily two-storey buildings with minimal heritage value. The arts precinct lining St Kilda Road to the east comprising the gallery and arts college was seen as an area with an urban character worth preserving and developing. The early strategy was to use leverage on public land to ensure some housing near the waterfront despite the resistance of the market. The market desire at that time was for commercial towers.

The urban design strategy for the hinterland was first developed in the 1986 study and then elaborated in a set of detailed guidelines in 1992. It included the development of the new Southbank Boulevard, creating open access between the Arts Centre and the river, and generating a series of new sites that were developed in the early 1990s. Building heights were to be limited to eight storeys (twenty-four metres) throughout most of the hinterland area. To limit the damage from parking and blank walls, active frontages were to be enforced on all streets (70 per cent on main streets, 50 per cent to minor streets).[2] New pedestrian laneways were to penetrate some of the larger blocks to enhance the permeability of the pedestrian network. The functional mix was to incorporate industry, arts, retail and showrooms, as well as residential uses. A range of new buildings at four to eight storeys, both commercial and housing, were constructed along the new Southbank Boulevard in the early 1990s.

Waterfront housing, however, was difficult to get started; in both the Riverside Quay and SouthGate projects the housing component was delayed or abandoned. While the Yarra bank waterfront to the west was initially intended for housing, this plan was replaced by the Casino. The only housing that was developed by the early 1990s emerged in the most southern section of Southbank, well away from the river. Most of this housing was undertaken by developers Central Equity who led the market for inexpensive apartment living with a formularised adoption of tilt-slab construction techniques. The first such schemes in Southbank were two- to four-storey perimeter blocks in neo-Georgian style with a gym and swimming pool in the central courtyard. The quality of this housing in both urban design and architectural terms was very poor. While there was an attempt to produce active frontages on major streets, these projects were also subject to the proliferation of blank walls and car parks that the urban design guidelines had tried to control.

BOOM

By the mid-1990s, with the economic recession over and crowds flooding to the new waterfront, market resistance to housing vanished and Southbank became a new hotspot for apartment construction. The change of government saw the rolling back of height limits as the area became 'market-led'. What the 'market' wanted was a complicated mix: walkable access to the new waterfront and central city; private facilities (pool and gym; secure on-site parking); and most importantly, commanding views. Planning Minister Maclellan promised a new urban future and warned that it might not be to everyone's taste. He derided the conservative suburbanites, whom he termed the 'wheely-bin set' and suggested that the future lay in high-density living close to the city. Shadows from high-rise towers would not be a problem he said because it rains in winter anyway.[3]

At this time there was also a complete rethink of the transport infrastructure of the Southbank district. This had been rendered necessary in part because the boulevard connection to Port Melbourne had been abandoned to make way for the Casino. The Southbank Boulevard, already fully constructed and lined with new buildings, was also partially abandoned in the mid-1990s when the decision was made to turn it into a cul-de-sac, where it meets the river at Queensbridge Square. Crown Casino was granted the right to claim public land under Queensbridge Square and to feed the boulevard traffic directly into its underground parking lot (Figure 5.1). With an audacity that would have appeared startling if the public had known about it, a major new boulevard constructed with public funds was appropriated primarily for private use. Only when the Casino was completed in 1997 did it become apparent that the central lanes of the boulevard had been swallowed by the casino car park entrance. There was however another and more sensible reason for the termination of the boulevard. The design of Queensbridge Square as a round-about and node point of the two boulevards was based on a different strategy for the waterfront: one that presumed a higher level of public access to the waterfront and a lower level of pressure for development of it. By the mid-1990s it was apparent that new developments on the waterfront lacked the north–south pedestrian permeability necessary to create good walkable access from the south. No provision was made for an overpass from SouthGate across City Road, despite the fact that the levels were ideal; the project was designed as a 'gate' to the shopping mall and corporate towers but no further. And far worse than this, Crown Casino had not only displaced waterfront housing, but had closed access completely to an entire half kilometre of riverfront, virtually killing off the urban design potential to the south. Thus the forms of the waterfront development seriously compromised walkable access from the south.

An analysis of the spatial structure of Southbank shows that those parts of the accessible pedestrian network within a 500-metre walk of the river frontage are very unevenly distributed.[4] Some areas immediately to the south of the Casino and many Southbank projects are within 200–300 metres of the river (as the crow flies) yet over a 500-metre walk (Figure 5.2). Major traffic flows accentuate this effect, leaving the only areas of good walkable access focused on the Queensbridge Square gap between precincts. When the hinterland area was opened up to the market in the mid-1990s the demand for housing was concentrated into the few blocks just

Figure 5.1
Southbank Boulevard becomes Crown
Casino (2003)

Figure 5.2
Pedestrian network within 500 metres
of the river with towers approved
from 1995–2003.

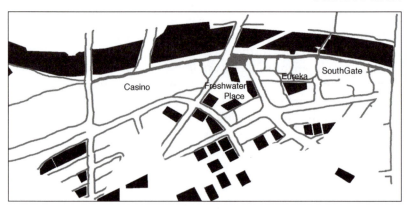

south of Queensbridge Square. The importance of walkability to this market is evident in the advertising for the housing, which lists the distances and times for walkable access to a range of amenities, and the waterfront is the top priority. The impermeability of the early waterfront projects funnelled the desire for housing into the Queensbridge Square area and the termination of Southbank Boulevard was in large part a way of responding to this new flow of desire. The termination of the boulevard has enabled a new waterfront plaza and the giant Freshwater Place development with direct river access. While the grand vision of the 1980s boulevard has now been reduced to a car park entrance, and the traffic flow has become convoluted, the city will soon have a new public plaza to complete this gap in the riverscape.

By 1998 the boom in Southbank housing was well under way with 770 new apartments completed and another 2600 approved in high-rise developments of twenty to twenty-eight storeys (Figure 5.3). Central Equity was again the major developer; the mock-historic style was abandoned for these towers and the design quality improved somewhat. There was, however, no plan until the Southbank Structure Plan of 1998.[5] This plan explored the built form options for the area through three models: the 'perimeter block', the 'tower + podium' and the 'perimeter block + tower'. It argued that the low-rise perimeter block: '... offers relatively low density living for this area and limited opportunities for views. Market demands do not favour this model in the long term.'[6] The 'tower + podium' model was presented as '... popular with the market and developers. This model offers best exposure to views (at least until a similar development appears next door).' The problems and contradictions of car parking consuming the street frontages, of towers overshading and blocking views were all acknowledged. The preferred model was a combination of the two which would magically resolve them: a high-density (four- to eight-storey) perimeter block podium with towers in the corners. Car parking was to be hidden behind active street frontages and the problems of towers blocking each other and overshading their own courtyards was to be solved by spacing the towers. As if to violate its own arguments the plan argued: 'There is no residential tower format that really works over time, as each new tower puts the amenity of the previous one at risk'.[7] The plan also called for new pedestrian linkages through existing blocks to increase permeability. It called for the inclusion of community facilities, such as child-care and preschools, although census data showed that Southbank was becoming a relatively childless zone of the city.

One of the interesting layers of urban analysis through which to examine this transformation is that of urban character. The 1986 study had divided the Southbank area into nine different urban character precincts of six to ten hectares, based on analysis of the existing industrial urban character. The 1998 study by contrast has both an 'urban character analysis' (with six precincts) and a proposal (with three precincts). None of these precincts are congruent with earlier analyses or proposals. The three proposed precincts are the river corridor, the arts precinct and 'city living'.

The river corridor was complete by this stage and the arts precinct was to be kept low rise with a six-storey limit. The 'city living' precinct, however, was to be an amalgam of many different precincts united only by being opened up to high-rise redevelopment. Urban character as an analytic category became fluid as differences between districts melted into a generic space of flows. Those parts of the Southbank hinterland, which were not identified with the river frontage or arts area, were 'deterritorialised' and rendered open to new flows of capital and desire. 'Urban character' became an effect of the market, relatively ungrounded from site conditions; the height limits and the urban 'identity' was to be whatever the market produces.

MARKET LEVELS

Height limits were deemed necessary to protect streetscape amenity throughout this development precinct and a limit of twenty-eight storeys (ninety metres) was proposed, rising to forty-six storeys (150 metres) on the river frontage. The twenty-eight-storey limit was established by the height of the only

Figure 5.3
Southbank hinterland (2003)

completed residential tower when this plan was written. The twenty-four-metre height controls, which had covered the vast majority of the hinterland area, had been rendered completely fictional by the crop of towers already completed or approved. The Planning Scheme that followed in 1999, labelled the 'New Format Planning Scheme', simply abolished height limits completely in the Southbank hinterland.[8]

The 1998 plan is a useful guide to the forms of urban thinking prevalent at that time. However, it was primarily a legitimation of what had already occurred coupled with some wishful thinking. It was couched in the 'preferred' and 'desirable' language of fluid planning discourse rather than the 'requirements' of urban regulation. Planning and urban design principles were following the flows of desire and investment, which in turn were already moving on. While the mid-1990s projects approved at twenty to twenty-eight storeys were already under construction, they were soon followed by thirty- to 44-storey projects in the 28-storey precinct. In 1999 Freshwater Place was approved on the southern edge of Queensbridge Square, peaking at sixty storeys (200 metres). Later that year the Eureka Tower was approved at eighty storeys, later raised to eighty-eight storeys (300 metres) to become the world's tallest residential tower. The site, ironically, was the original sixteen-storey housing component of Riverside Quay, which had remained vacant for a decade after the developers reneged due to lack of market demand. By 2003, ten towers were complete in the Southbank hinterland area, ranging from nineteen to thirty-two floors (60–106 metres). A further twenty towers were under construction or approved, ranging from twenty-eight to eighty-eight floors (90–300 metres) at an average of forty floors (132 metres).[9] The average heights of these approvals gradually rose from twenty-five storeys in the mid-1990s to over forty floors after the millennium.

It was the market, rather than the 'plan', which established the successive increases in height. Planning as 'forward thinking' became a 'backward-looking' documentation of what had already happened. However, the market also relied on a perception of forward planning, a stable framework for investment. The earlier projects were often named in a manner that suggested they would be the tallest building in their neighbourhood: the 'Summit' was completed in 2002 at twenty-six storeys, named and advertised to establish the symbolic capital that flows towards height and dominance. The brochures showed the commanding views across the rooftops (and into the courtyards of the early perimeter blocks). The

'Sentinel' next door followed at thirty-five storeys and again the advertising showed the commanding views, now across the top of the earlier towers. Across the street the 'Imperium Tower' will soon look down on the 'Summit' and 'Sentinel' from forty-four storeys; all of them will be in the shade of the sixty-storey Freshwater Place and the eighty-storey 'Eureka Tower' to the north. The market was determining heights and the planning controls were trying to catch up. In 2002 height limits were reintroduced, but raising them to 160 metres in areas of high demand and 100 metres further from the river.[10] It remains to be seen whether such limits can be enforced because the 160-metre zone already has buildings at 200 to 300 metres and it is difficult to argue that they should retain such a monopoly on the view and skyline.

The strategy of allowing greater height closer to the river, coupled with the funnelling of this investment into one piece of riverbank will produce a cluster of 200- to 300-metre towers casting shadows across most of the Southbank hinterland for about six months of the year. The tall waterfront towers all have prime riverfront access and cannot be overshaded, but they in turn will reduce the amenity of all the projects to the south. The four-storey perimeter block of Southside Gardens on Southbank Boulevard already has its central pool and garden area plunged into the shade of two new thirty-storey towers across the street. Both the courtyard housing and these towers will in turn soon be in the shade of others up to three times their height. The four- to eight-storey developments, which emerged from the first Southbank plan along Southbank Boulevard, are now juxtaposed against totally differently scaled projects and rendered economi-cally and aesthetically obsolete (Figure 5.4). The eight-storey Riverside Apartments project on the site that fills the gap between eighty-eight- and sixty-storey towers is a case in point. A level-playing field would suggest that this block be redeveloped at up to ten times the current height, yet any such proposal would bring opposition from the giant neighbours due to their loss of view and symbolic capital.

CONTRADICTORY DESIRES

The development of the riverscape has produced a flow of desire for property with views and good access to the waterfront. These desires are mediated by flows of capital, constrained both by urban morphology and planning restrictions. The built form and urban morphology has huge inertia; the impermeable morphology of SouthGate and Crown have funnelled these flows into Queensbridge. The planning context by contrast is fluid, constrained only by the loss of public legitimacy: has the 'public interest' been abandoned or superseded by the 'market'? The 'market' wants it all: an apartment with a view of the river, parks, city and bay; secure drive-in/out parking; high-style design; semi-private pool and sunny landscaped garden; a short walk to the river along safe well-designed streets; and access to a lively and diverse neighbourhood with a plethora of cafes and shops. It is in the attempt to give the 'market' what it wants that contradictions emerge, nowhere more apparent than the blank street facades of so many of the new projects where the 'guidelines' for active edges

Figure 5.4
Conflicting visions on
Southbank Boulevard:
1993 (front) and
2002 (rear)

Figure 5.5
'Active' frontages
(2003)

have been quite unsuccessful (Figure 5.5). What the market wants now is the destruction of the previous layer of development; many of the low-rise developments of the early 1990s will probably be demolished and redeveloped at a higher density. Such 'creative destruction' is the antithesis of the sustainable city. While it will take some time for this precinct to fill out, it cannot now be redeemed as a medium-rise district. The only hope is that it can become a more vital high-rise district.

While the market indicates a desire for diverse forms of urban living, this is a desire for diversity without difference of social class. There is little doubt that the housing boom in Southbank has produced an oversupply of apartment accommodation driven by a combination of factors. Primary among them is a capacity for small investors to borrow at low interest rates, claim tax savings produced by buying 'off the plan' and then claim further tax benefits through negative gearing.[11] The new housing is primarily for the rental market, and while none of it is 'affordable' to those in housing difficulty, the oversupply would appear to offer hope for greater affordability in the long term. The housing ranges in apartment size from about forty-five square metres up to giant penthouses; in a free market with an oversupply one would expect the small apartments at lower levels, where views have been built out, to become affordable. This market, however, is insulated against affordability. As the price drops with the oversupply the tax benefits of negative gearing rise; much of the housing is then left empty because the tax benefits and the capital gains provide sufficient return. And to allow these apartments to slide down-market would have collateral effects on the image of the neighbourhood as the 'wrong' kind of people move in. What the market wants is diversity without class differences. Neither investors nor residents want Southbank to become 'affordable'. The fluid city is effectively insulated against the desires of the poor.

The desire for waterfront living is a contradictory desire for place, identity, amenity, community, urbanity and escape. The Freshwater Place project is advertised as 'redefining what a city can be', where one lives up to sixty floors above an 'urban village' on the waterfront.[12] The Eureka Tower nearby is advertised as a 'city within the city', although with residential floors beginning above the eleventh floor it is somewhat detached from the city. One illustration shows a fish-eye view of the city from a great height – the city becomes a distant planet as the resident becomes a global subject (Figure 5.6). In another the tower appears on the moon as if it has taken flight; the earth appears over the lunar landscape, which is shot through with lines of light. The lines of desire here flow not only towards the waterfront, but into the stratosphere. The desire is to both become the city and to escape the city.

Figure 5.6
Eureka Tower – city becomes planet
(*Hocking Stuart/Grocon P/L*)

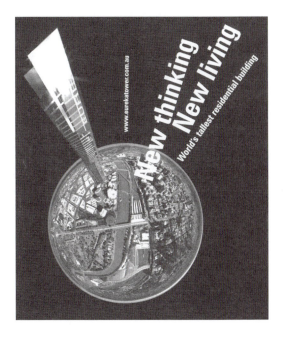

Walking around the Southbank hinterland area one sees some of the worst results of market 'rationality'. The exhortations to developers to provide active edges on the street walls have been hopelessly ineffective. As towers grew taller and parking require-ments expanded, the housing became further separated from the street and the damaging effects of parking garages became worse. Residents drive in and out of a series of largely blank walls forming a local neighbourhood which has yet to develop substan-tial street life or any sense of urbanity. The appalling paradox is that this is becoming one of the densest neighbourhoods in Australia in terms of built form, yet its pedestrian density remains lower than most of Melbourne's inner city. The attraction of course is the river, but to walk to it requires negotiating a series of dull and empty streets; for some residents it is surely easier to take a 300-metre drive down the former boulevard until it disappears into the casino car park. The Southbank precinct also remains somewhat impermeable since none of the new pedestrian links have been implemented. The residential population has risen from eighty-five to 6000 since 1990, and many of the new residents are not pleased.[13] Residents complain of a lack of parks, shops, community life, street amenity and walkability. Some residents are selling when they realise their views are being built out. Southbank is too important to the ongoing viability of the central city to be left to decline, and the call is now out for considerable public funds to be invested in the attempt to redeem the quality of the public realm in this area.

To summarise this process, a new desire for high-rise inner city living with walkable access to the riverscape has been unleashed. The desire for walkability was severely constrained by the impermeability created by the earlier projects, funnelling the housing into the Queensbridge zone. This stimulated ever-increasing desires for height that were progressively approved and the Southbank Structure Plan of 1998 operated to legitimate them after the event; regulation operated retrospectively. Having achieved the heights, the market then focuses on resolving the problems caused by them: the loss of views, the lack of diversity, the dead street frontages. Local government, which had minimal control over development, is left to pick up the pieces.

The development of urban living at Southbank has paradoxically been one of its great successes and failures. Given the proliferation of parking garages, the low level of pedestrian amenity and the impermeability of urban structure, it remains to be seen just how walkable this neighbourhood will become. The density of urban living (net densities of up to about 600 dwelling units per hectare) is totally unprecedented for Melbourne and has established a major alternative to the conservative suburban mentality of urban development. While it cannot be redeemed in urban design terms, if the traffic can be tamed, if a sensible urban planning and design framework can be re-established, then the Southbank hinterland has some hope of becoming a vital, if somewhat shady, urban district.

CHAPTER SIX

FEDERATION

Kim Dovey and Ian Woodcock

The river and the civic axis of St Kilda Road/ Swanston Street are the two primary linear elements of Melbourne's urban morphology, with the intersection long regarded as both the key node point and entry to the city. Princes Bridge is the urban threshold and has been the site for a long series of temporary archways that celebrate this flow of movement into the city; the grandest being the opening of the first federal parliament in 1901, celebrating independence from Britain and the birth of the Australian nation. A century later the south-eastern corner of this intersection has become the site of Federation Square (Figure 2.4). The city has long had an ambivalent relationship to its river landscape, both turning away from and yet facing the river. On the one hand, the first layer of development on the south-eastern corner was the city morgue, discharging its waste into the river. The neo-Gothic St Paul's cathedral by British architect William Butterfield replaced an earlier church on the north-east corner in the 1880s; although its spires were not completed until 1928. When Flinders Street Station was built on the south-west corner in 1901 it established the intersection of Flinders and Swanston as the busiest in town, as it further severed the city from the river. On the other hand, this southern view of the city with the cathedral as centrepiece became an iconic image as the 'face' of the city. While such images were crucial in the construction of Melbourne's identity, they were rarely photographs because the actual view in everyday life did not give the desired level of prominence to the cathedral; most postcard images are close-up three-quarter views (Figure 6.1). Early paintings and drawings often produced the illusion of a prominent cathedral, showing spires (which did not yet exist) and exaggerated vertically to dominate the city skyline.

In 1967 the south-east corner of Flinders Street and Swanston Street was redeveloped as the Princes Gate Project: two 23-storey office towers that were to dominate views of the city from the south for thirty years. While most of the bulk was set back from Swanston Street to allow views of the upper part of the cathedral,

Figure 6.1
St Pauls Cathedral and railway station – postcard 1930s
(*LaTrobe Picture Collection/State Library of Victoria*)

these slabs formed a sheer wall between the city and the river. Known as the Gas and Fuel towers after their major tenant, they were to become the most hated buildings in the city. While the design was mediocre, the key problem was urban rather than architectural – these slabs presented a highly visible, boring and monolithic face. There were uglier buildings in the city, yet none intruded so much upon its everyday image. The desire to be rid of them was shared by all but the most blind of modernist ideologues. Between these buildings and the river lay the broad swathe of railway yards well below street level. The prospect of demolishing the towers, bridging the railyards and reconnecting the city to the river was long regarded as one of the city's greatest development opportunities.

In 1985 the Labor government commissioned a detailed urban design study from architects Denton Corker Marshall (DCM), which explored the constraints and opportunities of the site and a range of options for its development.[1] The site was conceived as a gateway to the city, as a part of the civic axis, as a new urban precinct and as a linkage to the river. The report concluded that the area in front of the cathedral should be cleared to become an open plaza connecting the city to the river: 'The Plaza is a finger of the city floor reaching out to the river's edge. The river is a linear element that slices through the suburbs and gardens, and touches the central business district as it passes by'.[2] There were, however, two conditions that made this connection difficult: a steep change of level from above the railway lines to river level; and a series of 1880s bluestone vaults with some heritage value that formed a blockage on the riverbank. The vaults served as retaining wall, toilets and ferry booking service. The report concluded that an effective connection of the city to the river required demolition of the vaults. The preferred design option was for a dauntingly vast open civic plaza extending south from St Paul's and stepping down to the river, bounded by new commercial development to the east.

The value of the DCM study lay in the depth of analysis and the range of options pursued. Yet all of them were based on the premise that the 23-storey Gas and Fuel towers would remain on the north of the site casting much of the new plaza and commercial development into deep shade during the winter. Notably for what follows, options that obscured views of St. Paul's Cathedral were rejected in favour of ones that opened up the 'face' of the city. Other proposals for development of the site were entertained during the 1980s but came to nothing.[3] In 1994 the new Liberal government announced plans to buy and demolish the towers. This was a fortunate confluence of events: the buildings came on the market for the first time in decades; the price was low ($7 million) because the buildings were badly in need of refurbishment and the office market was in recession; and the public purse was flush with tax funds from the Casino and a broad sell-off of public utilities. But the kick-start that made it possible was the forthcoming centenary of Federation in 2001 with the prospect of federal funding for major urban projects the project was duly called 'Federation Square'.

PROGRAMMING

At this stage there were few ideas about the design, but there were several imperatives: it must be geared to Melbourne's new global role, transform the image of the city, celebrate the ideals of federation and independence, and connect the city to the river and to the parkland to the east. The Premier vowed that the vista of the cathedral from the south, once cleared of the Gas and Fuel towers, would remain unobstructed. The presumption that the site should be largely urban open space or 'square' was never seriously debated. Being on the edge of the city grid, many argued that the site was not a naturally advantageous location for urban open space and was in need of a major magnet to draw urban life to it and through it. The best prospect for such a magnet (the new museum) had already been relocated to a park outside the city. The project became an open space in search of functions that might make it useful; early ideas included a transport interchange, tourist information centre, multimedia centre, wintergarden, contemporary art museum and a theme park of Australian landscapes. This quest was conducted within a rather curious exclusion of the private sector. At a time when most major public utilities in the city were being privatised (including the railways underneath the site), when the largest collection of cinemas, nightclubs and entertainment facilities the city had ever seen were being approved for the Casino, no major private investment or usage was considered for Federation Square. While urban design and planning had become more flexible and privatisation mania raged, this project remained exclusively public.

The budget and the program for Federation Square were, however, highly fluid. The earliest budget mentioned was $150 million with the thought that the city, state and federal governments might contribute $50 million each.[4] To secure federal funding the project needed to be complete by 2001 and the programming task was accelerated. Possible functions were proposed, shuffled and rejected up to and beyond the announcement of the brief for an international design competition in late 1996. The brief at that point included four major components: the plaza; a wintergarden with ancillary retail space; performance and exhibition areas; and a cinemedia centre. Buildings were to be constrained to the height of the Flinders Street Station and the area in front of St Paul's cathedral was to be kept largely open. The project was to ensure a good connection to the river with active edges on all its frontages. And in addition to the transformative and celebratory imperatives mentioned above, the symbolic components of the brief were broadened to include a focus on 'multicultural themes' and 'indigenous contributions to Australia'. However, the glaring problem with the brief from its inception was that it lacked any crowd-pulling attractions. The cinemedia centre was not for popular movies, and the performance and exhibition spaces were not well developed. The wintergarden had good prospects, given Melbourne's winter climate, but they were not improved when the Planning Minister approved a development to the north that would have plunged it into winter shadow.[5] It was paradoxically a highly civic project but without civic institutions. With over three hectares in a prime location it was in many ways an underdevelopment of the site.

What the Federation site needed was a series of major attractors with the power to draw crowds of people – young and old, day and night, weekday and weekend. The project went to competition under-programmed and the urban design was partially dictated by the lack of buildings – vast areas of open space were incorporated into all competition entries. During judging a decision was made to incorporate a major Museum of Australian Art into the project. This was not a part of the first stage brief, yet judging was undertaken with an understanding that the largest single piece of program in the project would have to be added later. The addition of the museum after the competition added a much needed program, and to some this change was indicative of an appalling lack of planning.

The most significant program in this project was symbolic programming: the capacity of such a project to transform the image of the city, and to create a genuinely public space for a multicultural society. The project was to make a contemporary architectural statement; as Premier Kennett put it: 'We want to have a building that will actually encourage us to take our minds forward 100 years'.[6] While there was clearly an eye on the global market and urban brand identification, the audience was also a local one. The brief called for a design that 'stimulates the imagination, feeds the soul and lifts the spirit'.[7]

JUDGEMENTS

The judging panel comprised professional, community, business and government representatives; it included three architects and a landscape architect, but, at the height of anti-planning ideology, no urban planners.[8] The only practising architect and the most powerful member was internationally famed architect Daniel Libeskind. Entries closed in February 1997 with a shortlist announced in March followed by a final submission in May and judging in June.[9] The winning scheme, by LAB architects (Peter Davidson and Donald Bates), was presented to Premier Kennett who was horrified and privately declared it to be 'rubbish'. The decision remained unannounced for six weeks while the architects were asked to produce drawings with a little more political capital.[10] Kennett thrived on a contemporary and adventurous image, but this one did not meet expectations and the competition had kept it out of his design control. He much admired the Exhibition Centre and other projects by DCM, whose design was rumoured to have come second. By the time the result was announced Kennett became supportive. The design, he said, was: 'almost multicultural ... It is the coming together of a whole range of parts ... and that's what Federation is all about, it's also what Melbourne and Australia is all about'.[11] This was a remark that resonated with Kennett's other portfolio as the Minister for Multicultural Affairs. The design was clearly and strongly influenced by the work of Libeskind and the gossip networks soon spread the fact that one of the architects (Bates) had previously worked in Libeskind's office.[12] Libeskind is a radically innovative architect whose work is loosely classified with the 'deconstructionist' school. He has a fine sensitivity to the production of meaning in built form, with a particular focus on issues of nationalism, politics and culture. He also has a penchant for a very particular aesthetic language and to anyone who knows his work there could have been little doubt which of the shortlisted projects would gain his support.

There was, however, a far more practical reason for the choice of the winning project. As noted earlier, an entire new building had been added to the program since the competition began and the

judges were looking for a design with the flexibility to incorporate
a major art museum without losing its integrity. In other words, the
project needed a design with a fluidity to match that of its program.
The competing schemes were all infused with a stronger sense of
closure. While many aspects of the LAB scheme can be construed
as architecturally derivative of Libeskind's work, it was the best of
the shortlisted projects in urban design terms. Its main competitors
were Melbourne firms Denton Corker Marshall and Ashton
Raggatt Macdougall (ARM). The DCM scheme continued the
heroic late-modernist theme evident in the Exhibition Centre, and
included a 100-metre high leaning tower inscribed with a century
of federation history. It was regarded by the judges as being somewhat 'inflexible' – whether in function or symbolism is unclear.[13]
The ARM proposal was the most imageable of the projects, with a
giant looped ribbon of steel dominating the front of the site and
framing the view of St Paul's. Much of the formal language was
generated from loops, folds and cursive script as if the idea of
'federation' were to be written on the city. There were some strong
parallels between this design and that which later emerged in their
design for the National Museum of Australia in Canberra, which
depicts the nation as a kind of 'knot' or 'tangle' to be decoded. The
jury saw it as a design that promised: 'entertainment, humour,
spatial complexity and decorative festivity', but lacking 'coherence
and harmony'.[14] The ARM design was indeed a critique of the illusions of 'coherence and harmony' that are framed by nationalism.
What this design really lacked was a depth of urban spatial (as
opposed to textual) thinking – it remained an essentially architectural object without the spatial complexity or structure of a vital
urban precinct. The other shortlisted projects showed a lack of
understanding of the site and the Melbourne context. They were
variously described by the jury as 'daunting' and 'bleak' – one
wonders why they were shortlisted.

The winning design was a collection of crystalline structures
with diversely cranked plan forms and inclined walls clad in a
mosaic of sandstone, zinc and glass (Figures 6.2 and 6.3). The
project is conceived as a field of forms rather than an object, with
no singular central symbol or icon. The architects described it as
a 'tectonic aggregation':

> ...the bringing together of singularities, differences and
> unique entities without the imposition of a centralizing or
> subsuming authority. Rather than relying on classical
> geometries or historic clichés the organisation and order

which has been designed is emergent, becoming more visible and more apparent with time and experience. This design eschews the notion that experience and engagement with an urban milieu should be absolute and unambiguous upon first contact ... The project is not a representation of disorder ... [it seeks] to produce coherence out of difference and to materialize the cross-affiliations so essential to a dynamic urban ensemble.[15]

The project brought together issues of urban permeability and diversity with newer theories of cities of difference, hybridity and fluid meanings:

Rather than establishing an enclave of regulated activities and controlled participation, this project activates an aggregation of vital, emotive and enlightening experiences. The buildings and their corresponding courtyards, gardens, open plazas and circulation routes produce an array of vistas, framings and contingent relationships.[16]

Much of this discourse was for professional rather than public consumption; the winning scheme was presented to the public as a contextual design that picked up and extended the lanes and arcades of Melbourne's grid. The competition judges described it as 'the architectural equivalent of a federation ... an exciting, original and clever complex of buildings and spaces that will enrich the city, engage the public with witty and sympathetic architecture and provide an inspiration to Melbourne's heritage'.[17] There was some talk of how this would be the landmark Melbourne 'lacked', meeting a global market, helping to define the city and nation. Yet this was a market for a certain closure of identity and meaning, an ease of identification as symbolic capital, a logo for the corporate state. The design of Federation Square did not easily submit to this global 'gaze', a characteristic first identified by the Premier. Public response to the winning design ranged from horror to delight. With the exception of the losing firms, the architectural critique was generally supportive. However, there was trenchant criticism from conservative quarters. John Carroll called it: 'an architectural tantrum' and 'a crime on the long-term aesthetics and morale of Melbourne'.[18] Expatriate comedian Barry Humphries wrote to both major newspapers from London, accusing the project of urban vandalism, a 'provincial kitsch' soon to be riddled with

Figure 6.2 (Above)
Federation Square (*Courtesy of LAB Architecture Studio*)

Figure 6.3 (Above)
Anti-war protest at Federation Square, February 2003
(*Simon Schluter*, The Age, *15 February 2003*)

Figure 6.4 (Below)
Federation Square from St Paul's Court

'aromas of fast food and urine'.[19] Having based his career on Melbourne's supposed provincialism, this desire to preserve it was understandable. The most significant opposition came from the National Trust and the Anglican Church, who joined forces to oppose one piece of the design – the way one of the fragments or 'shards' partially blocked the view of the cathedral from the south. While the competition brief had called for a clear view to the cathedral from the south, it did not specifically require that the entire area be vacant. This desire to clear and clarify the 'face' of the city eventually erupted into a major political dispute to which we will return. When Federation Square was opened in late 2002 a clear transformation in public attitudes to the image of the project was evident as allegations of aesthetic vandalism became muted and scepticism was replaced by a broader sense of appreciation. Former Premier Kennett, initially among the horrified, was photographed in front of the tesselated panels like a proud father. The square attracted over a million visitors in the first three months and in February 2003 it was occupied by over 140 000 people protesting against Australia's participation in the illegal war against Iraq (Figure 6.3).[20] The square has been broadly popular and has produced a subtle transformation of Melbourne's image together with a re-imagining of what it is to be a Melburnian (Figure 6.4).

DIFFERENCES

Most of the discussion on the meaning of Federation focused on the idea of joining together rather than splitting apart; yet more important than the disputes between states, 1901 was the primary moment of Australia's independence from Britain – a 'becoming' of the nation. However, a dark side to the birth of the nation was that one of the first acts of independence comprised the infamous White Australia Policy, constructing Australia as a white enclave. Just as the political connection to the mother country was practically severed, the cultural connection was knotted together more tightly. With the postwar unravelling of the White Australia policy and its replacement with multiculturalism has emerged a deep concern about the unravelling of Australian identity among large sections of the Australian-born community.[21] However, the great symbolic opportunity here was to open up the meaning of 'Federation', not just as a federation of states but a federation of differences in a broader sense. The project was identified earlier as: 'an opportunity to rethink the way we program public life, public space and public buildings. To program the project in terms of a conjunction of differences ... to think in terms of a multiplicity of functions and meanings in space and time'.[22] At the end of the twentieth century it was cultural difference, a 'federation of cultures', that for many marked Australia and Melbourne as a multiplicitous democracy. Yet the official discourse of multiculturalism was, as elsewhere, infused with a superficial tolerance for diverse traditions coupled with a deeper resistance to change – a multicultural mosaic framed by White Anglo-Saxon Protestant dominance.[23] John Rawls clarifies this question of difference when he asks: 'How is it possible that there may exist over time a stable and just society of free and equal citizens profoundly divided by reasonable though incompatible religious, philosophical and moral doctrines?'[24] The production of urban civic space must engage critically with this question, and while there is no suggestion that urban design can produce justice, it inevitably provides a relatively stable 'ground' for the mediation of difference. While Federation Square celebrates the unity of the nation/continent, it is also a serious and revealing attempt to design a unified public space for a 'profoundly divided' society.

GROUNDS

The variegated redness of the ground surface and the relative lack of planting in the 'square' are clearly redolent of the desert, Australia's red centre. A widespread and longstanding desire for more greenery in the city was ignored in favour of a hard expansive plaza. While there is no suggestion that this desert metaphor is intended to refer to Aboriginality, there was a requirement in the competition brief for the design to acknowledge and celebrate indigenous contributions to Australia. The sense of the square as a synthetic landscape is reinforced by the slope of the ground plane and by the form and materials of the surrounding buildings. The facades have a geological character, lending the more enclosed parts the sense of a ravine or canyon. There were initial concerns that the open space was too vast to be consistently occupied, and indeed it is at times (like the desert) a harsh and glary space to cross. However, like the desert, in everyday life it requires relatively small numbers of people to feel occupied. The figure of the square is turned to some degree into a 'ground'; both the buildings and the pavement are constructed as a landscape of federation. One response from architecture students is that the buildings resemble the synthetic rock faces of rock-climbing venues. This artificial landscape is complemented by an artificial 'starry' sky at night time with an array of small lights fixed to a lattice of wires stretched across the square. Mythical identifications of Australia as outback desert and as beach culture are merged as stone from the outback is brought to the city to become cobblestones in swirl patterns, which many might link to both Aboriginal landscape paintings and the swirls of surf on sand.

The sloping stone pavement of the square is also the site of a constellation of nine pavement artworks by Paul Carter.[25] These works, collectively called 'Nearamnew', involve an exploration of a broad range of possible meanings linked to Federation – Aboriginality, history, governance and globalisation (Figure 6.5). At once pavement art and concrete poetry, 'Nearamnew' is a very fine, if esoteric, work that explores and challenges the ways meaning is found and constructed in public life and public space. It is a surface of juxtaposed texts, partial utterances inscribed in the stone pavement, the new synthetic 'ground' of federated meanings and practices; exploring ways in which language grounds existence; mediating between 'treading' and 'reading', between art and everyday life. This is a microcosmic set of the federated differences, unravelling questions for an often bewildered public. Along with some aspects of the larger square as an elite cultural acropolis, there is an appeal to certain forms of class identity, an affirmation of the social distinction between those who do and don't understand and appreciate.[26]

Figure 6.5
Uncertain grounds – 'Nearamnew'
(*Artist: Paul Carter*)

SKIN/FACE/MASK

The synthetic landscape effect is accentuated to some degree by the way that the facades of many of the buildings have a skin or surface that leaps representational scales from the molecular, through human and landscape scales to the cosmic (Figure 6.6). These facades are often blatantly represented as a 'skin' detached from the 'body' of the buildings. Mitchell likens the facade effects to 'patches of varied fleshtone, the effect of tanlines on bared summer skin'; a merging of body with landscape'.[27] Most of the façade is composed using a 'fractal' repetition of a single shape (a right-angled triangle) via a pinwheel grid into self-similar panels of varying size and material composition. The surface of the facades works as an abstract artwork as the tessellated surface folds into three-dimensional space-frames lining the atrium and auditorium.[28]

The stone, glass and zinc tiling has also been likened to a form of camouflage.[29] Camouflage is the deliberate frustration of the identifying gaze that enables us to establish the difference between figure and ground. Although it does not work here in the mode of traditional camouflage, it is a part of the visual effect that makes the surfaces seem uncertain and blurs the boundaries between buildings, and between buildings and landscape. The facades have been linked to the visual effects of an Escher drawing where crows metamorphose into fields and floor tile.[30] To some degree these façades frustrate the gaze that seeks to stabilise identities. The fractal screens, blatantly detached from the buildings, can be seen as a kind of mask or 'burqa' that obscures the identity behind it and fixes it externally. While most of the buildings are screened in this way, only one of them is clearly identified by signage: the multicultural Special Broadcasting Service (Figure 6.7). The word 'special' here operates as code for 'difference'. The SBS logo is proudly displayed on this facade in a context where all other identities and logos are downplayed or camouflaged. The 'other' migrates from the margin to the centre; a generic brand of difference ironically cuts across the camouflage; national and urban identity is asserted as impure, hybrid and multiplicitous.[31]

Federation Square constructs a new 'face' for the city. On one hand, this is a face that disrupts received views of Australian or Melbourne identity: its differences unsettle older notions of public space like a face with an occasional 'tic', a voice with a stutter, a step that is almost a stumble.[32] The facades show a series of tensions between a conservatively organised idea of Melbourne and Australia's identity, and a series of differences that work against this organised whole. On the other hand, this new 'face' responds to the flows of desire for the new and *avant garde*, and for Melbourne and Australia to have a new iconic face for the global gaze to add to the well-known iconic 'faces' of Sydney and Uluru. To meet this desire, this skin wraps the whole development and constructs a new organisation of identity, which is suitably consistent and thus acquires the requisite symbolic capital. The whole is composed of differences that are in turn contained by the larger resolution of the design.

Figure 6.6
Fractal facades – geology, face, skin, mask, camouflage

Figure 6.7
Masking difference

Figure 6.8
Atrium – virtual connections
(*Courtesy of LAB Architecture Studio*)

VIRTUAL/ACTUAL

The sense of one thing becoming another extends to a series of juxtapositions between the virtual and actual. The 'atrium', oddly named since it is neither lit from above nor surrounded by buildings, was depicted from early on as one of the key sites within the project. This remnant of the 'wintergarden' idea is formed of an elaborate steel space-frame supporting glass walls and an opaque roof. Early representations of this space show it like a street inhabited by a high density of pedestrians (Figure 6.8). This is a new kind of public space, neither plaza nor sidewalk; people are walking in different directions among filtered sunlight and palm trees with no seating. While the illustrations hint at the street, mall and corporate atrium they also suggest a new kind of urban subjectivity: a population on the move, a 'space of flows' in a fluid city. The space-frame of steel sections dramatically frames this space from above and casts a virtual 'forest' of shadows. However, it does not follow structural imperatives so much as it symbolises the interconnectivity of an information age; a virtual space framing the public space. The citizen moves through a kind of idealised 'non-place' for the globally connected subject. The three major institutions housed in the square are all involved in the production of virtual reality through broadcasting (SBS), film (Australian Centre for the Moving Image, or ACMI) and art (Potter Gallery). Juxtapositions of virtual/actual are constructed throughout the square. ACMI occasionally screens movies juxtaposed against the public life of the square and the giant screen fronting the main open plaza is programmed with a continuous sequence of images; a virtual log fire often turns the winter square into a virtual living room.

In setting out such a litany of possible interpretations we are not suggesting that Melburnians or tourists necessarily or consciously experience the square in this way. To some degree the quest to disclose meanings and identities is a distraction from the success of the square in frustrating attempts to grasp it. Federation Square is what you make of it; it invites a remaking of identity. Each attempt to make sense of it leads to a metamorphosis of meaning; like the Escher drawings it becomes something else. Pavement becomes landscape, desert, beach and artwork; the fractal geometry becomes skin, mask, camouflage, rockwall, forest and cyberspace. In this sense, the design is deconstructive in that there is an attempt to keep the meaning of the place fluid, to keep interpretation in play. This fluidity is a desirable quality for a multicultural society in transition. However, one of the most common critiques of the square from architectural critics is that parts of the project are 'unresolved' or seem 'unfinished'; evoking the ideal of design as embodying 'resolution' of difference. While there are formal details of the project that are disturbing in this regard, this desire for resolution is also linked to the desire for closure of identity: the desire to restabilise the face of the city.

GLOBAL GAZE

Federation Square has also become a virtual space within the field of architectural critique. In his 2002 book *The New Paradigm in Architecture*, and a series of related journal articles, Charles Jencks uses Federation Square as a primary example of a new paradigm based on self-regulating systems, complexity theory and an aesthetic linked to nature.[33] Writing for global consumption, Jencks welcomes such a movement where he suggests '... a new urban order is possible, one closer to the ever-varying patterns of nature ...'[34] The use of wave-like forms, synthetic landscapes and fractal geometries are linked to an architectural iconography based on the idea of the earth as organism. The challenge for major public buildings such as Federation Square, Jencks suggests, lies in the production of 'enigmatic signifiers': 'The injunction is: you must design an extraordinary landmark, but it must not look like anything seen before and refer to no known religion, ideology or set of conventions.'[35] This, of course, was precisely the project of modernity, before its images became clichéd. It is also a very good description of the production of symbolic capital. The idea of a new architecture with forms derived from nature, which has autonomy from authoritarian politics and crass commercialism, has always set mouths watering in the architectural field, but it does have its critics. Peter Davey, editor of the (globally circulated) British journal *Architectural Review*, uses Federation Square as his target. While praising the brief and the plan he says: 'the great problem with Federation Square is what it looks like ... (the) geometry is frantic yet fuzzy ... everything at Federation Square seems blurred; there is no evidence of human scale ...'[36] He suggests that the fractal geometries of the facades are 'frightening, unwelcoming and off-putting to most of us', although it is not at all clear who 'us' includes. The project, he argues, has an 'anti-urban, anti-civic geometry', indeed a 'wilfully anti-human geometry' and that the design 'tries to copy an abstracted notion of nature'. Furthermore, his architectural critique is infused with an anachronistic imperial gaze: he laments that Melbourne, long regarded as a 'seat of provincial respectability' seems to have fallen into the grip of fashion. He points out that Libeskind was the only practising architect on the jury and adds: 'which in itself says quite a lot about Melbourne civilization'.[37]

While at one level this is an internecine squabble within the architecture profession, the persistence of a neo-colonial gaze shows how enmeshed the project is in the postcolonial conditions it seeks to address. The view from the 'provinces' is rather different to that of Davey. While the scheme still has detractors, John MacArthur reflects a broader view in suggesting that: 'The people of Melbourne are, by all accounts, pleasantly shocked.' The result is what he calls a 'liberating bewilderment ... It opens a space for the public to feel that "we" might be something else.'[38] What is constructed is, in part, a difference between Britain and Australia, which resonates with the moment of independence a hundred years earlier. At the same time, the critiques of those such as Humphries, Carroll and Davey line up with a desire to keep Australia and Melbourne in their place, and the angst of those who feel they might lose their place in the fluid city, wherever they may call home.

EXCLUSIONS

There are problems and shortcomings with Federation Square, but they are not found in the geometry. One of them is that the architecture of Federation Square tends to assimilate its differences under a single skin, akin to what Ghassan Hage has called 'white multiculturalism', a kind of assimilation into middle-class values and tastes, camouflaged by the rhetoric of 'tolerance' and 'diversity'.[39] For Hage, cultural difference is constructed in terms of aesthetic appreciation by the dominant culture, rather than mutual engagement on common ground. The skin, while constructing fluid meanings as outlined above, also reduces them into one voice rather than many. The fractal facades become a kind of architectural Esperanto – this tongue of tessellated triangles is an artificial voice from 'above' the fray. There is no dialogue or tension between different voices, but rather the artful composition of an orchestrated 'mix'. Difference is contained for middle-class aesthetic consumption of cultural pluralism. The total control of the large site was written into the competition program that demanded a single architect to oversee both urban design and detailed architectural vision. With about ten semi-separate buildings all controlled within this singular vision the design retains a whiff of the totalising modernist desire to order the city from a single hand and to order society under a single culture. While the architects could have engaged other architects to work on different parts of the project, this in turn would have cut across the imperative to produce the kind of iconic imagery that constructs symbolic capital in the global market. Federation Square is indeed an attempt to produce an 'enigmatic signifier' and to a considerable degree it succeeds, along with the production of significant symbolic capital. In this regard the square establishes a brand identity for the city in both global and local markets. To achieve this iconic imageability, differences must be collapsed into a singular image (the 'enigmatic signifier'), which in turn becomes available as symbolic capital.

This production of symbolic capital in turn becomes problematic in other ways as the square becomes subject to corporate expropriation. The atrium space was closed for a Mercedes-Benz fashion show just a week after it was opened to the public – blocked by security guards and temporary walls with access for VIPs and 'designer guests' only (Figure 6.9). This new fluid space becomes literally stabilised, creating a serious disruption to the flows of life through the square. Many parts of it have since been used for

Figure 6.9
Atrium – 'Designer Guests' only, 2002

commercial promotions and signs have appeared claiming that the square is private property. This is at once technically true yet quite false: ownership of the square has been legally transferred to a 'private' management company that is wholly owned by the state. Thus public control can be maintained at the same time as the square has the autonomy to respond to the market. The 'private' company promotes the square as an 'events space' and records show that it housed about 340 events in the first year of operation with about 80 per cent open to the public. The great majority of closed events were held in the main auditorium where naming rights have been leased as 'BMW Edge'; the Atrium is also popular for private launches, functions and parties.[40] The square is particularly popular for up-market cutting-edge events that link art with advertising. The giant screen facing the plaza runs a regular video sequence that appears as an artwork with a giant eye becoming a series of urban scenes: a liquid car morphs into a human body that then takes off in flight through a rocky desert landscape similar to that evoked by the red square (Figure 6.10). The sequence finally stabilises on the BMW logo. Just as the advertising appears in the square, so the architecture of the square is insinuated into the advertising; a billboard opposite it depicts a vodka bottle, where the fractal architecture becomes the drug with the caption 'absolut pulse.'

Figure 6.10
One eye to the market, 2003

This use of the square for private functions is, in part, a response to the considerable cost overruns with early estimates more than trebling, and final costs approaching $500 million. Projects such as this, however, do not operate within the conventional economics of property development; their benefits to the public are measured (as much as they can be measured) in symbolic and social capital. While this can be partially cashed in the short term, as Federation Square Management appear intent to do, this also diminishes the public value of the project. While economists tend not to measure such things, there is a good chance that the real costs of Federation Square will be returned to the public many times over.

There are other forms of exclusion that operate in the square, often linked to the quasi-privatised management. The square is policed by security guards who enforce a set of normalised behaviours not unlike those enforced elsewhere in the city, yet here they are legitimated on the false premise of the square being private property. Cyclists are regularly asked to dismount and rights of assembly are dependent on written agreement and payment of a fee. There have been some minor protests over this issue.[41] There have also been complaints that parts of the square are inaccessible and dangerous for wheelchairs, despite meeting legal standards.[42] This problem is largely due to the slightly uneven surface and unmarked access routes for wheelchairs; it is currently being addressed by marking and surface-smoothing of such routes.

In a more general sense the sophisticated focus on flows of meaning and desire has not been matched by the design of the spatial structure that mediates flows of everyday life. Spatial practices have not received the same attention as formal imagery. The labyrinthine spatial structure of the square was inspired in part by the rhizomatic structure of Melbourne's central city laneways: the errant flows of everyday life that by-pass the rigid grid and give the city so much of its urban character. Yet here these flows rarely lead through the project as the laneways lead through the city. While Federation Square is not a cul-de-sac in the urban fabric, it is very much a place that one goes 'to' rather than 'through', and this lends it the feel of a cultural acropolis, somewhat set apart from the city. One of the most obvious ways to have guaranteed a continuous flow of people through parts of the square would have been to have connected it directly to the railway platforms below. Most tragically, however, the spatial structure of the square still sets the city apart from the river; the original ideal of 'the city floor reaching out to the river's edge' has not been realised. The square is raised well above the level necessary to clear the trains, gaining some wonderful views, but the price is a steep climb from the riverbank. The architects were required to preserve the heritage bluestone vaults lining the riverbank, some of which they had wanted to excavate as open archways for access to the river. This has not occurred, however, and the project re-enacts the oldest of sins in turning away from the river. Yet urban life abhors a vacuum and the largely derelict vaults were inhabited in 2003 by a group of (largely Aboriginal) squatters (Figure 6.11).[43] While the artworks above engage with an excavation of a lost Aboriginal history, down in the vaults it is still being lived. The management of the vaults has been transferred to Federation Square Management who have evicted the squatters in order to tidy up the vaults and to make them 'safe for everybody who uses the area'.[44] These vaults are of minimal heritage value and should probably be demolished, in which case the opportunity emerges for a second phase of the project that draws people through the square, connects it to the river and remakes the imagery of the waterfront.

Figure 6.11
Squatting in the vaults, 2003
(*Joe Armao* The Age, *19 August 2003*)

SHARDS

While the river was largely forgotten, the corner of Swanston and Flinders streets was for a long time the centre of attention and with its severely stunted shard is now for many the least successful part of the square. The 'shards' were the designers' response to one of the most difficult problems of the site and its greatest opportunity to animate the corner of Flinders and Swanston streets where the civic axis penetrates the grid. The shard on the south-east corner was designed to supplement the railway station, pub and church with a thin four-storey information hub that would overlook the new square, the cathedral and the civic axis. One of the key tactics in achieving an image of multiplicity, a federation of differences, was to juxtapose the new against the old and particularly the shard against the cathedral. When viewed from the open space of Federation Square, the two shards were to frame the view of the cathedral from the south – a new vista made available by opening up the square. The approach across Princes Bridge, however, would produce an urban experience where the western shard would move across the facade of the cathedral, a continuous image of juxtaposition (Figure 6.12).

Figure 6.12
Proposed shard
(*Courtesy of LAB Architecture Studio*)

Figure 6.13
Original shards proposal
(*Courtesy of LAB Architecture Studio*)

With construction of the square well under way in late 1999 the new Bracks Labor government was elected by a very slim majority with an agenda to put an end to the excesses of the Kennett regime. Within three months of taking office the new government initiated a swift review (by former Planning Minister Evan Walker) and decided to delete the western shard in order to open up the 'historic vista' to the cathedral. While public opinion on the issue was evenly split, there was powerful lobbying from both the Anglican Church and the National Trust. It has also been alleged that the decision was a payback for the Kennett decision to scrap Labor's museum and a chance for the new government to leave its mark on what may otherwise be seen as a Liberal project. The Minister for Major Projects is reported to have told the architects that Liberal interference on the Museum was a precedent that legitimates Labor's interference on Federation Square.[45] The irony here is that Federation Square suffered the least political interference of any major project of the Liberal era. The competition rules ensured that the choice of architects and design imagery was relatively free of such political control. There was no secrecy about the decision-making or the design once the competition was announced; and once the Walker review commenced the architects engaged willingly in a robust, and ultimately bitter, public debate.

The decision to eliminate the shard rested upon the premise that a long and clear vista of the south facade of St Paul's from Princes Bridge has important heritage value. Yet while the cathedral has become part of the face of the city, it does not face the site of the shard, which has long been occupied by a sequence of buildings, including a morgue, railway station and shops. The heritage view is largely myth, stronger in the contemporary postcolonial imagination than the everyday lifeworld. Butterfield's original design imagined the cathedral emerging from the urban fabric in a neighbourly rather than a dominating manner; it was first designed on an east–west axis facing Swanston Street, then rotated through 90 degrees due to site restrictions, leaving the entry on Swanston Street. The long view of the cathedral from the south was always interrupted by buildings at its base until the site was cleared for Federation Square. The history of the cathedral is a cobbled sequence of turns and interruptions, and it was a violation of that heritage to reinvent St Paul's as the precious object of the long gaze. A myth was constructed of a white Protestant community settling the banks of the Yarra with the cathedral as the 'face' of the city. The shard design interrupted this with a new story that stands in dialectic tension with the cathedral. This is what Walter Benjamin calls a 'dialectic image', where the tensions and contradictions of the city are exploited for aesthetic effect. While the story of political payback cannot be discounted, we suggest that a deeper, perhaps unconscious, conservatism was at work. While the cherished view was largely myth, it was the disruption of this myth that gave the shard its symbolic and political charge. The shard disrupted a worldview – the Christian ideal of one nation under God.

The shortlisted design by LAB (Figure 6.13), which was not originally publicised, shows four shards facing the cathedral along the Flinders Street frontage; the vista from the square was a concession made during the second stage of the competition. One defence of the shards was that traditional Gothic cathedrals sit tightly within medieval street systems and long axial vistas are impossible; the aesthetic release is associated with the 'surprise' of coming across the cathedral almost by accident as one turns a corner. These arguments worked better for the shortlisted design, than for the winning entry, which was amended to open up and to frame the full frontal view of the cathedral from the new square, part of which had diplomatically acquired the name of St Paul's Court. The winning design was already a compromise.

The decision to eliminate the shard tarnished Evan Walker's considerable reputation, put the arts community severely off-side and stamped the new government with an image of conservatism.

While the cathedral had never had an unobstructed ground-level view, it had long been prominent on the skyline. Yet ironically, this prominence had recently been destroyed by a new hotel to the north – an effect of the collapse of public planning in the 1990s. The same view of the cathedral, which was being cleared at ground level, was now marred above by a widely disparaged building with its 'Westin' logo shining between the spires. While the church and National Trust were focused on preventing a small public building being constructed on one side, a far more damaging private one was constructed on the other.

When the shard was deleted from the project, the major counterargument from its defenders was to appeal to the authority of the competition process – the shard had been properly 'authorised' and its deletion was therefore illegitimate. Aesthetic autonomy was affirmed against the charge of political interference. The architects suggested that the deletion of the shard violated the 'integrity' of the scheme, a seemingly sound argument that did not work either politically or theoretically. To use it was to affirm the design as a purified totality that is inviolable and fixed rather than an 'aggregation'. The deletion of the shard was seen by many as a tragedy, not because it violated the integrity of the design, but because it affirmed the myth of the univalent city, and because it marginalised the future in favour of this mythical past. The tragedy is not that the architecture became embroiled in politics. The shard was always political, to suggest otherwise is to rob it of its primary power as a dialectic image.

A severely stunted shard was eventually constructed on the site as an entry to an underground information centre. Many regard this as an embarrassing outcome for all concerned and the pressure to address it will hopefully continue (Box 6.1). The opportunity and the challenge of the shard lies in an engagement with the desire to liberate architecture from its static role in the preservation and stabilisation of identity and meaning. Is it possible to design a 'shard' as a conduit for ever-changing flows of desire and meaning; a form of place-making that truly engages with the fluid city? A large part of the success of the square lies in its capacity to enfold differences rather than confront. The shard was in some ways too stable a form, establishing a rather old-fashioned figure/ground relationship; a giant finger held up to the establishment. Perhaps Walker had it partly right when he argued that leaving the corner vacant was better than a stunted shard. Perhaps a large hole in the ground would have been better still: a giant question mark, an excavation and an opportunity.

Box 6.1
PROGRAM FOR A NEW SHARD

1   The shard must occupy the site, but must not resemble the design, of the original shard.

2   The height of the shard may range from -10 metres to + 50 metres with an average maximum of 15 metres over any season.

3   The shard must take the form and meaning of a bridge, stair, ladder, well, windmill, rocket, pool, stage, tunnel, cloud, telescope, tree, umbrella, monument, magnet, hall, flagpole, lookout, website, garden, keyboard and clocktower.

4   The shard must dissolve boundaries between part/whole, virtual/real, solid/void, global/local, architecture/landscape, transparent/opaque, finished/unfinished.

5   The shard must be based in at least Aboriginal, British, Greek, American, Irish, Italian, Jewish, Japanese, Indian, Vietnamese, Chinese, Islamic and Buddhist antecedents.

6   The shard must change from day to night, week to week, season to season: it must change with light and shade, rain and sun, peace and war. The shard must flap and fold; it must grow fruit and shed seeds (shardlings). The shard must be festive, sombre, angry, sad, intelligent, simple and complex. The shard can be swept aside.

7   The shard shall be constructed of earth, steel, glass, stone, concrete, timber, plastic, fabric, water, air, light, noise, scent and heat.

8   The shard shall be programmable by the collective desires of any group of more than ten people on location at any time. Public organizations will be granted programming rights. The shard cannot be censored by the state.

9   There shall be no privacy in or near the shard. It must celebrate views of the cathedral, station, river, civic axis and boulevard. The shard shall interrupt every viewpoint and create a new viewpoint for every interruption.

10 The shard is to be a place for traffic in people and ideas; a node of both the city and the world wide web. The public must be able to surf, climb, slide, ride, shelter, write and walk in, on and through the shard. The shard shall be the heart and head of the city, the blood and the brain; it is a node for flows of desire.

BIRRARUNG MARR PARK

While Federation Square has failed to connect successfully with the river, this riverscape is redeemed to a large degree by the addition of the adjacent Birrarung Marr park completed at roughly the same time to become the first new park close to the city in over a century. The eight-hectare park is on former railways shunting yards lining 400 metres of riverbank where the riverside avenue was closed for the Federation Square project. The existing mature fig and elm trees now shade a new waterfront promenade between Federation Square and the Tennis Centre. One grove of elms has a social heritage value based on its use as a 'speakers corner'. This was a centre of radical debate from the 1890s to 1970s, when the riverbank was clearly outside the urban order of the city.[46] Speakers' Corner has now been preserved as a landscaped artwork in a series of mounds and has ironically become a favourite location for corporate functions and private parties.

The park is primarily conceived in terms of a series of lines of movement connecting the global events of the MCG and Tennis Centre to the city. Provision is made for a future connection from the city to the Alexandra Gardens across the river to the south. The park is a new public space around the intersections of these pathways formed in a series of huge terraces connected by bridges. The upper terrace is raised with fill well above the level of the former railyards, and at its peak is an installation of Federation Bells creating, on occasion, a soundscape to go with the landscape (Figure 6.14).[47] The field of thirty-nine bells are at once urban design, public sculpture and public music; they are computer controlled and linked to a web site where the public is invited to submit compositions.

This is a site that generates a high level of visibility towards a large constellation of urban landmarks around Melbourne – Government House, the Arts Centre Spire, Federation Square, the corporate towers of the city grid and the sporting and entertainment stadia to the east. The inverted bells on top of the hill operate a little like a secular cathedral, but unlike the enclosure of both space and meaning in the traditional cathedral this is a place characterised by movement and connection. Visitors are often in transit and the crowd that gathers is, in Canetti's terms, an 'open crowd'. The site has a high level of urban iconic value and symbolic capital that is frequently cashed when corporate or government leaders use it as a stage set. This sense of open visibility was in part enforced by Premier Kennett who declared the terraces of an earlier design 'too cluttered' until trees were removed.

Figure 6.14
Federation Bells

Birrarung Marr park is a fine addition to the city, creating new pathways, visions and opportunities for public life; showing a high level of integration between different levels and types of design. It is used formally during arts and cultural festivals, fun-runs and staged events, and has assumed some of the carnivalesque aspects of traditional festivals such as New Years Eve, when it becomes a spill-over space for events at Federation Square. Yet here the collaboration failed. Federation Square and Birrarung Marr Park are two very finely conceived and adjacent projects, but are poorly connected via a car park. Another problem has emerged on the eastern edge of the park where the new walkway to the MCG was to connect with the valley pathway between terraces, which were in turn to be protected from such traffic. Yet the state government has now committed to a pedestrian overpass connecting directly to one of the terraces, cutting across the original plan.

One of the effects of increasing fluidity was to conceive of the park primarily in terms of flows of people, multiplicitous lines of connection in terms of both vision and walkability. Yet another effect was the erosion of the planning and urban design framework that would have enforced better connections with adjacent projects. However, when the connections across the river and to the MCG are constructed, and if the adjacent railways land is well developed, the park will come into its own as one of the finest projects of its era. We see here the glimmerings of a new integration of comprehensive planning with the production of design imagery – of social and symbolic capital. The park design eschews both formal and picturesque precedents and utilises the flows of pedestrian traffic and the visibility of urban iconography as primary design generators. While the park is an attraction in its own right, it has been largely organised as a place to pass through and to accommodate programmed events. It connects the city as a network of work and leisure, business and sport, urban and arcadian pursuits. And it works economically to add capital value to the public railway land to the north and north-east, where the cost of roofing the railyards makes development difficult. Birrarung Marr is still a work in progress and is becoming known among Melburnians and visitors in a far less sensational way than its contentious neighbour. However, as a connector for actual and potential flows in this part of the city, it is a key piece of the riverscape in the 'fluid city' yet to come.

PART B

DOCKSCAPES

CHAPTER SEVEN

DOCKSCAPES I – OVERVIEW

As Melbourne's earliest port along the Yarra River expanded downstream in the late nineteenth century, the swampy land to the west of the central city grid was excavated to form a large harbour that soon developed into one of the largest ports in the southern hemisphere. With containerisation and larger ships in the late twentieth century, new docks were built further downstream and by the 1980s the docklands close to the city became available for redevelopment. The site comprised about 150 hectares of publicly owned land lining seventy hectares of river and harbour with seven kilometres of water frontage (Figure 7.1). The major harbour waterfront is 600 metres from the city grid, offering forms of amenity the inner city has never had – a large body of water and a new view of the city. The harbour, however, was largely hidden from the everyday lifeworld of the city and did not feature on the collective cognitive map. To those who knew it, who walked out along the pier and wharves to gaze back at the city across the water, this was the greatest waterfront opportunity Melbourne would ever see.

Figure 7.1 (*Opposite*)
Melbourne Docklands, 1993

Large parts of the wharf were lined with huge warehouse sheds. Since their dock functions ceased the vast interiors of the sheds had been used for a variety of marginal urban functions, including maritime, light industrial and arts workshops and entertainment functions – most famously the use of Shed 14 for all-night rave parties. The harbour is in the shape of a two-pronged fork with a finger pier between the forks, all separated from the river by a narrow peninsula of land. The harbour had been excavated from a silty swamp; indeed, the course of the river was also changed in the late nineteenth century to reduce the distance from the mouth. None of this landscape is 'natural' and while it holds significant maritime heritage, the boundary between water and land has long been conceived as fluid ground.

KICK-STARTING

By the late 1980s, with the Southbank strategy in place, the opportunity of developing the Docklands rose high on the state government agenda. This was, however, a much more difficult redevelopment than Southbank. The city was severely cut off from the water: first, by the Spencer Street railway station and goods yards; second, by the major arterial by-pass of Footscray Road (Figure 7.2). Spencer Street Station had long been the major inter-state railways node and goods station, and also a key part of the city loop commuter network forming a major blockage at the edge of the grid. The other major blockage was Footscray Road, a major north–south artery that carried 48 000 vehicles per day. This was projected to increase to 81 000 by 2001 and a third of it was heavy haulage. Footscray Road was the only western by-pass around the city centre and there had long been plans to replace it with either a bridge or a tunnel; however, there was no funding available. Finally, one of the city's major container ports, Webb Dock, was connected with a single rail line along the waterfront, which needed to be relocated. Only one of the city grid streets (Flinders Street) continued into the docks and there was no public transport. Some of the land was contaminated by a former gasworks and much of the former swamp had poor soil conditions requiring piles for buildings over two storeys. Much of the wharf infrastructure was in such poor condition that the required investment exceeded the raw valuation of the site, leading some property consultants to suggest that the site had 'negative value'.

Much of the early feasibility thinking on Docklands was done in terms of how the property values of the city grid could be

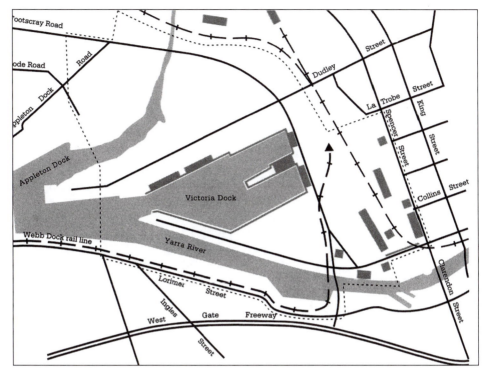

Figure 7.2
Existing infrastructure and heritage buildings
(Docklands Strategy, *1992*)

extended into the docks. There are five major streets forming the
city grid with highly differentiated property values. At the top of
this hierarchy were Collins and Bourke streets, which formed the
heart of the financial district at the western end of the city grid,
followed by Lonsdale and then La Trobe and Flinders streets
(Figure 7.2). The ease of access into Docklands was almost the
exact reverse of these property values. Collins and Bourke streets
were thoroughly blocked by the train lines. Neither street was
aligned with the harbour with no possibility of view lines to the
water. Both Lonsdale and La Trobe streets were aligned directly
with the harbour and bridges could give both direct views and
access to the water within 500 metres of the grid.

Early discussion on Docklands development focused on a
perceived need for a 'kick-start' and in 1987 a bid was mounted

Figure 7.3
Olympic Village proposal, 1987
(Docklands Strategy, *1992*;
Architects: *Daryl Jackson Associates*)

to host the 1996 Olympic Games with the Docklands as the key
site for housing and a media centre.[1] While ultimately unsuccessful, the Olympic bid was a seminal phase in the development
of ideas for the Docklands, leading to the first strategic planning
framework in 1989. The peninsula of land between the river and
harbour was chosen as the village site and a vision was developed
by architect Daryl Jackson (Figure 7.3). The vision showed all of
the major city streets being extended to the water as if the railways
lines were not an issue. Bourke Street was to terminate in a round-
about and Collins Street at a small boat harbour. New pedestrian
bridges were proposed to connect the isolated peninsula across the
river. The scheme reshaped the water's edge in many places with
canals and piers. This design would have distributed two- to six-
storey housing across the site with a few ten-storey buildings.

The planning framework incorporated a vision of mixed-use development, including residential, commercial, hotel and retail. There were to be lively waterfront promenades, water taxis, protected pedestrian environments and easy access to the water. The train station was to become a transport interchange. La Trobe Street was to be extended to the water with a tramway loop past the harbour to return on Flinders Street. A land-use plan was established for the major zones between the city and the water with a marina and varied waterfront developments. Building heights were to step down from the city to the water to avoid over-shading of waterfronts. Waterfront promenades were to be fully public and human-scaled with a rich and varied architecture. Landmark buildings were to terminate or frame important axes, but not overshade water or pedestrian areas. The planning frame-work also examined a series of options for the existing truck route of Footscray Road – realigning, sinking or reconstructing it. The problem was finally wished away with a plan to 'upgrade' it to a 'boulevard'.

Melbourne's Olympic bid was wrapped up with the desire to reorient, reface and globalise Melbourne. A major conference in 1989 was addressed by Premier Cain: 'The development of the site', he said, 'can reorient the city towards the west – and the water. We've had our back turned on the west for too long'.[2] The 'west' in this context was a reference to the working-class suburbs beyond the docks; the intimation was that Docklands was an opportunity for both facing the water and facing up to social disadvantage. The conference was sponsored by the property development industry, whose agenda was made quite clear – to establish a semiautonomous development authority as a channel for private investment, separated from political interference and modelled on the London Docklands.

The Olympics bid became a lesson in global inter-city rivalry. Competing against Atlanta, Toronto and Athens produced the realisation that this global market is a time/space phenomenon linked to the capacity to deliver live coverage of Olympic events to the most lucrative markets in Europe and North America. The television rights for Melbourne were worth significantly less than for competitors. It was also a lesson in how much was at stake in local inter-city rivalries; the bid was allegedly sabotaged by Sydney-based Olympic officials who realised that a Melbourne win would have eliminated Sydney's chances for 2000.[3] The language of globalisation was very much to the fore in the strategic planning framework: 'Melbourne joins other great cities of the world which are using the transformation of redundant port and railway areas to create new vigor, growth and economic activity.'[4] The site was seen as a tourist destination and developments such as Fisherman's Wharf in San Francisco, Catharine Dock in London and South Street Seaport in New York were listed as models. The body of water was to operate as it does globally – as a leisure landscape and a theatre of desire.

TASK FORCE

In 1990 a Docklands Task Force was established within the Office for Major Projects to develop the infrastructure strategy and manage public consultation. From 1990–93 three major policy documents were published by the Task Force.[5] Urban design principles were further developed, based on the ideas of theorists such as Lynch and Jacobs with a focus on mixed use, human scale, legibility, permeability and livability. Over twenty major consultant's reports were commissioned, including studies of ground conditions, heritage, traffic, finance, telecommunication, development costs, bridges, the transport interchange, soil contamination and property development options.[6] A report by Yencken for the Ministry of Transport was crucial in clarifying that burying or moving the railway lines was prohibitively expensive. It established the costs of extending Collins, Lonsdale and LaTrobe streets and the impossibility of extending Bourke Street. The proposed street layout was to extend Collins and La Trobe streets into the Docklands with a tram loop and a small grid of new streets producing land parcels of a marketable size. The street plan diverted waterfront traffic away from the waterfront and the major through traffic was to be taken by a new bridge to the west of the docks (Figure 7.4). The crucial funding for this Western By-pass, however, was not available. The Task Force also engaged in a long-term consultation process through a series of public seminars attended by over 400 people.[7] There was a good deal of community concern and involvement on issues such as urban design, public transport, the Western By-pass, housing, public access to the waterfront, heritage and height control. This planning process was also subject to considerable debate and a range of critical views was published in 1991.[8] The broadest concern was that this was not the only planning process, that the public agenda was being hijacked. By 1991 the Olympics proposal had failed, the global recession was biting hard and the stocks of the state Labor government were in terminal decline.

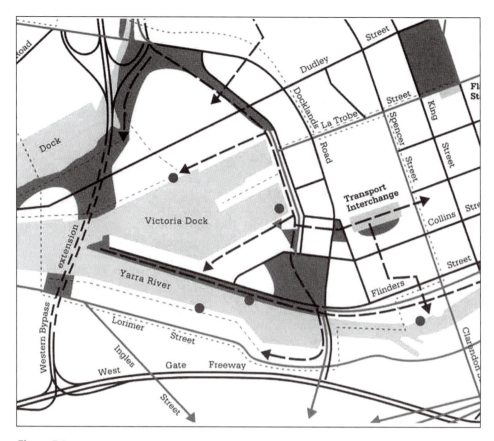

Figure 7.4
Docklands Task Force plan, 1992
(*Docklands Task Force,*
Docklands Strategy, *1992*)

COMMITTEE FOR MELBOURNE

While the work of the Docklands Task Force proceeded, a quite separate planning strategy was being pursued by the 'Committee for Melbourne', a group of civic boosters, funded and controlled by corporate interests with a select membership from both the public and private sector. This was the city's major lobby group for the formation of public–private partnerships and by 1990 it was playing a key role in state planning. The Committee for Melbourne had been pursuing Docklands strategies for some years, triggered in part by a proposal known as the Multi-Function Polis (MFP). This was a proposition by the Japanese

Ministry for International Trade and Industry in 1987 to invest $12 billion in a new 'city' of up to 200 000 people to be sited somewhere in Australia. All major Australian cities competed for this investment and the Committee for Melbourne took the running in pursuing this option for the Docklands.[9]

According to the feasibility studies and discussion papers commissioned or published by the Committee for Melbourne, the MFP was to be a concentration of high-tech (biotechnology, infotech) and 'high-touch' industries (conventions, resorts) on a new site near a major city and airport. Its population of highly skilled international workers was to form 'a substantial semi-residential community of researchers, designers, technologists and managers from Japan, Australia and other nations'.[10] There was also a strong focus on leisure and entertainment. A key synergy here was that Australia shares a time zone with Japan but with reverse seasons, cheaper land, more space and better recreational opportunities. The Japanese would gain exposure to the English language and a culture of creativity within a controlled zone of intercultural contact. However, it was unclear what the Japanese government expected for a $12 billion investment; suggestions that the MFP should have its own medical services and security forces stimulated concern that it would become a private enclave for stressed Japanese executives.[11]

In May 1990 the Committee for Melbourne released its MFP proposal and a discussion paper on the Docklands, which canvassed the development options with regard to both the Olympics and the MFP.[12] These documents also had a broad agenda to refocus Melbourne on the global market. Melbourne's survival in the twenty-first century was depicted as depending upon gearing its planning processes to a global economy moving from an industrial to an informational base. The advantages of an advanced English-speaking nation on the rim of the Asia-Pacific were highlighted in terms of building intellectual resources and producing intellectual capital. The eighty-page colour booklet resembled an advertising brochure and contained no substantive proposal. It sketched a very glossy future vision for the Docklands, but there was no planning or urban design framework. A few indicative maps contained stylish scribbles indicating possible functional zones, character areas and 'optical fibre connections'.

There were many pages of collage creating composite pictures where all of the finest aspects of Melbourne (Victorian architecture, parks and gardens) were to be extended and embellished in a place of science, technology, commerce, leisure and nature. Images of laboratories and information technology were meshed with those of water, recreation, wildlife and postmodern architecture; multicultural Australians mixed with stockbrokers and satellites. Docklands was presented as a future where healthy, happy people live a life of pleasure and leisure in an information economy. These collages offered a seductive future without social problems; they constructed desires without possibility of debate since there was no content. This was the 'fluid city' in discursive form; the flows of people, ideas, water, money and culture were represented in images, circuit boards, numbers and arrows (Figure 7.5). This construction of desire linked sport, art, culture and play with new forms of post-industrial labour. The city was presented as the 'engine room' of growth where opportunities for new alliances of culture and capital must be harnessed to secure footloose global investment. While there were no 'plans' in this document, a diagram published in the newspaper at the time showed the Docklands as a constellation of 'precincts' outlined as fluid blobs with indistinct boundaries labelled 'world education', 'cultural venues', 'bio-health', 'recreation' and 'advanced transport'. The Committee for Melbourne report concluded with a proposal to set up a Docklands Authority with high levels of autonomy from government.

Figure 7.5
Committee for Melbourne 'plan', 1990
(*Courtesy of Committee for Melbourne*, Melbourne Docklands, *1990*)

DOCKLANDS AUTHORITY

In late 1990 Melbourne's Olympic games and MFP bids for the Docklands both failed.[13] Strategies for Docklands development proceeded, however, and the Committee for Melbourne approach became the preferred model. The Docklands Authority was formed in July 1991, based on the model outlined by the Committee for Melbourne. The Board was dominated by corporate interests, a majority were also members of the Committee for Melbourne and not one member directly represented the community. The Docklands Authority Bill was passed by parliament in the face of criticism that it contained the potential of a sovereign state within the city.[14] The Bill gave the Authority the power to enter joint ventures, borrow, set up tax-free havens, compulsorily acquire land and levy development charges. The first CEO (Robert Annells) was appointed in January 1992 and was immediately dismissive of the Task Force strategy as too prescriptive and inflexible: 'I'm a hands-on man and I get things done'.[15] A decision was made to proceed with the $40 million Collins Street extension as the first stage. The plan was attacked in the press where a leading property consultant suggested that: 'The surplus of office and retail space and the economic downturn will not make Docklands feasible for another decade'.[16]

With the economy in recession and the public purse empty, nothing happened before November 1992 when the Liberal coalition government was elected under Premier Kennett. The new Premier soon announced that a 'Living Museum of Aboriginal Culture' would be built in the Docklands as a tourist attraction.[17] This strategy to put live Aborigines on display for tourists was quietly scuttled and Kennett switched attention to other projects. The first CEO of the Authority (Robert Annals) left in 1993 and was replaced by Doug Daines, a private-sector planner with an imperative to get projects on the ground before the next election. In late 1993 the Authority adopted a document entitled 'Docklands Plan' and the following Annual Report listed this as the Authority's primary achievement for the year. The 'plan' was notable for its complete abandonment of any infrastructure proposal; replaced by a division of the site into six large precincts and the proclamation of a series of principles.[18] The precinct map was labelled 'Proactive Context Map: Not a Master Plan' (Figure 7.6); precinct sizes and boundaries appeared to have their sources in earlier Olympic and MFP proposals. Primary among the principles was that all design and funding of infrastructure was to be

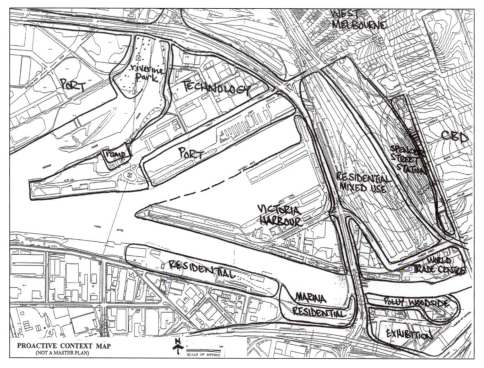

Figure 7.6
'Proactive Context Map: Not a Master Plan', 1993
(*Docklands Authority*, Docklands Plan, *1993*)

undertaken by developers; market forces were to 'dictate' what unfolds. The Task Force work, including the substantial database, analysis and consultation process was abandoned. The argumentation was shallow and vacuous; a section on 'sustainability' listed 'personal security' and an 'attractive pedestrian environment' as key issues. The problem of the traffic by-pass remained unsolved. There was no comment on public consultation, which was replaced by the need for public 'awareness'. An anti-planning ideology spread through the Authority who: 'Adopted a policy that the Authority should be a development agency, not a planning agency ...'.[19] The words 'plan' and 'planning' were systematically replaced with 'development', 'co-ordination' and 'promotion' of the Docklands. This was the 'real -world' perspective that was cast against the world of public planning.

Proclaiming that no market analysis had been done, the Authority commissioned a report from the same consultant who 18 months earlier had written off the Docklands development for a decade. 'I am confident' he now argued, 'that the market will find the Docklands investment opportunities very attractive'.[20] While the recession was now over, the primary change was political – the new government undertook to create the conditions and the price necessary to get development on the ground in a hurry. Despite the rhetoric of becoming 'market-driven', the driving force was the political desire to produce instant projects. The Premier set up and chaired a working group of senior cabinet members and public servants to ensure government control as the Docklands project gradually rose to the top of the new government's *Agenda 21* program of major projects. The most important of the other *Agenda 21* projects, the CityLink freeway, was contracted at this time and included a bridge across the western edge of the Docklands site. The by-pass problem was thus considered solved and Footscray Road, named after the working-class suburb it led to, was renamed Docklands Boulevard.

MILLENNIAL VISION

With the by-pass problem solved all was ready for the precincts to go to tender. However, the Authority lost its second CEO in three years when Daines departed in early 1995 and control shifted to the office of Planning Minister Maclellan. In August 1995 a key brochure entitled 'Melbourne Docklands: Towards the 21st Century' was released. It proclaimed: 'For decades, grand plans for Melbourne Docklands were held out to the people of Victoria – but nothing happened. Now that has changed.'[21] Together with a new range of collages was a pen-picture of the millennial vision: 'A Day in the Life of Docklands: 2000 ... With its growing residential population and daily workforce, Melbourne Docklands is now a living community.'

Two plans were presented: a precinct plan and a fully developed vision. The precinct plan was a more sophisticated development of the 'Non-Master Plan' from 1993 with the site divided into seven precincts ranging in size from 6.5 to 40 hectares (Figure 7.7). The precincts were presented as blank sites to be filled in by the market. While initially labelled with functions they were progressively renamed to reflect the fact that they were available for whatever the market chose to fill them with. The 'Towards the 21st Century' brochure was updated after four months and the only change was to rename precincts: from 'River Residential' to 'Yarra

Waters'; from 'Heritage Mixed Use' to 'Batman's Hill'. The boundaries between precincts were largely grounded in the existing site and its (largely obsolete) infrastructure. The average precinct size of twenty hectares made it clear that only major consortia of development interests would be interested. The second image was a fully developed infrastructure plan with a tree-lined street grid and a tram loop from the city, labelled an 'artist's impression'. This was a recycled version of the 1992 Task Force infrastructure plan. Ironically, this was one of the disparaged 'grand plans' of the past held out again but with a new twist. Here it operated as a 'possible' vision that was actually rendered practically impossible by the precinct plan. While it was not a real plan it legitimated the 'real-world' perspective, like the 'day-in-the-life' pen pictures, it grounded the project in an imaginary everyday life. At the same time as the vision fixed an image of a future Docklands, the precinct plan rendered this future increasingly blank.

Figure 7.7
Precinct diagram, 1996
(*Docklands Authority*, Melbourne Docklands:
Towards the 21st Century, *December 1995*)

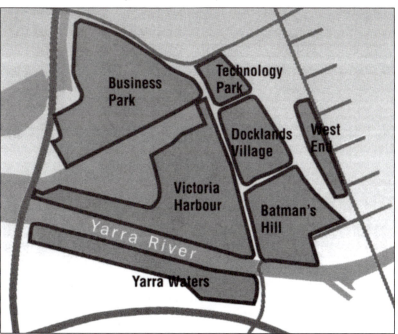

In late 1995 a legislative framework was put in place in the form of a Planning Scheme amendment for the Docklands area.[22] On the face of it this was a return to comprehensive infrastructure planning based on the Task Force material, adjusted for consistency with the new precinct boundaries. It certified roadways and land parcels of about one to five hectares with up to twenty parcels in each precinct. A set of height limits ranging from fourteen to sixty metres were designed to protect the waterfront from overshading (Figure 7.8). The Act was referenced to a volume of urban design guidelines, which incorporated significant public interest controls.[23] Heritage sites were to be protected, single-use developments avoided and public transport links provided to the city. Landmark sites were identified to establish legibility, create view lines and vistas. There was to be public access on all waterfronts. However, there was no clear commitment to construct or enforce this plan. The Act included a key clause which legislated that permits may be granted to any development deemed to make a 'positive contribution' to the Docklands. This was a Planning Scheme with which compliance was voluntary. The Act was released for a short period of public comment on Christmas eve 1995 – a well-known and successful tactic for avoiding public debate.

Effective control moved back to the Docklands Authority in early 1996 when John Tabart was appointed CEO, introducing a higher level of entrepreneurial leadership and a focus on marketing. Tabart had a strong background in property develop-ment and marketing, having overseen the Brisbane Airport and Mirage hotel developments. 'The Time is Now' was the title of a major forum of property developers where the tender process was relaunched in May 1996; the imperative was to get projects on the ground in four years to become 'Melbourne's Millennium Mark'. In his speech, via giant video screen, Premier Kennett argued that Docklands had been 'ignored by our predecessors' and Planning Minister Maclellan explained how the system of government designed and funded infrastructure, filled with private projects, was gone. Docklands was to be more 'strategic and innovative', a 'user-friendly development process' where the design of the city was all 'up to the people with ideas' – and he did not mean the government.[24] Docklands was to become a 'global landmark development' that would create a 'waterfront signature' for Melbourne. The financial consultant explained how urban design and finance were to be combined – projects were to be 'design-led'. Privatisation of the water's edge was raised as an 'interesting possibility'. The property consultant suggested that land prices

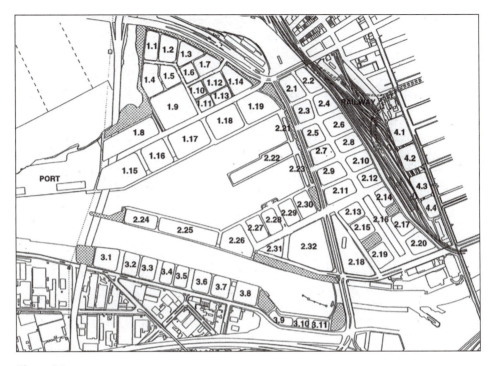

Figure 7.8
Voluntary Planning Scheme L202, 1996
(Melbourne Planning Scheme Amendment L202, *1996*)

would be 'competitive' and full development of Docklands was viable in ten to twelve years.[25] Everything was to be flexible except the time lines; project completion was to be strictly enforced by Development Agreements. The key criterion for a successful bid was to be consistency with the 'vision'. For an understanding of this vision developers were referred to the 1995 brochure with its 'day-in-the-life' pen sketches and recycled but obsolete imagery. A discursive loop was set up whereby developers were to bid to fill in the blanks of the precinct plan, yet the key criteria for success were consistency with the precinct plan and to ensure projects on the ground by 2000. Docklands was available for 'whatever'.

It slowly dawned on developers that there really was no infrastructure plan; the role of government was to be that of co-ordinating the integration of different precincts. The chance to acquire freehold title to large precincts and to design the infra-structure in accordance with private interests was to be a key lure for developers. Some developers raised the crucial question: why should they invest in public infrastructure (such as open space or city connections) where the value would accrue to adjacent precincts? Put another way, since good urban design and planning creates wealth well beyond its boundaries, how might they capture such flows of capital? The Minister and the Authority initially seemed stumped by this issue and said they would get on to it. Tabart later responded by conceding that perhaps the government may retain a role in funding infrastructure, but only as a means of facilitating private infrastructure development:

> The concept of a back-to-back contract, where a number of development proposals are agreed with developers and at that time certain infrastructure is provided by govern-ment to service those developments, is a real possibility … We need to see what developments are on foot before we consider how we might fund and co-charge, if you like, the cost of that infrastructure.[26]

This made it clear that infrastructure funding was negotiable, that developers may be able to secure government funding to facilitate the construction of their designs. A global advertising drive was launched with presentations by property consultants throughout Europe, North American and Asia.[27]

In late 1996 it was announced that a private football stadium would be built in the docks. It was to be coupled with a television studio headquarters and occupy the precinct labelled 'Docklands Village', formerly slated for a residential and commercial mix. The stadium (to be discussed in detail in chapter 8) had been a prospect for some time on a range of sites around the city. The reason for this site was the close proximity to both Spencer Street Station and the water, and it was a badly needed kick-start for Docklands. The downside was that it introduced a huge barrier between the city and the water, and eliminated any possible exten-sion of Lonsdale Street.

WATERWORLD

In 1996 the Docklands Authority also commissioned a new and dramatic urban design vision from *avant garde* architects Ashton

Raggatt Macdougall (ARM) in order to stimulate the thinking of the development community, to fill the vacuum in the public imagination and to generate public credibility for the project. The results were published to great fanfare in late 1996.[28] The report begins:

> In preliminary discussions, many developers indicated that although they appreciate the flexible approach provided under the Melbourne Planning Scheme for the Docklands area, they are seeking clearer guidance on the key elements and visions of development ... The intent of this document is to assist invited developers in the preparation of creative and viable development proposals.[29]

The document comprised both a planning/urban design 'framework' and a futuristic 'vision' portrayed in elaborate computer graphics (Figure 7.9). The framework represented a return to infrastructure planning and the vision was highly imaginative. At its centre was a dramatic idea for a large egg-shaped central park that would create open space at the termination of the Bourke Street axis, connecting the city to the harbour, adding value to surrounding properties. The five-hectare Docklands Park was located within a giant traffic roundabout with view lines and roads radiating in many directions – north to the harbour and stadium, south to the river and east to the city. Described as a 'Central Park for the 21st Century'; it was to be bounded by tall buildings to the south (but not overshadowed), connected by a pedestrian overpass to the stadium and with views opening to the harbour. Existing streets were to extend from the city grid before deflecting into fluid forms.

In these images there is a sense of a city that had turned its back to the water now literally turning *into* water. This fluidity of urban form extended to curvilinear streets and buildings with kidney, cylinder and ribbon shapes that loop, fold and twist in three dimensions. The waterfront was scattered with tensile structures, folded roofs and a string of ovoid islands. The vision set up a contrast between the new Docklands and the old city whereby the city was expanding, deflecting, becoming flexible and dynamic. The traditional image of the city was destabilised, melted, stretched and inflected. These images constructed an imaginative future of hyper-modernity where, in that famous phrase, 'all that is solid melts into air'.[30] They also reflect some key

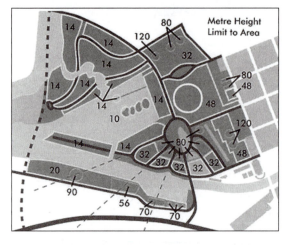

Figure 7.9
Fictional vision, 1996
(*Docklands Authority*,
Conceptual Planning
and Design Framework
and Visions, *1996*)

conceptions in current urban and architectural theory – the 'space of flows' in an information economy and the 'flexible accumulation' of global capital; a focus on 'smooth space' and on folding and curving images that defy stable significations.[31] This was an image of a future city where time speeds and space flows; a city of hypersurfaces where axes deflect and forms fold, a city where developers make a splash.

This was an imaginative framework and vision with considerable concern for the public interest; the waterfront promenades indeed had an excess of public space. 'The area should give accessibility and public ownership to the water edge' the document argued, 'much as the public zone of the Australian beach does'.[32] The harbour was treated in an integrated manner, although its opportunities for capital gain were not exploited. Block sizes were very large and overall densities were unsustainably low – this was not a diverse nor walkable city. The orientation to the street was largely replaced by a series of buildings as objects. Urban design principles of permeability, mixed-use and active frontages were largely subsumed by the focus on dynamic and fluid imagery. Viewlines remained important, but the stabilised gaze upon fixed vistas terminated by landmarks was gone in favour of movement and flow in a virtual 'waterworld'.

ARM is an architecture firm with a reputation based on a series of buildings that adopt a strongly textual approach to architecture: Storey Hall in Melbourne and the National Museum in Canberra are multiply coded with architectural, local, historical and popular references. The work is often laced with cynicism, a deconstructive resistance to singular meanings and a difficult beauty in the challenging tradition of the *avant garde*. The firm is not well known in planning and urban design fields. In this case architectural skills were called upon to produce an instant city. The buildings were entirely fictional and the infrastructure plan was in complete contradiction to the legislated Planning Scheme and the precinct plan which was already out to tender. The existing confusion between the precinct plan and the Planning Scheme was now compounded with a third scheme. This was not the kind of city that a market-led approach might generate; yet as advertising imagery and symbolic capital it did indeed meet its market with immediate and powerful effects on public credibility.

The futuristic vision received almost universal acclaim in the press. The highly influential editors of *The Age* appeared to confuse the fictional vision with a real plan and decided to get behind it: 'Anyone who has visited London's docklands – the newly pulsating heart of that centuries old city ... will applaud the latest plans ... the government appears to have backed a winner.'[33] *The Age* at this time was suffering badly from Kennett's intimidations, including interference at board level; however, it is difficult to imagine just what part of London Docklands they were thinking of.[34] In the absence of a 'plan' these images both sold newspapers and legitimated the lack of planning. The previous Labor government had produced plans from 1988–1992, but nothing happened and they were seen to have failed. After four years of the Kennett government little further had happened and the credibility gap was opening again. The ARM vision fulfilled a widespread need to believe in the ideology of the state *'on the move'*.

With three plans operating in parallel and substantial blurring between them, with the mass media confused, intimidated and eager for simple slogans and sound-bites, genuine public debate disintegrated. This was compounded by the fact that everyone involved with the Authority had signed secrecy agreements. Elected Councillors of the City of Melbourne were excluded from the process on the spurious basis that they had a 'conflict of interest'. As Tabart put it: '... to have Councils involved in selecting bidders, while at the same time they've got responsibilities to their own constituents is a problem.'[35] This severing of urban planning from public accountability was justified on the basis that commercial confidentiality needed to be protected from open governance. Commercial confidentiality in turn was used to protect private interests from public scrutiny.

There was, however, one major public forum organised by the People's Committee for Melbourne, a community-based group that emerged in response to privatised planning. The Minister, the Docklands Authority and their architects were all enticed to attend, producing a rare moment of genuine public debate. Architect Ian MacDougall explained the vision: '... our brief has been ... to essentially put flesh on the bones of the planning material that has already been prepared by the Authority ... What we have done is develop a skeleton ... and it is called the Framework Diagram'.[36] The confusion here between the infrastructural 'skeleton' and the urban design 'flesh', reflected a real confusion – both flesh and skeleton were fiction and neither bore any relation to the Planning Scheme that in turn was voluntary. To compound the confusion, Tabart suggested that the new framework was identical to the Planning Scheme and would be implemented: '... every bid ... will have to comply with the Planning Scheme, it will have to comply with the framework which [the architect] has explained here today.

It is a framework, it nominates the streets, the public space areas that bidders will have to comply with ...'.[37] This made little sense since the precinct diagram was the only real 'plan'. Planning practice had been largely displaced by urban design imagery and the architects had discovered a new role as propagandists.

'REAL' DOLLARS

In the lead up to the deadline for tender submissions in early 1997, developers were reportedly suffering both confused heads and cold feet as they tried to calculate the risks and benefits for large precincts without precedents.[38] There were reports of developers submitting low bids in order to shift the risk back on to the government. The difficulty for developers lay in analysing the ways the infrastructure, character and function of adjacent precincts would clearly add or subtract capital value and potential. The various teams of consortia began to form alliances and expand their bids to better integrate the infrastructure and control the uncertainties of adjacent precincts.[39] The development process eliminated small investors, privileged the largest of those who remained and stimulated fears that the entire 200 hectares might be monopolised under single corporate ownership.

Preferred bidders were first announced in September 1997, a moment of triumph for the Authority Chairman who proclaimed 'real dollars-on-the-table' at last.[40] Two shortlisted proposals were published for each of four precincts, plus a single proposal for the technology park (although subject to further approval). The development of each of these precincts will be described in more detail in the following chapter. For the moment it suffices to note that the initial round of bids included a business park, theme park, shopping mall, housing, commerce, hotels, cinemas, marinas, technology park and exhibition centre. Many of the proposals were couched in terms of new place-types such as the 'Centre for the Future', 'Export City Square', 'Cyberia' and '24 Hour City', all constructing the global image of a new form of urbanity linked to new perceptions of space and time.

The detail released to the public at this stage comprised a brief summary of proposed functions, amounts of investment and a range of images. The shortlisted bids were combined to form two composite schemes, each of which showed the entire 200 hectares completely developed (figures 7.10 and 7.11). These images were prepared by the Authority rather than the winning bidders to ensure that each bid was in the same graphic language and the

Figure 7.10
Composite Vision of Winning Bids, 1997 – Scheme A
(*Docklands Authority*, Annual Report *1997*)

Figure 7.11
Composite Vision of Winning Bids, 1997 – Scheme B
(*Docklands Authority*, Annual Report *1997*)

whole Docklands landscape would appear integrated. The attempt to read these images as firm plans was difficult, since they resembled the cut-and-paste collage effects of advertising with little consistency from one image to the next. There were a series of gaps in most precincts where the proposals failed to fill the precinct and pieces of the fluid ARM vision were patched in. These fictional patches comprised about a third of the total area – generating the illusion of a fully developed and integrated site full of 'real' proposals. The images, however, did successfully construct a public narrative of global investment flooding into the Docklands; the myth of 'real dollars on the table' was largely and successfully constructed by the computer graphics.

In public debate the glossy images of the completed Docklands were widely reproduced as lead stories in the mass media and accepted without question as real projects subject to final decision. At this stage, however, there was only one firm contract for one part of one precinct – the stadium. The pledge that Docklands would be free of public cost was quietly abandoned as $71 million of public investment was provided for bridges and related infrastructure necessary to connect the stadium to the city.[41] This confirmed developers' hopes that in the end government would fund the infrastructure necessary to seal a deal.

The Docklands Authority, like the state government it served, was highly media savvy, and unlike many public authorities, it did not leak. The shortlisted projects included a bid for the world's tallest building – the Grollo Tower. This project will be discussed in detail later but for now it is important to note that it served a key role in capturing the public debate and media focus. With an opaque and complex planning process the media needed an 'angle', a point of contention that was provided by the Grollo Tower. Everyone either loved or hated it and the Minister welcomed a vigorous public debate on such an adventurous project. Paradoxically, the most outrageous of proposals enabled him to rise above the fray with a patrician air and declare that the tower would be properly considered along with other bids as part of a thoroughly legitimate approval process.

What should have been apparent at this stage was that the bidding consortia were finding it difficult to find enough investment to cover the site. Most proposals broke the height limits of both the Planning Scheme and the ARM framework, yet remained at an overall low density. While the constraints of the Planning Scheme were widely recognised by developers as meaningless, the imperative to guarantee buildings on the ground within a couple of years followed by full development in ten to twelve years was seen as non-negotiable. To win the bid and gain freehold title to a full precinct required a minimum of instant investment. It is difficult to avoid the conclusion that the urban density was effectively set by the development timeframe – the market had simply spread the prospective investment for that period very thinly across the site. The potential density (and therefore sustainability) of the Docklands was being comprised by short-term imperatives.

While some schemes took cues from the urban design guidelines and the ARM scheme, none followed either of the two available infrastructure plans. On careful examination, every precinct was underdeveloped. The theme park that was shortlisted for the Business Park precinct lining the north of the harbour (Figure 7.10) had so little need for waterfront that it was lined with car park (and coloured green). Problems were also apparent in a lack of integration between precincts. The egg-shaped 'central park' of the ARM framework, which straddled the precinct boundary between Batman's Hill and Victoria Harbour, was incorporated by some winning bids and ignored by others. One of the composite visions (Figure 7.11) showed a 'boiled egg' park – provided in one proposal yet sliced off in the other. The Victoria Harbour bidders had no idea whether Collins Street would be extended and it is hard to imagine how they could calculate their risks. Those bidding on the Business Park had no idea what might happen on the central pier directly in front. Without any certainty as to context, developers appear to have covered their risks by minimising investment. The precinct which made most sense, and ultimately the first to reach a firm deal, was Yarra Waters on the south of the river because it shared no boundaries; the infrastructure and external conditions were relatively stable.

CROSS TRAFFIC

The CityLink project incorporating the Bolte Bridge was first announced in May 1995. This was a major linkage of three freeways that had been on the state government agenda for many years and predated the Kennett regime. A full account of this project is outside the scope of this book but it played a key role in Docklands. Most importantly, CityLink was to be the long-planned Western By-pass that would take through traffic off the waterfront and enable integration of the city with the harbour. By redirecting traffic across the elevated bridge, CityLink was also conceived as a way to bring the image of the docks to the foreground of public consciousness as the new 'face' of the city. A government brochure argued that: 'the bridge will provide an entirely new view of the city skyline against Docklands'.[42] Such a view, foregrounding the docks against the city figured prominently in both the fictional 'water world' vision and in the graphics publicising the shortlisted schemes.

The CityLink project was designed to connect three existing freeways with the bridge across the Yarra and a tunnel under it at another point. Docklands was adjacent to this intersection with the airport fifteen minutes away. This was a complex deal whereby ownership of the public freeway to the airport, the city's 'front door', was ceded to private interests for thirty years in order to generate new flows of traffic. To make the deal viable without 'cost' to the public purse, the government agreed to restrict traffic on competing roads – to stop toll-avoiders using the 'back door'. This privatisation of a public freeway stretched the credibility of the state to be acting in the public interest, a problem that was addressed in part by the design of the freeway experience. The journey from the airport and past Docklands enters a kind of 'speedscape' that culminates in the views of city and Docklands from the bridge. This speedscape is an aestheticised and enjoyable freeway experience that has markedly changed the image of the city and its waterfront.[43]

The CityLink bridge was opened to traffic in 1998 and its role as a by-pass for the Docklands was soon in doubt. Footscray Road on the harbour's edge remained busy and noisy because the new bridge had been built at a grade too steep for heavy haulage vehicles. It was not in the interest of freeway operators to have them slowing down the flow of toll-payers. To make matters worse, Footscray Road was one of the competing roads that the government had contracted to narrow in order to prevent toll avoidance. Never one to fret over a mistake, the Premier declared that a new by-pass would be constructed through the Docklands, but set back from the water and behind the stadium. This was politically astute since the problem was declared solved before it became a scandal. However, this option had been canvassed in the early 1990s and rejected because it simply severs the city from the docks in a new manner. Furthermore, the precinct plan rendered it more difficult to achieve. In order to connect across the river, the new by-pass required a complete reconstruction of the Grimes Bridge into a swerve shape, cutting off valuable waterfront (Figure 7.12). Threading around the Batman's Hill precinct wasn't quite possible so the by-pass literally sliced across it, damaging its connections with the river and the city. The shortlisted bidders were required to redesign their schemes around and over the expressway. One of these bids was strongly integrated with the Trade and Convention Centre to the south-east, and it eventually became the losing bid (see chapter 8). Some plans from this time showed the by-pass slicing through this proposal with remnants left on either side.

The by-pass was completed in 2000 and given the Aboriginal name of Wurundjeri Way, after the original inhabitants of the site. A 25-metre high sculpture entitled 'Bunjil' was later added to the broad median strip. Representing the eagle totem and 'spirit creator' of the Wurundjeri, it was undertaken by a non-Aboriginal sculptor (Bruce Armstrong). The serpentine path of the by-pass as it weaves around the stadium became Aboriginalised as the Wurundjeri way; insulated against criticism and rooted in authentic history. The by-pass was the nadir of urban design and planning in Docklands, 'the after-thought of all after-thoughts' as one developer later claimed.[44] It was arguably unnecessary since constraining traffic on the Docklands Boulevard would have tamed the heavy haulage and squeezed some of it on to the bridge. To cap it off the by-pass was in clear violation of the contract with CityLink developers, since it was used to by-pass the toll bridge; the state was later sued for loss of revenue.[45]

The by-pass was difficult to sell to an increasingly sceptical public, and ARM were commissioned in advance for a new round of propaganda. The new bridge was announced together with a fictional proposal for a new icon, ostensibly intended to inspire the bridge tenderers to better design. The design was in the form of a slender yellow steel arc that spanned the river landing on the city side in a crown-shaped splash. 'City Faces a Bright Future' proclaimed the headlines in the *Herald Sun* and architects praised the design as reflecting 'a city feeling confident about its future and willing to experiment in design'.[46] The imagery did its job in capturing public debate, but was never seriously intended for construction. It was, however, a fine design that showed a talent for capturing the spirit of the times. It melded echoes of the Southbank pedestrian bridge and Crown Casino logo with images of developers making a splash. Its chances of being built were not helped, however, when a letter to the editor suggested that: 'The symbolism of the yellow stream arcing across the Yarra, then splashing down in a welter of foam on the other side is unmistakable'.[47] This fine memorial to public pissing was not built, but the symbolic capital did not go to waste since the design was later adapted by the adjacent Yarra's Edge (Yarra Waters) project as a logo.

And here lay another glitch in transport planning. Webb Dock, a container terminal with a crucial role in maintaining Melbourne's role as Australia's largest port, was connected by a railway that ran through the Yarra Waters precinct (Figure 7.2). In order to make the precinct available for new development, the railway connection was simply taken out of commission with no alternative connection in place. The obvious solution was to combine a new rail connection with the new bridge. This was an integral part of the early public strategy, but was abandoned when the private CityLink deal was negotiated in 1995. The former CEO of the freight authority put the issue well: 'We are very visionary here in Victoria: we moved the port downstream, we dredged, we built Webb Dock ... So here we are with a world-class port that is trying to be world competitive – and we take the railway away'.[48] Replacement of the Webb Dock link is now slated to cost about $80 million.[49]

POST-HOC PLANNING

From 1997–99 winners were announced and re-announced for five precincts totalling up to $4 billion of investment. However, during 1998 and 1999 winning bids collapsed on every precinct except Yarra Waters. This period coincided to some degree with the collapse of credibility of the Kennett government, which was voted out of office in October 1999. These projects had been publicly announced so many times the images were now part of the public imagination and there was some sense of disbelief as the visions evaporated. The planning process had become media-driven and image-focused, firmly geared to the construction of political legitimation as evidence of a state 'on the move'. The steady supply of colourful visions from the Authority was designed to capture the public imagination and fuel the mass media thirst for iconic imagery. The *Herald Sun* promoted government propaganda and reinforced the advertising with headlines such as: 'Great Moment in History', 'Blossoming of a Wasteland' and 'Our Waterfront Wonder'.[50] Community concerns about the prospect of private governance of the Docklands were portrayed by the editors as 'sectional interests', from which the Docklands must be defended.[51] In mid-1999, while schemes were stalling or collapsing on three precincts, the *Herald Sun* narrative remained one of 'Docklands Vision Unfolds' and 'Pieces Fitting into Waterfront Jigsaw'.[52] The reasons for these collapses are often unclear due to secrecy provisions, however, I will return to such issues after examining the precinct proposals in more detail in the forthcoming chapter.

The new Premier, Steve Bracks, was cast in opposition to his predecessor – concerned with community issues, long-term infrastructure planning, consultation and a focus away from the production of urban spectacle and iconography. By mid-2000 the directions of the Authority had moved with the political pendulum. A booklet entitled *Integration and Design Excellence* listed the key goals as: 'to facilitate the integration of all developments within Docklands, and with adjacent areas, and to sustain design excellence and public amenity ...'. There was an attempt to reconcile flexibility with certainty: '... the design principles and frameworks ... are dynamic. They provide a high degree of certainty and a useful tool that will evolve and be refined as precinct design and development evolves'.[53]

The decision to remove all-through traffic from the waterfront was made in the context of great uncertainty about the future of both Batman's Hill and Victoria Harbour precincts. As the first round of possible projects had demonstrated, neither of the selected tenderers for either precinct had much idea what to do about the zone between them that had long been suggested as a park. With the traffic removed, the strip of land formerly consumed by Footscray Road became available for a linear open space extending from the Grimes Bridge to the harbour (Figure 7.12). The idea of a large park in this vicinity, protected by diverting traffic off the waterfront, goes back to the Task Force plan of 1992. During the early period of precinct tendering the Authority lived in hope that tenderers would collaborate to produce an integrated open space system. By 2000 it was clear that any such plan would need to be led by the Authority who embarked on a genuine public plan for the area.[54] This was the first major piece of infrastructure design engaged in by the Authority; made possible by shaving significant amounts of land from the Victoria Harbour precinct, which in turn was made possible by the collapse of the winning bid for that precinct.

This strip of new public space is designed as a mix of park, plaza and esplanade about a hundred metres wide and a kilometre long. It forms a central spine connecting all six major precincts from the northern edge of the harbour to the Yarra where it connects to Yarra Waters with a new pedestrian bridge. By 2000 the Wurundjeri Way by-pass had forcibly shifted all-through traffic off the newly renamed 'Docklands Boulevard', which was then renamed again as 'Harbour Esplanade'. The old warehouse buildings along the water in front of the stadium were demolished to create a large new public open space called 'Grand Plaza'. Conceived as a 'meeting place', 'event space' and water taxi access to the stadium, it remains to be seen just how this area might be used. The new esplanade and plaza are designed with a vast pavement design based on the bold colour effects of a waterfront container terminal – stripes of coloured pavement mark out giant numbered bays that are labelled 'event spaces'.[55] This conception of 'event spaces' derives from the work of architects and urban

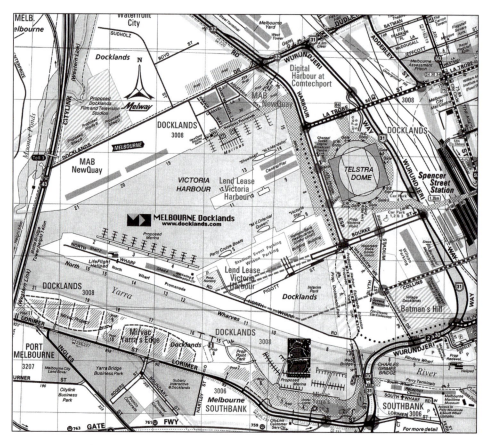

Figure 7.12
Melways map of Docklands, 2003
(*Courtesy of* Melways Street Directory, *Edition 30, 2003;*
Melway Publishing P/L)

designers infused with a desire to produce new forms of public space freed from the supposedly over-determined and formularised choreography of the city.[56] These are fine imperatives, yet here the coloured stripes and numbers are overwhelmed by the emptiness of the open space and the barrenness of the stadium frontage with its corporate landscaping. The vision is that crowds attracted to the football will spill out on to the 'Grand Plaza' and esplanade with its unpredictable 'events'. For the moment this vast space remains barren and it is difficult to imagine that it can ever become a consistently vital public space.

While the park remains under construction and the design is unclear, it will in effect be two parks since the extensions to Collins and Bourke streets will produce major boundaries. The strategy for linear strips of public open space is generally based on the capacity to create a continuous pedestrian and bicycle flow through the urban fabric and to generate new forms of access. This 'linear' park runs against the flow of traffic from the city to the Docklands; it privileges the flow of pedestrians from the precincts to the harbour and each other, rather than from the city to the harbour. While this string of highly contemporary public spaces will add substantially to Melbourne's public realm, it also adds substantially to the capital gains on the newly privatised waterfront.

After the millennium the forms of representation changed as the Authority began to show plans of the Docklands in the graphic language of the popular Melways street maps. Here the precinct boundaries were erased and the site was portrayed in the language of the familiar and everyday rather than the futuristic. The Docklands were portrayed as a real and integrated extension of the city grid. With a focus on certainty rather than flexibility, infrastructure plans became clear rather than fluid. Investors could be certain the park and plaza would happen; Wurundjeri Way by-pass was in place, together with city connections and a tram loop. The decision was made to extend Collins Street, a commitment first made by the Labor government in 1992. The imaginary city of the future became the real city of the present. This sense of the virtual turning into the actual through the Melways representation worked both ways as the actual Melways street map began to feature the new Docklands (Figure 7.12). While the street plan remains uncertain the Melways map functions to advertise the Docklands precincts with brand names, corporate logo and web site address.

With the idea of public infrastructure back on the agenda, in 2001 the Authority announced that the Docklands would be digitally networked to provide all Docklands residents with high bandwidth infrastructure. This was a sensible strategy to attract the wealth-creating synergies of information-intensive industries and populations. Yet again these public funds will boost the value of waterfront property after it has already been sold. In 2001 a community services plan was released that layered a range of community services on to the private precincts. A medical centre was to be attached to the stadium, a high school and childcare centre were to be incorporated into the technology precinct with a library and youth park in Batman's Hill. A retail 'hub' was proposed for one of the least accessible locations near the western end of the peninsula. This plan was little more than an attempt to convince the new Minister that Docklands was to be a real community rather than a private enclave. Traditional community services such as childcare and health were to become add-ons to the digital high school and sports medicine facility. The 'plan' was welcomed by the new Minister: it demonstrated that the project had a 'heart and soul'.[57] Polls were produced showing 79 per cent community support for Docklands, almost identical to the 80 per cent 'support' for earlier fictitious 'plans'. 'Docklands is for Everyone' has become the new slogan, together with key words: 'sustainability', 'affordability' and 'community'. The integrated open space strategy was entitled 'Places for Everyone', based on 'community consultation' that consisted of asking for public approval of the glossy vision. As soon as the first residents moved in the Authority organised a community association and a community newsletter; guest lectures were organised on how to build social capital together with gardening sessions for high-rise balconies, dog-walking groups (no dog necessary) and fishing tips.

By 2003 the role of the Dockland Authority was much diminished, deals had been sealed on all major precincts, although the details remain confidential.[58] The Docklands Authority was merged with the state's major suburban land authority (ULA) to form 'Vicurban', with John Tabart as the new CEO. On the top of its agenda are 'sustainable development' and 'affordable housing'. Docklands has become the model for the larger city. I will return to a broader assessment of the Docklands after examining the story for each of the precincts in greater detail in chapter 8.

CHAPTER EIGHT

DOCKSCAPES II – PRECINCTS AND PROJECTS

STADIUM

The 'Docklands Village' precinct occupied the most central location in the Docklands, filling the gap between the railway station on the city grid and the harbour. Slated since the late 1980s as a residential and commercial mixed-use precinct, it never went to tender as such. The idea for a sports and concert stadium with a retractable roof in the Docklands first emerged in 1994 and was brought to fruition as the first real contract for the Docklands in 1996–97. The key market was to be the local Australian Football League (AFL) code, which draws an average of 40 000 people to each of its games during the winter. The proposal, which had been mooted for several sites around Melbourne, was for a stadium of 52 000 people. While the stadium is a private project it was a deal that was initially stitched together between the state and the AFL administrators before tenders were called from developers. This was to be the kick-start that Docklands badly needed. In 1996 the 'Docklands Village' precinct was chosen as the site, and the development was put out to tender. About 27 matches per year were to be moved to Docklands from other venues in order to guarantee the base revenue stream.

As developers were shortlisted in early 1997 another element was added to the negotiations – control over the telecasting rights to AFL football, worth $500 million over ten years. This ensured that all the major television networks became interested, bidding up the price until these rights were then withdrawn before the contract was settled. The other effect here was to entice television studios to the stadium precinct, which at thirteen hectares was too large for the stadium alone. The bidding process then became a much larger power play between consortia formed of construction, finance and television interests. The winning bid, by a mix of television and construction interests, was announced in September 1997 and construction began almost immediately.[1] The $386 million stadium was to be supplemented by an adjacent $50 million digital broadcast centre for the Channel 7 network.

While the stadium was proclaimed to be free of cost to the public purse, it could not proceed without major public infrastructure connecting it to the city and train station at a cost of $71 million: the La Trobe and Bourke Street bridges, which were built in conjunction with the stadium and without which the stadium cannot function (Figure 8.1).[2] These bridges are smart pieces of urban infrastructure that were proposed in every infrastructure plan ever produced for Docklands. The Bourke Street pedestrian bridge provides the major pedestrian access from the train station to the stadium. The urban design, by Wood Marsh Architects, rises from the edge of the city grid with a steep bank of steps and ramps giving access to a long broad walkway, lined with a series of curved red 'ribs' with spiked lighting elements (Figure 8.2). In formal terms this is a fine piece of urban design; its initial use, however, is limited to that of a stadium entry with throngs of one-way traffic before and after events. The willingness to invest in substantial public infrastructure was a welcome shift, even if it did contradict government rhetoric. It was, however, rather post-hoc, designed to make the stadium deal viable rather than part of an integrated Docklands plan.

The Docklands Stadium was completed in March 2000 and it was immediately apparent that this was a fundamentally different kind of sporting experience. With its very steeply raked tiers, the stadium achieves a remarkably close relationship of its audience to the playing field. One would hope this would translate into a strong sense of place and occasion but it doesn't. Saturated with advertising, playback screens and a deafening echo of crowd noise, the stadium creates the sense of a virtual world, as if one has entered a television set. This merging of real and virtual is accentuated when the roof is closed as it is for both sun and rain – the roof is closed on sunny days to control the light for television broadcasting. The stadium accentuates the enclosure of the 'crowd' against the city as theorised by Canetti:

Figure 8.1
Docklands panorama, 2003

Figure 8.2
Pedestrian bridge
(*Architects*: *Wood Marsh*)

> Outside, facing the city, the arena displays a lifeless wall;
> inside is a wall of people. The spectators turn their backs
> to the city ... for the duration of their time in the arena
> they do not care about anything which happens there; they
> have left behind all their associations, rules and habits ...
> the crowd is seated opposite itself ... exhibiting itself to
> itself ... this crowd is doubly closed, to the world outside
> and in itself.[3]

The game becomes an entirely internalised and relatively place-less
experience. The lack of sun has not helped the grass surface, which
resembles a patchwork quilt where some parts are replaced several
times each winter.

The merger of interests in the real (stadium) and the virtual (TV rights) reflects the conception of a single market; the spectacle of sport can be consumed via the stadium or television and the two markets flow into each other. A key strategy has been the siphoning of matches and events from the much larger and much-loved Melbourne Cricket Ground (MCG) to the Docklands stadium. When the Docklands stadium reaches capacity the excess demand stimulates the pay-TV market. There was some public debate about this private appropriation of the 'people's game' by a stadium where the public 'pay more to get into a venue where the sun never shines, the grass never grows, the footy atmosphere is muted at best and a pie costs the earth'.[4]

The stadium reflects the hybrid nature of so many recent mega-projects where the boundaries between different project types melt. With its corporate boxes wrapped around the playing field and seats with interactive gambling facilities the stadium is at once a playing field, TV studio, theatre, advertising billboard, casino and corporate office. As one developer put it: 'Bums on seats is now only a minor part of the big game.'[5] The first manager of the stadium was a former television director and theme park manager. One way of looking at this is that the television market takes control of the sport by means of the stadium. The stadium is no longer the field on which the game is played so much as the medium and the brand through which it is produced and identified. And the brand name, as a form of symbolic capital, is worth about $5 million/year – the 'Docklands Stadium' became 'Colonial Stadium' in 2000, selling finance until it moved into telecommunications as 'Telstra Dome' in 2002. The building is in no way dome-shaped but needs to be distinguished from the Telstra Stadium in Sydney (also known as the Olympic Stadium). The fluidity of the brand name is further confused because the public broadcasters (ABC) are not permitted to advertise and continue to call it 'Docklands Stadium'. The two Telstra stadia were the major venues for the 2003 Rugby World Cup; with a television audience of three billion, this was precisely the kind of event intended to capture attention for Melbourne on the global stage. Yet one primary result of selling naming rights to a fluid market is to confuse Melbourne with Sydney.

Despite the free-market ideology and hype, the stadium was essentially a government initiative hatched through the Docklands Authority who badly needed the credibility of a real project. The AFL was drawn in with the deal of a lifetime, receiving eventual ownership of a $300 million stadium for $30 million while being absolved of risk. The deal was propped up with public infrastructure and supplemented with discounted land taxes that normally apply only to non-profit venues.[6] The project was also subsidised by the siphoning of public life and economic viability from the MCG. Despite all this, in its first year the stadium lost $25 million followed by $40 million the following year, and major investors were threatening to sue the developers. The lack of profit was blamed on a combination of low bookings for concerts plus the slower than expected development of surrounding precincts. While the stadium was touted to embody 'concert-hall quality acoustics', echoes became apparent during the very first concert when Barbra Streisand interrupted her performance to proclaim: 'There must be two of me!'. Despite improvements the reputation as a poor concert venue has not recovered – the projected minimum was twelve major concerts per year but in 2001, there were two.[7]

The architectural design of the stadium by Daryl Jackson (in association with stadium specialists Blight Lobb) reflects the complex imperatives of the deal. The best aspect is urban rather than architectural – a broad and publicly accessible promenade encircles the stadium providing views across the harbour and back to the city. The promenade is the site of two major artworks. 'Threaded Field' by Simon Perry is a series of giant lime green 'threads' that loops through the stadium building and promenade. This is a fine piece of urban art that threads through the crowds and through which the crowds thread; it captures the dynamism of many kinds of playing field and carries hints of deals stitched together like precincts or patches of grass. 'Vox Lumiere' by Peter McNeill Stitt, is a laser-light installation on the external surfaces of the stadium, which changes colour and form in response to the crowd noise inside. The 'people's voice' is distilled into light, paralleling the ways in which the public popularity of football has become a form of advertising. The 'theatre' and the 'carnival 'were the advertising themes for the stadium, which was promoted through a collage of brightly painted faces as 'Melbourne's Centre Stage' (Figure 8.3). These images meshed ideas of theatre, carnival and football with the desire for new forms of identity, both personal and urban. This was in part a strategy to appropriate the symbolic capital embodied in the MCG, an echo of the casino advertising. The imagery of painted faces to construct a multiplicitous identity was an initiative of the Docklands Authority rather than the stadium developers; the masked faces also appeared on the cover of the Annual Report and as billboards in the vision for the new public park.

Figure 8.3
New identities on a new stage – stadium hoarding, 2000

Despite all its problems, the stadium was the kick-start Docklands needed. The bulk of the stadium stood out as a figure against the barren docks and quickly became a new landmark for the city. Together with the new bridges, which connect it to the city, the stadium became evidence of Docklands success. Football has a very deep and broad following in Melbourne, so the stadium drew many people to the docks who had never been there and never seen the enormous potential of the harbour on its doorstep. One can decry the way in which the stadium blocks the city from the harbour and what a waste it is to consume so much prime waterfront with such an internally focused building; yet this was the initial project that drew people to the docks and raised the everyday awareness of its opportunities. Before construction was completed the image of the stadium reflected in the waters of the harbour was used in Docklands publicity – a view that was enhanced when the heritage warehouses in front of the stadium were demolished. The stadium has become the magnet that attracts the people and generates the visibility, and it has been the billboard building which sells the larger Docklands development (Figure 8.4).

Docklands stadium encapsulates some of the broader changes afoot in the fluid city. The red spikes of the pedestrian overpass frame a throng of people 'on the move' to a new kind of football and a new kind of city. The stadium uproots the 'people's game' from the 'people's ground' and replants it in the docks. The social ground has been 'deterritorialised' and 'reterritorialised'. Here the 'people's voice' becomes an artwork and the new ground is stitched together like the larger precincts and deals. The mirage effect of the stadium with its blurred reflection in the harbour also mirrors the morphing of real into virtual and the blurring of identities. The painted faces of the carnivalesque advertising reinforce older tribal identities of football team followers (magpies, bulldogs, kangaroos) as they suggest a multiplicity of new ones. What seems true for the performer ('there must be two of me!') becomes so for the audience.

Figure 8.4
Docklands Stadium – not a mirage
(*Docklands Authority*, Melbourne Docklands 2000+, *2000*)

BUSINESS PARK

The idea for a 'Business Park' precinct in the Docklands first emerged in 1995 when the precincts were framed by property consultants. This 36-hectare precinct occupies the north-west area of Docklands lining the northern side of the harbour. With the potential to overshadow the water, height limits of fourteen metres on the waterfront were proposed in all urban design schemes. The first two shortlisted bids in 1997 were for 'Yarranova' and 'Entertainment City'. Yarranova Consortium proposed a '24-hour city' with a mix of residential, commercial, industrial, marina and retail uses (Figure 7.11).[8] The waterfront section of retail and residential was of a density and height consistent with a lively waterfront, protected from overshading. The rear section was to be a rather dull and low-density office park. The alternative vision, Entertainment City (Figure 7.10), was proposed by a consortium of theme park, film and cinema interests.[9] The vision was of a large lake in the centre of an adventure theme park (Adventure Harbour) with a working film studio (Paramount) at the rear.[10] An entertainment and leisure area on the waterfront was to be anchored by a cinema 'megaplex' and a themed resort hotel. A large section of the site was to be left undeveloped and a huge car park was to line a prime piece of the harbour edge.

Figure 8.5
Business Park – split decision, 1998
(*Docklands Authority* Annual Report *1997*)

Figure 8.6
New Quay – sailing through
the height limits
(*New Quay advertising 2000,
courtesy of MAB Corporation*)

It was apparent that both consortia had difficulty in filling such a large site and it was soon announced that the precinct would be subdivided – Yarranova would be given two separate pieces of waterfront while Entertainment City theme park would be given twenty-two hectares in the northern section of the site with a narrow harbour frontage (Figure 8.5). The business park was to be stripped from the Yarranova bid with much of the waterfront stripped from the Entertainment City proposal. This split decision was an obvious move since both proposals were underdevelopments of the site.[11] Yet it also demonstrated that the size, form and proposed functions of the precinct were arbitrary rather than market-driven – the market wanted smaller land parcels. While the first buildings were to be completed in 2000, there were no contracts or any firm plans in place at this stage.

In May 1999 a contract was concluded for the Yarranova sub-precincts that were renamed 'MAB Docklands' and then 'New Quay' before marketing began in late 1999.[12] As became apparent later, the height limits were raised from fourteen to eighty metres as part of this deal. The publicity images showed a row of towers set above a four-storey podium (Figure 8.6). The towers were

Living at the Conder you'll be surrounded by a decadent diversity of food, wine and style stretching along the city's only harbourside promenade.

Figure 8.7
New Quay – southern sunshine
and decadent diversity
(*New Quay advertising 2002,*
courtesy of MAB Corporation)

marketed off the plan one at a time.[13] The first stage of New Quay was opened in October 2002. The eighty-metre high towers plunge the harbour and the waterfront into shade for much of the year, a problem that is partially addressed by a thirty-metre setback and erased in the publicity images by showing the sun shining from the south (Figure 8.7). The waterfront promenade is not only shady but is also somewhat cut off from the harbour by a series of free-standing restaurants projecting over the water. This site is a good example of the way high-rise development can damage the very amenity that attracts it there, a form of place suicide that squanders the wealth creation opportunities of urban design.[14] Every urban design plan ever produced had recommended strict height limits for this site to protect the water and waterfront from overshading. The ARM scheme outlined earlier proposed a limit of fourteen metres and other schemes ranged from fourteen to twenty metres.

The project has a permeable street structure and an active waterfront lined with artworks and restaurants. The development is marketed through its connections with food, art and design, described in one advertisement as a 'decadent diversity': 'Living at the Conder you'll be surrounded by a decadent diversity of food, wine and style stretching along the city's only harbourside prome- nade'. The diversity, however, is formularised and controlled with little prospect of social mix. The development incorporates a contemporary art gallery, some of the city's best architects and landscape architects have been involved and the site is studded with contemporary artworks. The centrepiece by Adrian Mauricks is a small forest of organic sculpture through and under which pedestrians pass; its value limited by its function in stimulating the consumer mood.[15] The buildings projecting over the water create new scope for architectural creativity and the integration of artworks into the project is innovative. However, both the art and the architecture are reduced to instrumental components of the economic strategy. The scope for a genuinely challenging public art, indeed any art that does not stimulate consumption of the spectacle, is negligible.

The architects Nation Fender Katsalidis (NFK, now FK) have a reputation for innovative urban housing; their projects of the early 1990s set a new standard in Melbourne for high-density housing with a strong urban presence. They also developed a repu- tation for meshing fine art with architecture, and fine architecture with market sensitivity and popular taste. In the mid-1990s the Planning Minister called upon developers to disregard height limits if they could achieve higher standards and he used the work of NFK as an example.[16] Regulations such as height limits were portrayed as limits to creativity, a story readily accepted by many architects. For many, however, architecture became the 'Trojan horse' against statutory planning, opening the city to a free flow of desire and capital. This shattering of height limits is largely achieved by the production of symbolic capital. The soaring NFK towers engage with the modernist narrative of progress – height limits signify a past to be left behind. The imagery is heroic, bold and sophisticated, rather than *avant garde;* it meets a market for aesthetic distinction on the skyline. Each tower has a distinctive profile and identity – the 'Palladio', the 'Boyd', the 'Arkley'. The ship-shaped Palladio soars through the height limits like the plane taking off behind it (Figure 8.6). The architecture folds into the urban as art on the skyline; the licence to open the waterfront to market forces is a poetic licence. To oppose the height is to oppose the architecture. Here we see a trade between the public interest in urban amenity and the private interest in maximum height, a trade mediated by the architecture operating as a form of legitimating imagery. This is not to suggest there is not also a public interest in a dense waterfront; however, the dismantling of democratic planning ensured that there was no public debate.

The first phase of New Quay occupies about 10 per cent of the original Business Park precinct. With its proximity to the city and direct harbour frontage, this was always a prime prospect for early development once the extension to La Trobe Street was completed. Its development could have proceeded more quickly without the false hope of the 36-hectare precinct. If it had been divided into smaller lot sizes from the start, if the overshading of the water had been controlled, then the sunny waterfront with a 'decadent diversity' may have become more than advertising hype.

The Entertainment City precinct, the other half of this split decision, became a sad series of pie-in-the-sky visions that did not lead to a contract for over five years, despite being repeatedly announced as if they were certain. The key problem here was that the tender process produced completely unrealistic proposals with serious problems. Film studios and theme parks have little real connection to each other or to the water; they are entered via giant car parks. The global model is based on Universal Studios in Los Angeles, which attracts customers through the blurring of the boundary between theme park and studio – one can visit 'real' film locations. Here there could be no such illusion; and both studios and theme parks are sealed enclaves, so neither can claim any waterfront without privatising it. Despite the fact that no contract was sealed, the vision for 'Entertainment City' was re-announced several times in 1998 with headlines such as 'A Development of Paramount Import' and '$350m of Fun'.[17] In 1999 it was renamed 'Studio City', and the Premier tipped in $14 million in tax credits to render the film studios viable. The developers were granted more time to find the investment, but by early 2000 the deal collapsed. Interestingly, the glossy images of the scheme have a longer life than the deal they illustrate – the Docklands Authority publicity has regularly filled out the Docklands vision with the image of obsolete schemes.

In early 2001 the site was subdivided further and the new government increased the offer of public funding for film and television studios on one part of the rear section to $40 million; a move that eventually led to a contract and construction in 2003. The precinct was now in four parts. In late 2002 the remaining nineteen hectares was announced as 'Waterfront City': a mix of housing, retail and public entertainment on the water with discount factory retailing behind.[18] One of the selling points is a giant Ferris wheel – a remnant of both the theme park and the myopia of the

1990s. Another is the promise that the developers have agreed to incorporate affordable housing; given the contractual secrecy, the time to judge this claim is when it comes on the market. While the results in Waterfront City are not clear, it is clear that the New Quay model of towers overshading the waterfront has been abandoned in favour of a more sophisticated five-storey high-density development extending well back from the harbour.

TECHNOLOGY PARK

The Technology Precinct in the north-east corner of the site was conceived as a place for developing the kinds of innovative synergies at the cutting edge of information industries that are evident in places like the 'silicon valley' region of northern California. The idea was that Victoria's relative strengths in the university sector could be linked to the commercial world of IT firms and high-tech industry research to produce high levels of intellectual synergy. The first round of bidding in 1997 produced a single winning bid that remained subject to meeting certain undefined 'set conditions' before acceptance. The Tech 2000 consortium proposed a 'Centre for the Future' to be owned by four of Melbourne's six major universities – Monash, RMIT, Deakin and VUT. In urban design terms it was to be housed in a ring of towers up to twenty-four storeys high occupying about half the available precinct site.[19] This proposal adopted some of the ARM urban design framework, including the teardrop park on the extension of La Trobe Street. The first stage of the project was to be completed in 2000.

There were in fact no acceptable bids for this precinct but the Authority and the government badly needed a vision to legitimate the process – they could not afford to admit they had misconstrued the market. This was the only credible bid, and it had been put together with a very recent member of the Docklands Authority Board playing a leading role.[20] Universities generally understand the synergies of campus life, but in this case the urban context was quite uncertain and the bid devolved into little more than a crude property development. The Tech 2000 bid collapsed in1998 when the universities withdrew after coming to the conclusion that the deal could not be made to work without substantial public funding. Into the vacuum came a bizarre proposal from an Italian-Australian businessman and 'Count' who proposed a $200 million reproduction of 'Little Italy' with a 'colosseum', 'Trevi fountain', 'Spanish steps', 'Piazza Navona' and so on. He was initially taken seriously by the Authority, until it was discovered he was a former bankrupt.[21] Seed funding of $22 million was soon promised from the federal government, the name of the precinct was changed to ComTechPort and tenders were called again.

Despite the subsidy no new proposal was announced for the technology precinct until late 2000 when the 'Digital Harbour' consortium was announced as the winning bidder, but again no contract was finalised. This consortium included a range of IT, property and construction interests together with the University of Melbourne – one of only two universities not to have been burned in the first round.[22] The University later withdrew to a very minor role. The precinct has developed into a mix of commercial and residential accommodation including sports and conference centres, hotel and apartments, all with high-tech dressing (Figure 8.8).[23] The urban design is in some ways quite smart, organised as a loose perimeter block with considerable diversity of building form and opportunities for a diversity of enterprises and identities. The approved building heights range from 75 to 100 metres, consistent with New Quay next door and enough to cause serious overshadowing of the esplanade, harbour and finger pier every morning for much of the year. There is, of course, little point in constraining development on one precinct when the amenity has already been compromised on another. The building morphology has been organised, however, to ensure sunlight into the central courtyard with its 'digital garden' and 'digital landscape' – Digital Harbour is heavily hyped. The precinct is to be developed with a 'whole of precinct' approach and 'bundled infrastructure', which is surely what was once called 'planning'. It is to be a 'smart city' with high digital band-width in 'online office towers' surrounding a 'digital neighbourhood centre'. The 'waterfront youth incubator' seems to be what we once called a 'school'; presumably producing digital Marlon Brandos.

There is a coherent argument for the development of urban precincts with large digital bandwidth and high levels of interaction between industry clusters. As economist Peter Brain has argued:

> The knowledge economy concentrates innovation-intensive industries in places where people who are skilled in the technology of each industry can form and maintain loose, quasi-business, quasi-social networks. The interaction of people from different firms has become a critical determinant not only of regional competitiveness, but more importantly of firms' competitiveness.[24]

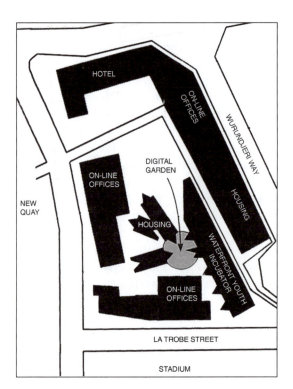

Figure 8.8
Digital Harbour
site map
(*redrawn from the
web site*
<www.Melbourne
docklands.com>
September 2003)

He is critical, however, of the belief that the market alone will provide such infrastructure. The planning of this technology precinct seems to lack a thorough understanding of how synergies of ideas work in the IT industry. The parallel with silicon valley is a poor one because the valley is a highly dispersed set of corporations based on freeways, parking lots and a traditional university campus (Stanford). And with the exception of the campus itself, in urban terms it is an awful model of a socially divided and car-based city with very poorly developed public spaces.[25] Boston is a model more akin to Melbourne, where the production of ideas is both campus-based and spread across a diverse but dense urban network. In 2001 the Authority announced that all of Docklands would be networked with an 'iPort Network' to provide all Docklands residents with high bandwidth infrastructure. This is a sensible strategy that seems likely to attract the kinds of people and firms necessary to generate wealth-creating synergies in information-intensive industries. It is advertised as a 'key value-adding feature for businesses locating at Melbourne Docklands'.[26] The problem again is that the state is adding the infrastructure after the deals have been done in most of these precincts. Public infrastructure investment is made on private land, too late to reap the capital gains for the public purse.

YARRA WATERS

Yarra Waters is a fourteen-hectare strip that lines one and a half kilometres of the southern bank of the river with fine city views and good potential for high-rise housing. This strip of land about 100 metres wide is separated from the rest of the Docklands by the river and therefore protected from the risks and uncertainties of the larger Docklands development. With north-facing water-frontages, clear city views and an existing harbour at the eastern end, it has always been the best prospect for high-rise high-density development. Serviced by an existing street to the south there were less infrastructure costs than in other precincts. With industrial land to the south there was little prospect of damage from high-rise development. The planning scheme had initially marked this site for a twenty-metre height limit while the ARM scheme suggested parts of it could go to seventy and ninety metres.

Both shortlisted projects in the first round of bidding proposed a mix of housing and waterfront retail in both low- and high-rise form with the small harbour at the eastern end utilised for a marina in both bids. The Melbourne Docklands Consortium proposed 930 low- and high-rise apartments and townhouses (Figure 8.9 top); the competing bid from the Yarranova consortium was similar, but at a much higher density with 2400 units (Figure 8.9 middle).[27] The major differences between the two bids were first in the pro-posed densities (64 versus 165 units per hectare) and second that Yarranova proposed to surround the small harbour with a wall of high-rise close to the city, while the other bid kept the dense develop-ment further down the river. One rarely finds a better site than this for high-rise development – a north-facing waterfront with great views to the city and the harbour, and a freeway to the south with little possibility of causing damage to existing neighbourhoods or future potential. The dramatic edge that a wall of development would provide to the river without overshading it, coupled with the massive capital gains flowing into the public purse, suggest that there was a public interest in developing this site at high density. Yet again the precinct size proved far too large for the available investment.

The Yarranova proposal to develop the city end at high density was clearly the more sensible but there were other factors under consideration and the bid was not successful. The contract was

Figure 8.9
Yarra Waters proposals, 1997–98
Top: Melbourne Docklands Corporation (Mirvac), 1997
Middle: Yarranova, 1997
Bottom: Revised Winning proposal, Mirvac 1998
(Docklands Authority, Annual Reports 1997, 1998)

awarded to Mirvac, one member of the Melbourne Docklands Consortium, in late 1997. This was a strange decision because the new vision then released closely resembled that of the losing Yarranova bid – the small harbour was now to be tightly enclosed with towers and the density raised to a similar level (Figure 8.9 bottom).[28] It was, however, a good decision in terms of urban design quality. The project was renamed 'Yarra 's Edge' and the waterfront was redesigned to incorporate a public waterfront park. Architects ARM were employed to give a stronger imagery to this waterfront spectacle, and some of the folded and fluid forms from their 1996 scheme began to appear in this vision (Figure 8.10). A string of housing towers are gradually enclosing the small marina and water body with towers being sold off-the-plan and built one at a time beginning from the eastern end and moving west. While the contract is secret, it is fluid enough to permit the heights of the towers to grow over time as the market has expanded. The towers begin at 100 metres (thirty-two floors) on the eastern end, increasing to 155 metres (forty-seven floors) with the later towers as they rise like a reverse line of steadily growing dominos. The waterfront

Figure 8.10
Mirvac vision, 1999
(*Docklands Authority,*
Annual Report, *1999*)

Figure 8.11
Webb Bridge
(*Artist*: Robert Owen;
Architects: Denton
Corker Marshall)

formula here is almost identical to New Quay on the north of the harbour; these two mini-precincts are in direct competition and the imagery of the architecture is a key part of this competition; the advertising describes one of the Yarra's Edge towers as: '... a gleaming sculpture that fulfils the splendour of its wondrous location'. However, with its sunny waterfront, Yarra's Edge is the more desirable development and apartments are selling at 30 per cent higher prices.

The Wurundjeri Way by-pass and the reconstruction of the Grimes Bridge has left this precinct disconnected from the Victoria Harbour precinct to the north. This problem has been addressed in part by the construction of a new pedestrian bridge – named the Webb Bridge after the former railway bridge that was demolished. The design, by artist Robert Owen with architects Denton Corker Marshall, is a serpentine loop of space-framed tunnel designed as an analogue of an Aboriginal fishing trap (Figure 8.11). Pedestrians flow 'fish-like' between the Southbank promenade and the emerging park to the north. Funded by both the state and the developers, this is a beautiful piece of urban design that generates better permeability across the river and adds significant symbolic capital to Yarra's Edge. In design terms it both compares and contrasts with the overpass to the stadium (Figure 8.2) and the earlier pedestrian bridges along the Yarra (Figures 3.2 and 3.6). Webb Bridge is a meandering bridge; a gentle flow of people and space that weaves, swells and contracts as it crosses the water. It connects the urban to the natural and Aboriginal; its web-like frame is at once World Wide Web and fishing net.

It is too early to judge this precinct in urban design terms, although it clearly shows more promise than the shady waters of New Quay (Figure 8.1). Since the contracts are secret it is impossible to say what the prospects for the larger precinct are, but only 20 per cent of the precinct has been developed and developers can offer no guarantees as to what will happen further down the river. It seems likely that Yarra's Edge will effectively become an up-market enclave because it has certain defences against access by outsiders: a main road to the south, a river to the north and negligible public transport. If all housing is up-market and if parking is expensive, then the new 'public' space on the river will deliver its benefits to a narrow sector of the population. The next stage of urban development here is to redevelop the street network to the south, yet such broader access to the river has not been thought through as part of this precinct. A combination of lack of access points and parking costs could still render this scheme a defacto privatisation of the waterfront. As a final point, the financial outcome for the state does not look good. Payments from developers for the entire precinct were projected to total $60 million, which is 4 per cent of the $1.5 billion project cost.[29] If we balance this against the public investments in Docklands and the likely lack of public access, this most marketable piece of riverscape appears to have been sold for a song.

BATMAN'S HILL

John Batman was an infamous drunkard and megalomaniac who, in 1835, first claimed the site of Melbourne with the declaration 'this will be the place for a village' (which he wanted to call 'Batmania'). He then organised the expulsion of the Wurundjeri people from what was to become central Melbourne. He lived on a small hill within this precinct, which became known as Batman's Hill before it was removed to make way for the railways. The Batman's Hill precinct caps the end of Collins Street adjacent to the city grid and is the key to linking the docks to the waterfront. It has no water frontage of its own, but is bordered by the financial district of the city, a convention centre to the south, train station and stadium to the north, and Victoria Harbour to the west. The two shortlisted proposals in 1997 were the Grollo Tower and Yarra City. The 560-metre Grollo Tower with residential, hotel and office functions was to be the 'world's tallest building' placed on alignment with an extension of Collins Street, surrounded by parkland above a large car park (Figure 7.11). The historic goods shed was to be largely demolished. On the same site the Malaysian-based YarraCity consortium was proposing 'Docklands Village', a low-rise multimedia-oriented commercial office development (entitled 'Cyberia'), an ice hockey stadium with a sports themed retail complex and home/office apartments (figures 7.10 and 8.12).[30] A 'TEC Shed' exhibition of multimedia technology was to be located in the historic goods shed. The Grollo Tower was a truly damaging proposal, an anti-urban scheme and paradoxically an under-development of the site – it will be dealt with at greater length in the following chapter. However, the tower was designed with a certain elegance and it captured the imagination of a public who were divided on its virtues.

As outlined in the previous chapter, the decision to build the Wurundjeri Way by-pass was made while the two shortlisted consortia were preparing their revised bid. This expressway sliced through the Batman's Hill precinct, cutting it off from both the city and the river, reducing its amenity and capital value. The short-listed proposals needed to be redesigned and the YarraCity consortium had the biggest problem since its scheme included a strong synergy with the existing convention centre from which it would now be separated. In December 1998 it was announced that the Grollo Tower was the approved winning bid for the precinct. The design had been somewhat transformed with the aim of 'enhancing Melbourne's multicultural character and liveability'. The tower now rose from a collection of low-rise buildings as an urban precinct rather than a single building. Despite the confident announcement there was no contract in place and negotiations continued until the deal collapsed in April 1999. The precinct was again put out to tender with the suggestion it be subdivided into 'bite-sized' pieces, the first public recognition of the urban indigestion that was painfully apparent in all precincts. When the new government decided to proceed with the extension to Collins Street in 2000 the Docklands Authority produced an infrastructure plan for the precinct, the first real plan since it was constituted in 1992. Utilising the alignments of Bourke and Collins streets together with the heritage goods shed as a framework, the plan carved the site into smaller land parcels of two to four hectares. The precinct was also revalued at this time by the development of the Docklands Park to line its western edge. This grid is currently being filled out one project at a time. The largest of them is called 'Village Docklands' an eight-stage $700 million mix of hotel and residential on a four-hectare site incorporating part of what remains of the historic Goods Shed after being sliced in two by Collins Street. This is also the only major flow of international capital in the Docklands, driven by the Asian-based Kuok consortium.

The design has some other similarities to the 'Docklands Village' proposal rejected earlier, albeit with a high-rise typology. The early stages will be 110 metres (thirty storeys) high and the later Shangri-La hotel on Collins Street will peak at 160 metres (sixty storeys). One rather disturbing proposal in this precinct is a network of street overpasses at podium level, connecting the pool deck, garden and recreation areas of a range of private housing projects. A private pedestrian network is to be superimposed above the public street network. This project is also the only one in Docklands to introduce questions of race; one key advertising image shows a white Western male eyeing off a beautiful Asian woman (Figure 8.13). What is being sold is a sequestered and semi-privatised realm where class differences are reinforced, yet racial differences are overcome.

Figure 8.12 (*top*)
Batman's Hill, YarraCity
proposal, 1997
(*Docklands Authority*,
Annual Report *1998*)

Figure 8.13 (*left*)
The multicultural 'village'
(*Courtesy of*
Village Docklands
P/L advertising, 2003)

The outcome for Batman's Hill precinct is by no means clear, although it is clear that the attempt to develop the precinct as an integrated whole has failed and the planning and urban design has been tragically piecemeal. The transport planning for the precinct has been comprehensively bungled by the Wurundjeri Way by-pass. In order to keep through traffic off the waterfront, access to the Batman's Hill precinct is severely restricted. We are creating a highly dense sector at the heart of Docklands, a new piece of Collins Street with building heights exceeding most of the central city. Yet in access terms it is something of a cul-de-sac. The great hope for Batman's Hill lies on its western edge where developments lining the park are yet to emerge.

VICTORIA HARBOUR

The Victoria Harbour precinct of thirty hectares in the heart of the docks encompasses the central peninsula of land between river and harbour, together with the harbour and finger pier. This has always been the key precinct for the success of Docklands as a whole, since it contains 3.7 kilometres of waterfrontage. This land was considered unsuitable for high-rise, both because of soil conditions and the inevitable overshading of the waterfront. Parts of the site had serious soil contamination from a former gasworks. The initial round of bids in 1997 produced a shortlist comprised of 'YarraCity' and 'Victoria Harbour Corporation'. The YarraCity Consortium proposed a mix of hotel, office, marina and residential development with 1500 dwelling units (Figure 7.11).[31] This vision maintained some of the heritage waterfront buildings and transformed the end of the pier into a semi-circular hotel as a harbour centrepiece, connected by a pedestrian bridge to the northern bank of the harbour. A canal was to be cut across the peninsula at the point where it narrows, creating an island. The proposal was essentially low-rise with a diversity of building types. The axis of Bourke Street was to be picked up in a boulevard that terminated in a tall landmark structure on the riverbank. The street layout was close to that suggested in the Planning Scheme but ignored the ARM scheme.

The alternate vision proposed by the Victoria Harbour Corporation centred on 'Export City Square', a 40 000 square metre shopping mall and exhibition centre with 1340 housing units and a marina (Figures 7.10 and 8.14 top).[32] This scheme also incorporated the Bourke Street alignment and allowed for the central park idea from the ARM framework. Canals were to cut across the peninsula in several places to form a string of islands and a highly impermeable urban fabric. All heritage buildings were demolished with the harbour frontage reshaped and the central pier re-formed into a hotel. The waterfront design made a public promenade impossible and the string of islands suggested a gated enclave.

A series of problems were common to both of these proposals. Each of them focused the urban vision on the southern half of the harbour that they controlled, turning away from the northern section that they did not. Neither project seemed to conceive of the harbour as a whole. In both cases the site was underdeveloped with relatively low residential densities of only forty to fifty units per hectare. And both projects restricted access to the peninsula, raising the prospect of a gated enclave. The idea of pedestrian bridges, which would render the peninsula permeable (first mooted in the Olympics vision, Figure 7.3), was not considered in either proposal.

In June 1998 the Victoria Harbour Corporation was announced as the winning bidder, with the first stage to be complete by 2001. There was, however, no contract as the project was subject to meeting certain conditions. The winner was soon announced again and an entirely different design was released (Figure 8.14 middle). A public promenade was now established on the waterfront with canals deleted. A thirty-storey tower rose from the 'export city' shopping mall and the remnant of Docklands Park disappeared in favour of a 'tree-lined civic plaza'. The density had been raised with a series of ten-storey buildings lining the river. The new proposal was infused with a shift towards the cheap and commercial, as if the developers had responded to the challenge of a more public vision with a loss of imagination. The success of this scheme was announced again in early 1999 as it became the subject of difficult negotiations over both public access to the waterfront and responsibility for clean-up costs.[33] While the secrecy provisions render this story somewhat hazy, the picture that emerges is that the developers wanted both a partially privatised waterfront and for the Authority to pick up contamination costs. Since private responsibility for the clean-up had been a key plank of the tender framework, this process raises questions about why they were shortlisted and then selected. It appears that political pressure to announce and re-announce winning projects was used as a lever by the developers to gain a premature commitment from the Authority that was then used to leverage public funds for the clean-up and approval for a privatised waterfront. The Authority finally agreed to pick up the decontamination costs, but held firm on a public waterfront. The proposal finally collapsed in October 1999, a month before the change of government.

New fictional visions and infrastructure plans for the precinct were developed by the Authority and used for marketing as the precinct was put out to tender for the second time in 2000 and then again in 2001. However, this was no longer the same precinct as that which had been put to tender four years earlier. The Wurundjeri Way by-pass had taken traffic away from the eastern edge of the precinct, some of which was shaved off to create the public spaces of Docklands Park and Grand Plaza. The tramways loop from the city and the Bourke Street overpass were complete and the decision had been made to extend Collins Street. The publicly funded decontamination of the gasworks site was in process. In sum, several hundred million dollars of investment had

Figure 8.14
Victoria Harbour winning bids
Top: 1997
Middle: 1998
Bottom: 2000
(*Docklands Authority* Annual Reports *1997, 1998, 2000*)

been committed in ways that added enormously to the potential and capital value of the Victoria Harbour precinct. The preferred developer was announced as Lend Lease with a proposal for residential, retail and commercial development, together with a new urban design vision (Figure 8.14 bottom).[34]

While Lend Lease was given a firm contract without any infrastructure plan being finalised, this brought a major improvement in urban design thinking to the precinct. The heritage sheds on the finger pier were to be upgraded for retail development with an 'architectural icon' on the end of the pier. The decision of the government to extend Collins Street was crucial in rendering this precinct more valuable. A further infrastructure plan was released in 2002, representing a return in many ways to the urban design principles of the early 1990s with low-rise replaced with high-rise. The extension of Collins Street is to curve to meet the extension of Bourke Street. The grid of streets creates a series of land parcels both on the waterfront and contained within a central 'village'. With its much finer grain-size coupled with an integrated plan across the giant precinct, this is developing as the best of the precinct plans. While there are detailed visions for the precinct, many of the details remain unclear. The low- to mid-rise central 'village' set back from the water offers a fine prospect to negotiate a mix of affordable housing, but it is too late to negotiate this into the contract. Some early images of this 'village' indicated that it may deploy the same formula as for Docklands Village in the Batman's hill precinct, with a privatised rooftop network connected by overpasses. Recent images are more promising, but the plan remains unclear.

Development has proceeded on a project-by-project basis, with the National Bank headquarters moving out of the central city and high-rise residential towers coming on to the market in 2002. The advertising is directed at middle-aged 'empty nesters' of Melbourne's eastern suburbs – 'Live in the City on the Water'. The 'Dock 5' tower offers the prospect of living 'in' the water, advertised as an architecture which 'appears to shimmer, weave and pirouette ... a narrow glass curtain wall shifts in both vertical and horizontal planes to generate a shimmer at the tower's edges, similar to that of the ripple the sun creates on moving water'.[35] And the architecture is not all that is fluid as the small print makes clear:

> While Lend Lease has prepared various concept plans ...
> they do not constitute a promise or representation on the
> part of Lend Lease that Victoria Harbour or any part of it
> will be developed as indicated in any such plans or at all.[36]

CHAPTER NINE

GROLLO TOWER

The Grollo Tower was the most adventurous and contentious of all Docklands proposals – a five-year saga with its roots in the migrant success story of the Grollo dynasty. Luigi Grollo, the family patriarch, migrated to Melbourne in 1928 where he built a family business from concreting gutters to become one of Australia's largest construction companies. In the early 1980s the Grollo company, by then in the control of sons Bruno and Rino Grollo, became the builder and part owner of the Rialto office tower, which remains Melbourne and Australia's tallest. The company was more than a family dynasty, however, including a large coterie of foremen and workers with enough loyalty to guarantee a performance that was rare in the industry – on time and on budget. This success was founded on Italian cultural and family bonds coupled with a masculine egalitarian ethos, mateship and hard work. These achievements and reputation were threatened in 1992–93 when a tax fraud investigation was launched and Bruno and Rino Grollo were charged with conspiracy to bribe a Federal Police officer.[1] The patriarch, Luigi Grollo, died in 1994 just before these charges came to court. Bruno Grollo's dream of building the world's tallest building first emerged around this time, partly as a monument to his father. Yet there was nothing sombre about Grollo's symbolic program: 'It would be a golden building for a golden city for the golden times to come ... it has to put the city on the world map'.[2]

GLOBAL VISION

After some measured support from Premier Kennett, Grollo commissioned the Sydney architect, Harry Seidler, to produce a design. Grollo had worked with Seidler before and admired his heroic architectural spirit. Grollo's brief, however, was not an easy one: 'I want it to represent the universe. I want it to represent the sun and the moon and the planets and the stars. I want it to represent humanity; you know, man and woman, love. There's too much negativity in the world today'.[3] This was to be a building for a global stage, not just the tallest, but a global landmark in both space and time: 'To do something for Melbourne that did what the pyramids did for Egypt, or the Collosseum did for Rome, or the Opera House and Harbour Bridge did for Sydney'.[4] The result, unveiled in mid-1995, was a 500-metre tower with a roughly hexagonal base and tapering profile (Figure 9.1). The glass walls were to be orange at the base representing the sunset, turning golden yellow at the top to represent the stars with white granite columns as silver 'moonbeams'. The project was depicted by Grollo as a gift to Melburnians: 'If they don't like it we won't build it', he said.[5]

The debate took off and almost everyone had a view, including Rino Grollo who described his brother as 'off the planet'.[6] Seidler's reputation for taking his critics to court was unlikely to encourage debate on the design of the building, but there was a broad condemnation of the potential urban damage. Architecture critics were generally supportive of a visionary approach while dismissing this particular vision and very tall buildings in general.[7] Haig Beck wrote that: 'One of the immediate effects would be to wipe out the surrounding street life. At half a kilometre high, this building would act like a straw, sucking the urban life far up into the sky.'[8] The vision both caught the public imagination and polarised the community. While some call-in surveys showed up to 66 per cent support, the professional polls showed about 40 per cent approval and 48 per cent opposition; support was strongest among the young and male populations.[9]

It soon became apparent that the quest for the 'world's tallest building' was by no means a simple race, being both difficult to define and a moveable feast. From 1973 the title of 'world's tallest' was held for over 20 years by Chicago's Sears Tower (443 metres).

Figure 9.1
Bruno Grollo with
the first tower, 1995
(*Photo: Michael Raynor/*
The Age, *27 April 1995*
Architect: Seidler)

Figure 9.2
Grollo Tower, Batman's Hill bid, 1997
(*Docklands Authority*, Annual Report, *1997*
Architects: Denton Corker Marshall)

Stimulated by conditions of globalisation and rapid growth in Asian economies, a crop of taller towers were planned for a range of Asian cities. The Petronas Towers in Kuala Lumpur, symbolic of both the nation and Islam, were almost complete at 452 metres and the Chinese were determined to claim the mantle before the millennium.[10] Clearly, 500 metres would not be enough, or not for long. Any such competition is further complicated by the construction of telecommunications masts and superstructure to claim extra height; while the Sears Tower is defined by its top floor, the Petronas has spires. According to the Council on Tall Buildings and

Urban Habitat, who have adjudicated on such matters, the height is determined by the structure of the building and can include 'spires' but not antennas. But what is a spire and indeed what is an inhabited building? The spectacular 'Pearl of the Orient' tower in Shanghai does not qualify in this race despite housing a hotel.

As a result of the debates and revelations, Grollo commissioned Melbourne architects, Denton Corker Marshall, to produce a new design. The architects were popular with the Kennett government and this was a move to increase political support.[11] The new design was released in December 1995 – now to rise 680 metres, 50 per cent higher than Petronas. It was in the shape of a slender and elegant silver obelisk, renamed the 'Melbourne Tower'. The building was to be in six parts stacked vertically: an underground parking garage with retail facilities; an open undercroft at ground level; an office section (200 000 square metres); a housing section (258 apartments); a 300-room hotel; and finally, a light pinnacle with observation deck (Figure 9.2). Multilevel external elevators on the corners of the building were to offer a 'thrill trip through the clouds' to break into sunlight during Melbourne's grey winters. In this design the symbolism was less literal, as one of the architects, Barrie Marshall, put it: '(Grollo) talked about the moon and the stars and the sun, but there was enough there for us to feel comfortable about taking on the job – there was no point doing it if it was going to be a dog – and I think the result is a tower of timeless quality.'[12] The building was to have an ethereal quality with the light beacon on top shining at night like a 'Melbourne Torch'. The 111 metre high beacon accounted for most of the additional height – it was uninhabited but technically a piece of the structure rather than an aerial, therefore counting as part of the building height.

After having expanded from 500 to 680 metres during 1995, the proposed height of the tower quietly shrank to 560 metres during 1996, before it was submitted with the first round of bids for the Batman's Hill precinct in May 1997 and shortlisted later that year (Figure 7.11). The tower was then presented as part of the broad range of precinct designs showing the entire Docklands developed in full. The images showed the tower rising from parkland like the Eiffel Tower, its shimmering silver surface giving it an ethereal presence. In early 1998, as time grew close for a final decision, a Ministerial Panel was appointed to consider whether the Planning Scheme should be amended from a notional height limit of 32 metres to 560 metres. This was an odd move since the Planning Scheme already had provision for height limits to be broken (see chapter 7). The formation of the Panel roughly coincided with the decision to build the Wurundjeri Way by-pass through the Docklands – the Panel hearings were useful for the Minister in diverting attention from a scandalous lack of transport planning. The Panel hearings also exposed arguments against the project, which were substantial both in terms of urban issues and imagery.

ANTI-URBANISM

The world's tallest buildings were limited during the nineteenth century, by a mix of fire regulations and elevator technologies, to about 40 metres. Melbourne briefly housed the world's tallest building in the 1890s before heights shot up during the early twentieth century and then flattened out at about 450 metres in the 1970s. There are some fundamental reasons for this flattening. While density and profit rises with height, these gains have limits since every tall building is effectively a cul-de-sac in the urban fabric, which becomes progressively less efficient with height. As the height of the building increases, the space required to get people and services in and out rises exponentially in relation to the useful floor area. Banks of elevators consume more and more of the building volume; and with ever-increasing trip times more elevators per floor are required. The question is not whether, but at what height, this becomes economically (and ecologically) unviable. The landmark status of tall buildings generates considerable symbolic capital that offsets these inefficiencies – 'prominence' still translates into 'dominance' in the corporate urban field.[13] However, beyond about 250 metres serious diseconomies set in and other tactics are needed to increase the height. The Petronas Towers are essentially public buildings, propped up with state finance. While the Grollo corporation were angling for a massive public subsidy, the major tactic for increasing the height was to reduce the lettable floor area. This reduces demand for elevators, parking and so on. The paradox is that the less habitable space, the higher you can go; the higher the building the lower the density. This is why nearly 30 per cent of the height of the tower was to be void – 50 metres at the base and 111 metres on top. The net floor area was to be about sixteen hectares on a thirteen-hectare site. This is a lower average density than most of the central city. Several times this amount of space could have been spread across the site within the 32-metre height limit; the Grollo Tower proposal was an underdevelopment of the site's potential. Many hectares of ground space were labelled as 'parkland', yet much of this was traffic islands determined by the imperative of getting massive volumes of vehicles in and out of the car park in peak periods.

The proponents of the tower stressed its economic benefits in attracting jobs and investment. This claim relied on the suggestion that the building would attract people to move to Melbourne simply to live in it; a claim unsupported by either evidence or common sense. Opponents countered that investment was simply being moved around the city, from many smaller projects to one large one, flooding the market with office space, housing and hotel rooms. Potential losers here included all the other construction companies, developers and architects. There were also arguments about the broader loss of urban diversity. Cities, like societies, are multiplicitous networks; their density is a richness of social connections, and beyond a certain height buildings cease to service this connectivity. No matter how good the design, what we get are singular visions, singular uses, singular classes of people and products. The paradox is that as we go higher we become less urban, less diverse; the elevator does not substitute for the street. The project was essentially anti-urban; it would have left a thirteen-hectare hole in the dense urban networks of central Melbourne. The tree-like structure of the building, with elevators as 'stems', can be contrasted with 'rhizomatic' or 'web-like' structures of dense urban networks; it controls and channels difference rather than nourishing the multiplicities of urban life.

The potential damage from the shadow of the tower also became a key issue. The developers argued that the shadow would be fast-moving, thin and diffuse; yet this was only true at the tip of the shadow several kilometres away. The greatest potential damage from the shadow was to the adjacent Docklands harbour and the newly developed public promenade along the nearby river. Diagrams showed that the fifty-metre wide shadow would have tracked across the Victoria Harbour and Yarra Waters precincts during the morning. While the graphic images issued by the Docklands Authority showed a foreshortened shadow, it was clear that the Yarra Waters marina about 300 metres to the south would be overshaded for much of the year. From noon onwards the shadow was to track along the already developed southern bank of the river (Exhibition Centre, Crown Casino and SouthGate), casting each part into shade for about fifteen to twenty minutes. For much of the year the late-afternoon shadows would have plunged up to half a kilometre of the most vital stretch of Southbank into simultaneous shade. On summer evenings the shade would swing around to align directly with prestigious Collins Street and plunge its entire two-kilometre length into shade for twenty minutes. Given how crucial sunshine is to the livability of public space in Melbourne, these issues were of vital concern. The tower would clearly damage the amenity of the city's most prestigious downtown street, its most successful riverscape developments and the prospects for some of the best opportunities in the Docklands.

While the architects had produced exact shadow diagrams, they lacked the drama to sell newspapers. The *Herald Sun* exaggerated the bulk of the tower to show it turning the city into a giant sundial (Figure 9.3). The fine print says 'not to scale', but it is the politics of the image that dominates in this context. Most of the imagery of the project was controlled by the developers and the Docklands Authority who ensured that the media were well supplied with images which evoked the chosen narrative – a bold and exciting vision of the shining silver obelisk seen from a distance. But the overshading issue created a market for a new kind of hyperbole. The developers and the Docklands Authority lost control of the imagery; the sundial and the shadow became a counter-narrative that did the project considerable damage. The politics of representation, more than rational argument, became the field upon which the issue was played out in the public realm.

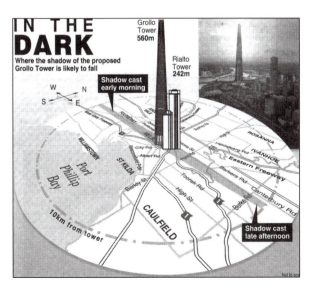

Figure 9.3
Tower as sundial
(*Courtesy of*
The Herald Sun,
26 June 1998)

As the issue developed, a range of further problems emerged. Batman's Hill is the site of one of the few pieces of valuable heritage in the Docklands – a 385-metre long goods shed formerly used for loading and unloading very long trains. Its primary value lay in the vast and sublime shaft of interior space rather than its architectural form. In some ways it is a counterpoint to the tower – internal and horizontal instead of external and vertical. The National Trust and several community groups opposed its demolition. A further problem emerged when it became apparent that the tower would interfere with the flight patterns at Melbourne airport, almost twenty kilometres away. 'It's no problem,' said Grollo, 'all they've got to do is change the flight path'.[14] The Federal Aviation Authority saw it differently – the tower would cause a loss of flexibility in assigning safe flight paths and the effect would be to bring forward the construction of a new runway by a decade.

SEDUCTIONS

Parallel with these debates on urban damage were those that focused on the building's image. Both the Seidler and Denton Corker Marshall designs were highly accomplished architecturally; however, the later design was seen as more attuned to Melbourne and its designers were more open to public debate. This was crucial since Seidler's reputation for litigation largely stifled debate on his designs and the DCM design succeeded in focusing critical attention on the quality of the architecture and away from its urban effects. Beck abandoned his potent urban critique ('like a straw, sucking the urban life far up into the sky') to declare the tower: 'the most elegant and exquisite high-rise building that has been designed in the past thirty years'.[15] The idea that one might trade off urban damage for good architecture became a particularly potent idea during this period, promoted by the Planning Minister who called on developers to disregard height limits if they were creative enough to produce 'landmark' designs. The developers exploited this idea of a one-off landmark that would not create a precedent; it was likened to the Eiffel Tower as a visionary public symbol that was initially opposed by those with no imagination but later loved by all. The other way of seeing this is as a claim for monopoly rights to symbolic capital on the public skyline. The city they desired was to be just fluid enough for one tower and no more.

There was no dispute that the tower would have transformed

Melbourne's image and drawn global attention to the city, but there was no consensus on the outcome. The contradiction is that the quest for attention through sheer size can produce a negative identity – trying too hard to be noticed can signify an inferiority complex. I outlined earlier the way Melbourne's multiplicitous urban character occasionally generates identity crises. This multiplicity is one of Melbourne's great strengths, and the periodic attempts to freeze, contain and stabilise it in simple images are a weakness. The Grollo Tower was competing in a competition that great global cities have largely abandoned. Some of the more potent cartoons of the tower hinted at an underlying dialectics of scale where large can mean small – the double meanings of a 'large complex' and the claim for a 'new world record for shallowness' (Figure 9.4 a & b). While the aspirations for a bigger global reputation, which drove the tower, were forward-looking and positive, one of its effects would have been to belittle the city and its reputation with a negative image.

A large part of the public fascination with the tower lay in the sensitive question of its deeper layers of meaning. The well-explicated links to the pyramidal tombs of the pharoahs, to the timeless qualities of sun, moon and stars, all suggested its beginnings as a memorial to the family patriarch. This is the age-old use of architecture in the quest for immortality – using space to hold back time. Many of the deeper meanings were difficult to speak or write about and were best articulated in cartoons that focused on the symbolic construction of political and sexual identities. Some identified the tower politically with a megalomanic Premier and as a counterpoint to widening social divisions within the city. The most prolific and suggestive cartoons were on the phallic meanings of the tower, depicting it as Grollo's Viagra, as a 'male thing' that 'needs an overcoat' (Figure 9.4 c & d). Many letters to the newspapers ridiculed the project on the basis that it was a private sexual fetish and one rather convoluted editorial called it a 'Freudian manifestation of tower envy'.[16] Having earlier allowed himself to be photographed with the tower between his legs, Bruno Grollo was disarmingly frank about this issue: 'We muse about why some people have such an obsessive aversion to phallic symbols and erections … erections are quite normal.'[17]

Some of Grollo's supporters were quite censorious about the phallic issue and accusations of puerility flew both ways.[18] Yet serious critique of the project could scarcely ignore a key dimension of its meaning from both the popular and theoretical view. Grollo is correct to see this as normal – all tall buildings engage a

certain sexuality that, within limits, enhances the city. At its
extreme, such critique can seem to reduce architecture to a sexual
urge, as Lefebvre puts it: 'Metaphorically (the tower) symbolizes
force, male fertility, masculine violence. Phallic erectility bestows
a special status on the perpendicular'.[19] The issue here, however,
is not sexuality but scale – is it sensible to surrender the city to a
boy's game of 'mine's bigger than yours' whether we are dealing
with buildings, monuments, penises, corporations or egos? This is
clearly linked to the broader quest for identity, power and legitimacy in which architecture has long had its roots. At every scale
from the house to the pyramids, architecture is a means of stabilising a fragile identity.[20] All tall buildings 'establish' metaphors of
'stature' and 'stability'; words that share the linguistic root 'sta'
(to stand). Physical prominence operates as a metaphor of dominance. The question was not whether the tower partook in such
symbolism, but the scale at which it did so and the extent to which
this project would have dominated and belittled the public city
with a private symbol.

To return now to the political narrative, the Ministerial Panel
recommended that the proposal be rejected on a range of grounds,
but the Minister in turn rejected his Panel's advice. The developers,
now led by Bruno's son Daniel Grollo, responded to the various
criticisms of the tower and a new vision was released in late 1998.
The tower remained identical but the site around the base was
transformed – no longer sitting in a park, but rising from a new
urban precinct with a multicultural food market, festival centre
and heritage museum. The heritage goods shed was to be retained
in two fragments, one on either side of the tower that was to 'merge
beautifully' with a neighbourhood of cobbled streets and 'multicultural trading mews'. A strange lack of conviction now infused the
proposal: the claim was made that it no longer needed the tower to
be viable, perhaps it would be added later and even then it may not
be the world's tallest.[21] Representations of the project now played
down the heroic tower in favour of small-scale liveability at its base
with the shrunken tower disappearing into the sky. Other advertising for the tower at this time shifted from showing its dominance
of the city and the docks to views, which portrayed it as if it were
merely the tallest of an urban cluster.

This latest version was finally selected by the Docklands
Authority, contingent only on final payment of $37 million for
off-site infrastructure – essentially payment for the land and development rights. The decision to approve the tower was made at a
political level and against the recommendation of the Design,

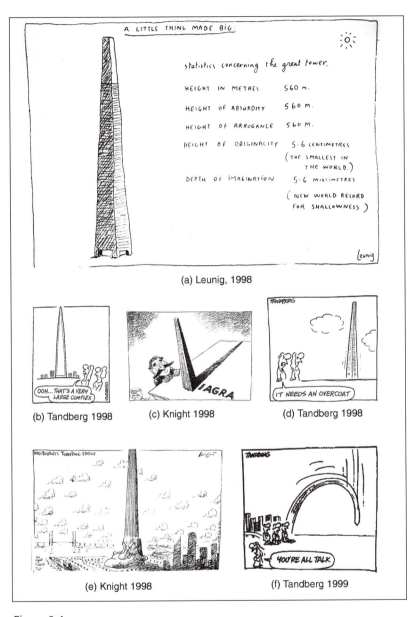

Figure 9.4
Psychology, sex and politics
(a) *Michael Leunig*, The Age, *9 December 1998*;
(b) *Ron Tandberg*/The Age, *12 October 1998*;
(c) *Mark Knight*, Herald Sun, *8 December 1998*;
(d) *Ron Tandberg*/The Age, *9 December 1998*;
(e) *Mark Knight*/Herald Sun, *9 December 1998*;
(f) *Ron Tandberg*/The Age, *14 April 1999*.

Amenity and Planning Committee of the Docklands Authority.[22] Yet within a few months the agreement was terminated when the developers refused to pay the infrastructure fee.[23] It is hard to imagine how a deal can collapse in dispute over about 0.1 per cent of the total project cost. One can only surmise that much more was really at stake, that the project had never been viable without massive public subsidy and had been kept artificially alive with hype and promise until trust collapsed. There was bitterness all round: 'Melbourne has turned the lights off on the new millennium', said Daniel Grollo and Premier Kennett called it a 'major loss of face for the Grollo organization', a tone reinforced by some cartoons (Figure 9.4 f).[24] Key decisions were primarily taken by the Premier who in turn had to weigh the political damage if the project collapsed against the loss of legitimacy as more and more concessions were made. The developers wanted the maximum level of government commitment with minimum financial commitment – the task was to win each round of bidding and sort out the financial details later when the political cost of allowing the project to collapse would be too great. The developers miscalculated the resolve of the government to enforce the agreement, yet in this they were also the victims of an overly fluid planning process. The uncertainty that permeated the entire process was exploited by developers at every stage. After this debacle the Docklands Authority released the precinct again for tender with suggestions that it might be subdivided. The Grollos resubmitted an identical proposal but there was then little hope that the tower would rise again.

It would be wrong to view this five-year saga simply in terms of the heroic quest for the world's tallest tower, thwarted by a combination of community resistance, common sense, politics and economic realism. Despite its demise, the proposal played a key role in the urban development of the Docklands as a whole, not just the Batman's Hill precinct. The first release of the tower proposal on the Docklands site coincided, to the day, with the release for public comment of the draft Planning Amendment L202 a few days before Christmas 1995. This was the Planning Scheme with which compliance was negotiable, the legislative basis for market-led design-driven development. It was astutely double-buried: first under the distractions and absences of Christmas and the holiday season; second under the debate over the Grollo Tower. This was but the first of many uses of the tower as a red herring to deflect debate away from the larger Docklands process. Every time there was a round of announcements on new developments in the Docklands the tower was among them. And the tower was always the centre of debate – a striking image guaranteed to deliver ratings and consume the attentions of the mass media. The Ministerial Panel set up in mid-1998 ensured that the tower debate was sustained during a period of declining credibility, when the precincts had been out for tender for nearly three years and no projects had been finalised. The Wurundjeri Way bypass had the potential to erupt as a major scandal if reasoned debate were to break out during any interruption to the flow of grand and contentious visions. The government had a motive for keeping the project alive despite its lack of economic viability and the damage it would cause.

There is no doubt that the tower would have had a dramatic effect on the image of Melbourne at a global scale, but the impact would have been short-lived and largely negative. Melbourne is inevitably enmeshed in global competition for investment and our urban image does make a difference. But the Grollo Tower was silly enough to do us damage, both locally and globally. It was a grossly over-scaled development that would have permanently belittled the Melbourne skyline; an anti-urban project sucking life out of the city while damaging existing amenity and heritage. The tower was an old-fashioned project masquerading as new and visionary; a variation of cultural cringe dressed as entrepreneurial spirit.

The postscript to this story is that the tower proposal was revived again in 2003 with the identical design to be constructed on a new site in Dubai – a 'city within a city', rising from a 'man made island', with 'open green spaces, water features, pedestrian boulevards, an "old town" and one of the world's largest shopping malls'.[25]

CHAPTER TEN

HYPE
AND
HOPE

By 2004, after eleven years of precinct-based development, agreements were in place for parts of all precincts with construction under way (Figure 8.1). However, a large number of proposals had collapsed, and there was no final plan for any full precinct. How are we to assess this process against the broad and long-term opportunities embodied in the Docklands?

'DOCKLANDS IS FOR EVERYONE'?

A first point to make is the degree to which the docks are set to become the residential preserve of a rather narrow social group of middle-aged empty-nesters and younger managerial classes. The issue of social mix in the Docklands vanished, even from the rhetoric, after 1993, only to reappear after the millennium when it was too late. While there were warnings about the forms of social polarisation that were likely to occur, such discussion was derided as an impediment to the flows of global capital that were assured if only one honoured the free flow of market forces. Concerns about the complete privatisation of the waterfront and the formation of gated communities have not, thus far, been borne out. While some doubts remain about undeveloped portions where no clear plans are in place, at least four kilometres of continuously accessible waterfront seems assured. However, almost all such waterfront is now freehold property with a caveat enabling public access and in many areas private control extends across the water. The social polarisation is constructed through a complex mix of controls over behaviour, design imagery and flows of traffic (both pedestrian and vehicular). The vast majority of the Melbourne population cannot afford to buy or rent Docklands housing and parking costs make a visit expensive.[1] As outlined at the end of chapter 7, the rhetoric of affordable housing rose to the top of the agenda of the Docklands Authority just after the final deals were being sealed without any such provisions. While most Melburnians will visit, and many will enjoy these new waterfronts, they cannot now become an integrated part of the inner city.

Docklands was declared to be both market-driven and design-driven, yet the market analyses and designs had a loose relation to reality. Docklands was treated as a state of mind, a matter of confidence and image; urban development became 'fiction-driven'. The economic fiction came in the form of unrealistic predictions by property consultants who imagined a flood of global investment sufficient to completely develop the 200 hectares in a decade. As public credibility diminished during the mid-1990s, the announcement of new projects took on increasing importance to sustain the narrative of a state '*on the move*'. Winning visions could only be re-announced and changed so many times before the public expected real projects on the ground. A 'mirage' was constructed on the waterfront, with fictional visions deployed to fill the credibility gap when real projects were unavailable. One of the lessons is that the public desire to believe the illusion proved stronger than the desire to understand what was happening. Docklands planning has been an extraordinarily successful exercise in myth-making. The public imagination has been saturated with largely fictional visions of a future that exceeds expectation – the hype exceeded the hope.

By 2001 the state had invested about $450 million over seven years in operating expenses, infrastructure and subsidies with a longer term projection of up to a billion dollars of public investment.[2] The early premise that the Docklands could be developed with minimal or no cost to the public purse was abandoned in order to attract the stadium. Public investment includes the bridge extensions of Bourke, La Trobe and Collins streets, as well as Docklands Park and Plaza, the new tramway, Wurundjeri Way, Grimes Bridge, Webb Bridge and decontamination costs. Other costs include operating expenses for the Docklands Authority, the broadband digital network and public subsidies to attract the technology park and the film studios. The need for a new rail bridge remains, along with possible recompense to the CityLink operators for construction of the by-pass. Some of this expenditure is expected to be repaid through developer contributions, but developers have proven extremely reluctant to contribute to infrastructure beyond that necessary to construct their own precinct. By 2001 such returns totalled $26 million.[3] Docklands development was premised on the prospect of little or no cost to the public purse. In reality the state has funded much of the project while ceding control to private interests.

Private investment in the Docklands is difficult to quantify since the contracts remain secret. The promises at various times have included $900 million at New Quay with a further $450 million on the studios nearby, $450 million for the stadium, $650 million on Yarra's Edge, $300 million on Digital Harbour and $1.8 billion on Victoria Harbour. Without even including Batman's Hill (now broken into small pieces) it is clear that long-term investment will be massive and will make the developer contributions look paltry. However, this investment is not occurring in the short term and it is primarily investment that would have occurred in other parts of Melbourne in any case. While the strategy was to attract global rather than local investment to the Docklands, nearly all projects are Australian owned and controlled. The stadium is based on the attraction of local football crowds; when it is used for global events, the stadium is not the attraction. The housing and waterfront restaurants compete with other housing developments in Melbourne. The only major office building in the docks is the National Australia Bank whose headquarters are being syphoned from the central city. The selected developers for five of the six precincts are Melbourne-based, and it has been the more globally based projects that have collapsed or been rejected. The Malaysian-based YarraNova and YarraCity consortia were shortlisted in four major precincts, but then rejected or sidelined at later stages, even when their ideas were adopted (Figure 8.9). In each case they submitted the better of the two shortlisted bids; one can only presume that the decisions were based on financial rather than urban design criteria.

As early as 1998, property analysts were ringing alarm bells about the potential of such a process to oversupply the market and drain investment from other parts of the city. As if to show that such analysis was as fluid as its advertising images, the Authority responded with a study from its property consultants who argued that the market-driven approach would prevent oversupply.[4] There were warnings that the new stadium would undermine the viability of other stadia, that oversupply of offices would threaten the central city and that flooding the docks with housing would drain the housing market in Southbank and elsewhere. The public subsidies are a crucial issue in this regard; if this investment is local, then where is the justification for subsidising it in one part of the city and not another? The hype suggested large amounts of global investment with no public cost under condition that the state largely surrender design control of the waterfront to that market. The result has been medium amounts of local investment at substantial public cost coupled with loss of control. Given the flexibility of global capital markets, this bias towards local capital would seem to indicate that the heavy politicisation of the process gave a certain advantage to local developers. The deal-making relied on certain levels of reciprocal trust and social capital based in local networks, and a sell-off of the docks to Australians is easier to manage politically than to foreigners. The more that capital flows are deregulated, the more the political flows need to be contained in other ways. If the locals always win then the global effect may be to damage Melbourne's reputation as a site for global investment.

THE TRAGEDY OF THE PRECINCTS

The fluidity and uncertainty characterising the planning and urban design process has seriously compromised the outcomes. Developers promised more than they could deliver in order to get to the next stage of negotiation, knowing that conditions remained fluid until a contract was signed. The amount of risk developers were asked to take was huge and the attempt to shift it back on to the government was understandable. Sensing the increasing need of the government to get firm contracts concluded, developers gained the impression that they could not only get in at a low price, but also force the government to pay for infrastructure. Government decisions to add infrastructure in an ad hoc manner reinforced this impression – the La Trobe Street extension, Bourke Street overpass, Wurundjeri Way and Grand Plaza all added value to the stadium after the deal was done, and other developers expected similar treatment. Yet the stadium deal only ever made sense as a 'kick-start' – the massive public subsidy could not be sustained for other precincts.

The fluidity of the development process has not met the approval of the development industry, many of whom have been privately critical of it: 'It was an extraordinarily long process. Incredibly expensive. We spen[t] a lot of time, energy, money on things that ended up not being relevant. The rules kept changing. We were given a set of goalposts, we got through them and then we found ourselves facing a new set.'[5] The lack of certainty about infrastructure was a key reason for some of the bids collapsing. Developers could not calculate risks without knowing how adjacent precincts would add or subtract value from theirs. The main harbour of Yarra Waters (now Yarra's Edge) precinct was about 200 metres south of the 600-metre Grollo Tower proposal, which would have cast the harbour into shade and diminished both the amenity and symbolic capital of the development. The risk of the Grollo Tower being constructed must surely have been factored into the price paid for control of Yarra Waters. It follows that the collapse of the Grollo Tower became a windfall capital gain to the developers. While the flexibility built into the Planning Scheme enabled developers to think outside the box, to engage new flows of desire and symbolic capital, the same flexibility on neighbouring precincts made this very risky. The desire for height and dominance in the Grollo Tower overshadowed and belittled the desire for a sunny harbour in Yarra Waters. The uncertainty about adjacent precincts lowers the price in all precincts, not only because of possible adverse effects, but also because no one wanted to be first. As one developer put it: 'We weren't prepared to be a shag on a rock in the middle of nowhere ...'.[6]

While developers were willing to pay for on-site infrastructure where they could control the design, they were less than eager to contribute additionally to off-site trunk infrastructure. More importantly, they realised that the politics of the situation could be manipulated to their advantage. Having proclaimed the Docklands development 'Melbourne's Millennium Mark', and with the millennium approaching, the government's credibility with the electorate was at stake. Developers used this situation as leverage to lock in tacit agreements, leaving the crucial details to be sorted at the next stage. As one developer put it: 'Understand how it works. You keep bidding until you win. Once you win you try to re-draw the boundaries a little bit. What the Authority has said, both to the Grollos and to Victoria Harbour where they were the preferred developer and they tried to claw back is: 'You're not going to do that. You're out'.[7] While developers are not risk averse, they need certainty about the framework within which they will calculate those risks. Initially there were well-expounded limits to such flexibility – developers would pay all infrastructure costs, proposals must involve high levels of new investment, and precincts must be fully developed within a decade. All of these requirements also turned out to be flexible. Planning law was being negotiated as the process unfolded. Certain conditions were ostensibly set by the Authority, yet many of them were as fluid as their advertising images. All infrastructure was to be designed and funded by developers, yet at certain moments the government stepped in with key funding for infrastructure. All clean-up costs were to be covered by developers, but when pushed, public investment was offered. The process was to be design-driven with strong imaginative visions, yet the precinct plan made an integrated vision almost impossible. Developers were to meet certain public interest provisions such as public access to the waterfront, but the Planning Scheme was widely disparaged by those responsible for implementing it.

The planning and urban design process was essentially being subcontracted to developers. To use an architectural analogy, it was as if the plans for an apartment block were developed by tendering it out for design one apartment at a time and hoping that the owners would see a collective interest in providing the lobbies and corridors. The size, shape and functions of the precincts were poorly conceived. They have, without exception, proven too large for the available investment – those that have proceeded have only done so on small portions of the precinct. Control over both the urban design and the rate of release of the land has been ceded over the whole precinct in order to achieve piecemeal development on a part of it. Yet the precincts were also too small for integrated development to occur, with a loss of opportunity for integration between precincts. Nowhere is this more apparent than in the failure to develop the harbour as the Docklands centrepiece. The harbour was originally excavated as an integrated body of water lined with wharves and warehouses. While there was a good deal of urban character and heritage embodied in this formation, there was no great imperative to preserve it. There was, however, a social and economic imperative to conceptualise the harbour in an integrated, creative and imaginative manner. The multiplicity of proposals and fictional visions, the computer graphics and repeated hyperbole generated an illusion of innovation and integration, but the result shows a dismal level of conceptual thinking.

The finger pier is a key to any such thinking; its visibility makes it a centrepiece and a major opportunity for a public site or structure that adds value to the harbour. It is the place for something out of the ordinary: a folly, a spectacular urban object, a place from which to view the city, a formal celebration of the new Docklands. Yet the precinct divisions rendered any integrated urban vision impossible since the harbour was surrounded by four precincts. This led inevitably to a precinct-centred focus rather than a water-centred one. While adjacent precincts were encouraged to collaborate, there was no firm infrastructural framework within which they could do so. When the deal was done for the stadium there was no vision in place for the adjacent waterfront. The busy road was later removed, the waterfront was excised from the Victoria Harbour precinct, warehouses were demolished and the Grand Plaza added – all at public expense. The stadium now monopolises several hundred metres of prime public plaza and waterfront for which it has little use.

The waterfront on the northern side of the harbour, which was first shortlisted as a car park, now has a row of eighty-metre towers casting the harbour into shade, or what remains of it after the marina, walkways and restaurants, which extend over the water. This is presumably what the market dictates – the towers maximise the private view and generate the highest short-term flows of capital. Yet it has always been (and remains) unclear just what this view of the harbour will eventually consist of. If the central finger pier were now to be developed with a highly imaginative design and new forms of public amenity, then this would add significant value to these apartments after the event. This flow of capital, which could have been used to produce public wealth, has been squandered. It is possible to argue that there would be no development in this precinct without permission to overshadow the water. Such assertions operate to clear the territory for radically market-driven policies but they defy credibility. Under a new government, Waterfront City proceeds next door without overshading the waterfront. An integrated urban design vision for the harbour would have generated different market conditions and a subdivision of smaller lots along the northern wharf would have been quickly snapped up by medium-scale developers who have been systematically excluded from all Docklands development. The future of Victoria Harbour remains partly in process and there are some promising signs since Lend Lease took over the precinct in 2000. Docklands will surely become a place that many Melburnians will enjoy, but those with imagination will also see what a marvellous opportunity was squandered here as the precinct focus led to a relative neglect of the harbour as a public place. Urban design is a wealth-creation task that relies upon an imaginative and integrated vision.

BURNOUT

In the end this analysis must turn to the opportunity represented by 200 hectares of public land and water directly adjacent to a major city centre. It would be wrong to suggest that public interests were ignored, rather they were equated with attracting global investment – what's good for the economy is good for the public. Yet the Docklands Authority also continuously espoused principles of public access to the waterfront, environmental sustainability, mixed use, height controls to protect amenity, heritage protection, public artworks, waterfront promenades, public open space, pedestrian/cycle networks and public transport. Developers were encouraged to design for such public interest provisions and all schemes were reviewed (in confidence) by the Authority according to them. However, at the same time, developers were encouraged to exceed height limits with 'adventurous' projects and many came to believe that all public interest provisions were negotiable.

It is possible to argue that the market-led approach we have seen was the only way to generate any development in Docklands. Yet there is a counter-view that the precincts currently being developed could have developed at a similar pace with a more imaginative and integrated infrastructure plan, with a greater social mix, creating opportunities for a vastly increased range of developers and project types; with greater architectural variety; and a far greater level of public wealth creation. It seems apparent in retrospect that a good market analysis would have shown that the docks would require a billion dollars of public investment over a decade in order to achieve current levels of investment. If it were designed with imagination and integration – with high waterfront amenity; with opportunities for private developers at a range of scales; with affordable housing; with a digital infrastructure to attract high-tech industry; with a diverse mix of people and place types – then not only would the long-term wealth be increased, but much more of it would flow back to the public purse through subsequent land sales.

'Burnout' was a performance art event, conceived by Ben Morieson and sponsored by the Docklands Authority, where high-powered cars laid rubber on the vast concrete surface of the docks. The work is listed in the Guinness Book of Records as the largest artwork created with tyre marks and the photographs became publicity for the Docklands Authority (Figure 10.1). In the uncanny way in which art tells a truth that is difficult to explain, the burnt rubber and smoke traces of these flows of adrenaline resemble both the early Committee for Melbourne 'plans' and the fictional 'water-world' of 1996 – Docklands as a place of transgression where one 'lets off steam', unleashing flows of desire. These traces of 'lines of flight' are echoes of the larger development process with its smell, smoke and noise; some of the more theoretical dimensions of this shift will be explored in the chapter 11.

Figure 10.1
Burnout 2001
(*Artist*: *Ben Morieson*; *Photo*: *John Donegan*/The Age)

CHAPTER ELEVEN

CONSTRUCTING DESIRES

Stephen Wood and Kim Dovey[1]

It is clear from the preceding chapters that urban planning processes associated with the Melbourne Docklands represent a radical departure from anything that might be regarded as a 'normal' planning process. This chapter will attempt to theorise these changes using concepts derived from the philosophy and social theory of Deleuze and Guattari. The contention here is that while one can legitimately critique such an urban planning process in terms of what it does *not* do (it is not rational, transparent, democratic, or participative), such an approach offers prospects for understanding what it *does* do. The challenging nature of such theory will render this chapter far more difficult than others in this book; we will avoid jargon where possible.

The Melbourne Docklands planning process may be construed as having three main phases, with certain overlaps, as outlined in Figure 11.1. Phase I, from 1989–1992, consisted of two parallel threads: the 'public' planning process undertaken in the context of the Olympics bid and Docklands Task Force, and the 'private' planning process, led by the Committee for Melbourne, focused on the Multi-Function Polis bid. The first of these threads embodied many of planning's traditional ideals, including 'social rationality', comprehensive analysis, public consultation and transparency. This process was strongly grounded in the existing site with distinct territories and strong boundary definitions. It identified the problems, goals and objectives; it undertook research and analysis; it identified alternatives and developed an infrastructure plan geared to a two-stage community consultation process. This was a process that was well-grounded in existing site conditions, the local community, transparent decision-making and the authority of the state.

The second thread of this early phase, focused on the Multi-Function Polis bid, operated to undermine the grounds of the first. It painted a portrait of a city in crisis where normal planning concerns were a brake on progress. This was a discourse of both fear and opportunity, which worked in direct opposition to the first thread: the threat of Melbourne becoming a 'backwater ... of declining significance' is contrasted with the 'opportunity to re-orient our whole urban planning process'.[2] This reorientation was to gear urban development objectives to global market forces. Within this thread, the future of Docklands could not be planned in advance of market determinations and proposals were consequently devoid of content. Boundaries became blurred and history was erased since

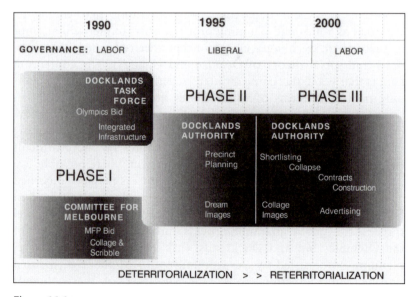

Figure 11.1
Phases of Docklands Planning

place identity was to emerge from the market. Infrastructure planning consisted of little more than a series of scribbles (Figure 7.5), and visions of the future were limited to collages that gestured towards how a market-driven development might 'feel'.

With the formation of the Docklands Authority, a second phase of planning may be identified, extending from 1993 to 1996, focused on the articulation of a 'real-world' market perspective. The Authority disavowed itself of the earlier public planning process and established criteria for a successful development in economic and financial terms. The 'plans' generated by this perspective systematically avoided 'grounding' the development process in anything other than flows of capital and the desires of investors. The earliest precinct diagram was labelled 'Not a Master Plan' and the successive precinct plans had fluid boundaries, functions and height limits (Figures 7.6 and 7.7). The legislated planning scheme of 1996 (Figure 7.8) was never intended for enforcement and was soon contradicted by an equally fictional but seductive, dream-like vision (Figure 7.9). The 'real world' became a 'dream world'.

From 1997 onwards, a third phase may be identified, as developers' proposals were shortlisted, contracts were awarded (and terminated), and construction was commenced in places. This phase was marked by a proliferation of visions as proposals were shortlisted, amended, abandoned and replaced. If there was a constant to this phase, it was the constant difficulty of forming any clear picture of what was being proposed for the Docklands. This difficulty stemmed not only from commercial-in-confidence clauses, but also from the way in which proposals were described. The discourse of the Docklands Authority resembled an advertising or marketing campaign with much less emphasis placed on 'what' was being proposed than was placed on the 'feel' of the projects. Different representations of projects appeared to contradict each other and the design was often changed radically after being approved. Until so many projects collapsed in 1999 this campaign may be regarded as very successful – in the public imagination a fantastic but real world was coming to the Docklands. Since the millennium, this phase has proceeded to contracts in most areas with outcomes described in chapter 8.

PLANNING, CAPITAL AND DESIRE

The dramatic departure from 'normal' paradigms for urban planning practice stands as one of the most striking features of the

Docklands planning process. While planning has 'traditionally' sought to pursue 'comprehensive' forms of analysis guided by 'social rationality', from the second thread of Phase I onwards the process came to be dominated by 'market rationality'.[3] This shift away from comprehensiveness and social rationality was accompanied by a heightened emphasis on the production of desire. Very few major decisions and proposals were accompanied by reasoned exposition, but they were all accompanied by affect-laden discourse – illustrations and visions that were less reliable descriptions of the future than they were imperatives to 'feel' positive about that future.

The planning process was not based upon the perceived interests of groups defined according to existing social distinctions, but instead worked to produce new desires and identities through the planning process itself. While it can be construed that one set of interests (community) was displaced by another (market), to reduce the process to this observation is to miss the significant manner in which the process sought to produce a *new* set of interests and desires. In this context, the affective dimension of the Docklands discourse may be regarded as critical, as is exemplified by the repeated use of the collage of masked faces (see Figure 8.3). Deployed initially as a form of advertising in the Authority's publications, these collages were subsequently used to promote the stadium, and then incorporated into the design of the park.

The move from social rationality to market rationality will not surprise neo-Marxist critics of the relationship between capital and urban planning. From such a view, the form taken by urban development is a reflection of market power, modes of production and class interests. An examination of the Docklands Authority board reveals the dominant interests of private capital in this regard. The imperative to use Docklands to help Melbourne shift its economy from manufacturing to knowledge industries, together with the need to market Melbourne to attract global investment, fits neatly with accounts of 'globalisation', which foreground changes in modes of production from 'Fordism' to 'post-Fordism'.

At the same time, when the Docklands planning process is examined through the lens of the social theory of Deleuze and Guattari an emphasis is placed on the way in which the planning process was 'driven' by desire, and was productive of desire. The interests and identities of social classes can be seen as the end-products of processes of new modes of production, the production of desire. For Deleuze and Guattari desire is a principle of creativity, invention, and connection that fuels all of life's processes. Desire is 'revolutionary in its essence' because it constantly unsettles stabilised identity (or 'being') in favour of new 'becomings'.[4] From this view the 'grounding' of urban development in market rationality is linked to the grounding of flows of desire in flows of capital. Before the market can play a determining role in urban development, flows of desire must be made to appear to derive from flows of capital.

This was achieved through the planning process by 'deterritorialising' desire (sweeping aside pre-existing desires) and then 'reterritorialising' desire (producing new desires which are indexed to capital). The 'private' planning thread of Phase I, together with much of Phase II, may be viewed as an expression of this movement of deterritorialisation. The second movement, reterritorialisation, ensures that consumption takes place and profit is realised. New desires are produced that are indexed to capitalisation processes. The later stages of Phase II, together with Phase III, may be viewed as an expression of this movement of reterritorialisation. This process of deterritorialisation–reterritorialisation relies on the simultaneous production of two different kinds of surplus value: quantitative and qualitative surplus values. On the one hand, the Docklands planning process was clearly concerned to ensure that the familiar surplus value of profit accrues to investors. On the other hand, it also produced a 'subjective' form of surplus value, which might be characterised in terms of an affective 'buzz-charge' or 'aura', comparable to what Bourdieu terms symbolic capital. That is to say, as the Docklands was being produced and consumed for profit, a symbolic surplus was concurrently being deposited in the hands of the government (as 'political kudos'), citizens of Melbourne (as 'civic pride'), prospective residents of the Docklands ('prestige'), and other consumers of the landscape (an 'aura' of 'style' or 'hipness'). Although these two types of surplus value are based in different flows of capital, they are co-dependent for their realisation.[5]

These observations suggest at least three important consequences for the theorisation of urban planning's role in society. First, the explanatory significance of such issues as 'class', 'need', 'use value', and pre-existing 'interests' would seem to be reduced. Identity becomes contingent on production and not the other way around. The Docklands planning process was far more concerned to produce *new* 'interests' and 'identities', than it was concerned to 'repress' old ones (which were, in any case, swept aside by the deterritorialisation process). 'Needs' and 'interests' were not given in advance, but were instead produced through the planning process as a form of 'lack' that Deleuze and Guattari regard as a perversion of desire: 'The deliberate creation of lack as a function of a market economy is the art of a dominant class. This involves deliberately organizing wants and needs amid an abundance of production; making all of desire teeter and fall victim to the great fear of not having one's needs satisfied.'[6]

Second, capital substitutes for the state as planning's dominant authority figure. During phases II and III, the state largely abandoned its responsibility for infrastructure development. It adopted the goal of avoiding government investment on the site, and its role as a framework of power receded. The interests of the state became tantamount to the interests of capital. To a significant degree, the state withdrew from its role of authorising and limiting what was unfolding in the name of 'higher' public goals or values.

Finally, when flows of desire were 'reduced' to flows of capital the process driving the production of urban space became disassociated from 'meaning' or 'content'. Throughout phases II and III, determinations about 'what' was to be produced at the Docklands were not made on the basis of existing qualitative values, but rather on the basis of quantitative, economic calculations. The form and style of so much of the Docklands discourse was without content; 'visions' were productive of desire rather than reasoned debate. It is not being suggested here that the Docklands planning process was without 'meaning', rather that the Docklands planning process 'meant' much the same thing as any advertisement 'means': '... that a company is trying to increase its profits'.[7] In this context, it is worth noting that the elision of sensible referents and detailed references to 'actual' proposals parallels contemporary advertising practices, where the nature of the 'product' is often of less consequence than its 'branding'.

POWER

We now want to briefly situate these issues in relation to Deleuzian conceptions of power, generally known as 'control power'. Traditional planning processes have deployed theories of power largely based in the rule of law with a focus on transparent and rational decision-making in a context of what Habermas terms an 'ideal speech situation'.[8] Power is largely conceived as a power 'over' others that is held by social agents and institutions subject to social control. While such understandings of power may be embodied in elements of the public consultation process associated with the first thread of the first phase of Docklands planning, later phases are characterised by opacity, confusion and distortion. Foucault has long argued for an alternative theory of power as a set of disciplinary micropractices dispersed throughout the social body, power is productive, it constructs us as subjects. 'Disciplinary power' functions to establish particular identity types and to cast others as 'deviant' and 'dysfunctional'.[9] The disciplinary institutions of civil society play a central role in this power regime to educate, order, and regulate individuals in the interests of the state.[10] However, in the later phases of Docklands planning most of the institutions of civil society became marginalised, established norms were swept aside and deviations were actively encouraged. The Deleuzian conception of power extends Foucault's critique from 'discipline' to 'control'.

Control power is predicated on a condition of groundlessness and does not begin with fixed social identities: 'it is oriented not toward position and identity but rather toward mobility and anonymity. It functions on the basis of 'the whatever', the flexible and mobile performance of contingent identities'.[11] The identity of the Docklands was rendered in a very loose and fluid fashion, descriptions were provided of what the Docklands 'could be' or 'might be', but there was a refusal to specify what it 'is' in advance of the determinations of investors and developers. Place identity was held in check as an unqualified, non-specified, indeterminate 'whatever'. Control power is not a 'power over' something that already exists, but instead is a 'power to' create its object; the object of control power emerges through its exercise.[12] As developers and investors made decisions, the previously unqualified, non-specified, indeterminate identity of the Docklands became qualified, specified and determinate. With control power, the 'normal' becomes fluid, at any given moment it becomes synonymous with whatever functions to aid capitalisation processes.[13] When, finally, determinations did begin to be made about the Docklands identity, they were accompanied by a barrage of seductive imagery and language that attempted to 'control' how these determinations were perceived. Flows of 'affect' were circulated as a normative control mechanism; a channelling of desire. Control power does not 'require' the disciplinary mediation of civil society and is not underwritten by any kind of morality or code: 'Any 'belief' can circulate if it sells, and any science will be supported if it produces a further flow of capital'.[14]

In so far as written publications from the Docklands Authority constituted the primary interface between the general public and the planning process, the so-called 'discursive turn' in urban studies is crucial to understanding this process. There are many kinds of discourse analyses, and from a Deleuzean perspective those approaches that focus on what a discourse 'means' are of less practical use than those that focus on what a discourse 'does' and on how it 'works'.[15] In contrast to the approach of Barthes, for instance, a Deleuzian approach would focus less on the way in which a discourse represents states of affairs and produces meanings or narratives, and more on the way in which it incites, induces, seduces, evokes and enables.[16] For Deleuze, any quest to expose the meaning or reality 'behind' a discourse is politically ineffective since that is not where the power of a discourse resides. It is akin to analysing an artwork without considering how it 'evokes' certain affects, or analysing an advertisement without considering how it 'induces' a certain purchase. As Colebrook argues: 'It is the desire for the image and affect itself, and not what it means, that is political'.[17] It follows that it is unhelpful to treat discourses as mere 're-presentations' of the 'real'. The Docklands discourse was in many instances directly productive of the 'real': constructing the public imagination; generating a 'real-world' perspective; and producing desires for a dream world predicated upon it.

As a final point here, this critique questions the politics of deconstructive approaches that seek to keep meaning in play. Some Deleuzean critics suggest that such approaches may support the exercise of control power.[18] The meanings of the Docklands discourse were already multiplicitous, fluid and slippery; and paradoxically some of the work of ARM appears inspired by Deleuzian conceptions of space.

TRANSCENDENCE AND IMMANENCE

Finally, it is worth considering the relevance to Docklands planning of Deleuze and Guattari's privileging of 'immanence' over 'transcendence'. The transcendent image is constructed when everyday experience or practice is 'grounded' in something outside; described or explained in terms of some underlying or more 'real' foundation. Deleuze and Guattari insist that life has no 'ground' outside itself, and such an approach points to the task of engaging with planning and design in an immanent manner. The first thread of Phase I included many appeals to transcendence (in so far as it was grounded in universal ideas of reason and knowledge, state authority, the notion of the public interest, and so forth), the remainder of the planning process was almost entirely ungrounded and, in many respects, approximated immanent engagement with the Docklands. That said, it must be stressed that this remained a tendency only, for these parts of the process still posited an abstraction as the foundation of flows of desire – capital. This grounding of life in capital is a peculiar one that has been described as a 'groundless ground'.[19]

From the perspective proposed by Deleuze and Guattari, there can be no return to the transcendent ideal of the 'state' to supplant the groundless ground of 'capital'; indeed, it might be argued that the 'problem' with the Docklands planning process was not that it was ungrounded, but that it was not ungrounded enough. As Colebrook puts it: 'The only way out of this is to push the deterritorialising tendency of capitalism ... to its limit'.[20] This, however, is a dilemma, rather than an easy solution. Urban planning and development, as the invention of a future, invariably embodies an imaginative 'line of flight', involving multiplicitous desires. The deterritorialising tendencies of the market are productive in this regard: to the extent that they potentially liberate desire from the domination of prevailing social codes and identities, they free all manner of creative energies. At the same time, capitalism always reterritorialises and re-codes that which it deterritorialises. The projects on the ground in Docklands do produce relatively stable territories and identities. The unleashed becomings and desires are marshalled to the ends of capital. How then, might one counteract planning processes that resemble Docklands, without constructing some other transcendent ground that involves established territories and identities? A key challenge for urban theory posed by the work of Deleuze and Guattari is that of producing a mode of planning and urban design which invents the future with imagination, but which does not have recourse to grounds outside of life. What are the possibilities for immanent engagement with the movements, rhythms and intensities of the various flows that converge to produce any place? What resonances might be established between these flows, such that an unending process of becoming is unleashed? There are more clues to these questions in the Federation Square project (chapter 6) than in anything that has or is likely to emerge in Docklands.

PART C

BAYSCAPES

CHAPTER TWELVE

CREATING AND DEFENDING URBAN CHARACTER

While the central city and the waterfronts we have discussed thus far are several kilometres inland, Melbourne has always been a city on a bay. Port Phillip Bay is the vast stretch of water protected from the sea by the Bellarine and Mornington peninsulas, which almost meet at the Port Phillip heads fifty kilometres to the south. Unlike the river and port, which were cut off from the city and largely forgotten, the bay has long been one of the city's prime residential locations and urban playgrounds. The stretch I am concerned with here is the four-kilometre frontage closest to the city from Port Melbourne to St Kilda.

The former working class suburb of Port Melbourne is about four kilometres as the crow flies from the Flinders Street station in the city (Figure 2.1), an alignment established in the early days of European settlement by the Sandridge railway – of which only the bridge across the Yarra now remains. The former seafaring town has two substantial piers, one of which retains a major function as the Tasmanian ferry dock. The town developed in the late nineteenth century within walking distance of the industrial port centred on the piers. The suburb was a grid of small streets and lanes with a rich mix of small housing types, supplemented in the 1940s by the Garden City development of public housing to the west. St Kilda is further from the city and developed in the nineteenth century as the city's major waterfront resort – a headland overlooking a string of waterfront parks and a long pier capped with a Victorian pavilion. St Kilda is one of the most high-profile districts within the Melbourne area, with a rich social and cultural mix and a thriving arts community. It has an edgy and somewhat transgressive urban character that is consistently under threat from new development.

The frontage of Port Phillip Bay from Port Melbourne to St Kilda (Beaconsfield Parade) is a four-kilometre stretch of palm-lined boulevard and waterfront promenade. The beach is almost continuously swimmable and the only buildings on the beach side of the boulevard are the occasional kiosk and change rooms. The boulevard is also an arterial road carrying heavy traffic that separates this housing and its hinterland from the beach. The suburban street grid to the north was fully developed in the nineteenth century, with a mixture of single- and two-storey housing. While a range of taller buildings from five to fourteen storeys have emerged along the waterfront since the 1960s, these are regarded as aberrations and the boulevard remains predominantly two storey with most under heritage control. The south-eastern section towards St Kilda is a mix of many architectural styles with building types ranging from single- and two-storey terraces to large detached Victorian and Edwardian mansions mixed with early twentieth-century apartments and a few high-rise towers. The north-western section towards Port Melbourne is generally lower in scale – primarily two-storey Victorian terraces. This waterfront from Port Melbourne to St Kilda is the only part of Melbourne that offers full beach frontage within ten minutes of the central city. The desire for access and consequent pressure for high-density development are immense.

SANDRIDGE CITY

In the mid-1980s about thirty hectares of disused industrial land adjacent to the piers at Port Melbourne became available for redevelopment. This became one of the first major public–private partnerships under the control of the state's new Major Projects Unit (developed in response to the Southbank initiatives). This government agency was designed to facilitate entrepreneurial governance by separating it from the development of planning policy and law. There was a broad perception that the planning system was unable to respond to the fluidity of the market in large-scale development. Public interest provisions were to be protected by a Development Brief; the aim was to: 'extend the Port Melbourne residential community … in an integrated development …'.[1] It also required the provision of 160 units of public housing. The selected proposal, called 'Sandridge City' (also known as 'Bayside'), was to excavate the waterfront site for a canal development with waterfront townhouses supplemented with high-rise housing, hotel, commercial and retail facilities on the bay frontage (Figure 12.1).[2] This was a fairly standard waterfront formula for its time with a 'festival market', fish market, cafes, piers and an aquarium. There seemed a good deal of potential for more public amenity here, but the local community was suspicious. The literature issued by the developers to describe the project was sharply divided into a seductive vision on the one hand and an almost unintelligible set of plans and provisions on the other. With the theory and rhetoric of 'place' gaining currency in the fields of architecture and urban planning, the publicity suggested that: 'The philosophical approach to the design has primarily been influenced by accepting the overall disciplines of a sense of place, scale and appropriateness'.[3] The developers suggested that: 'residential areas link in a friendly way with existing neighbourhoods … integrating it comfortably into the existing fabric of Port Melbourne'.[4]

This discourse of 'place' and 'integration', however, was deployed largely as legitimating rhetoric. The two thick volumes of the *Environmental Effects Statement* were almost impossible for the local community to understand and so riddled with contradiction and obfuscation that an accurate translation was not possible.[5] The simulations of the completed development supplied by developers as a basis for public debate were consistently underscaled. It was clear, however, that the proposal was to block the waterfront road in order to provide boat access for the canals and direct beach access for the new development. This disrupted both vehicle and pedestrian networks along the beachfront, leaving the Garden City neighbourhood to the west isolated from the traditional shopping precinct. It was difficult to imagine a proposal that could be less integrated with the existing community. There was a great deal of community resistance to the project and a collection of critical views on it were published.[6] It was clear that the site was to include new forms of private control over public open space and that many provisions of public planning were being dismantled to facilitate this.[7]

Figure 12.1
Sandridge City Proposal, 1987
(*Sandridge City Development Company,*
Landscape Australia, *4, 1987*)

When the project was set to proceed and came on the market in 1991 it became apparent that Sandridge City was to become Melbourne's first gated community. Two large portions of the site incorporating most of the waterfront housing were to have access restricted to owners by guards and gates. The project was marketed as: 'The most private and relaxed residential community ... a totally private, secure and secluded environment ... The Bayside Act and its associated by-laws give specific and powerful planning, security and environmental controls never before available to development in Victoria'.[8] While 'gated communities' have a very long history and had been proliferating in the United States and South-east Asia for some time, there was only one in Australia and none in Melbourne. In addition, all open space within the development, including the waterfront promenade, was to be subject to a dusk-to-dawn curfew. The proposed by-laws allowed private security guards to refuse admission to the site to: 'any persons that they consider will or may cause a nuisance ...'.[9] This enclave sealed off the beachfront to all public thoroughfare, protecting the new residents from the existing community. The revelations of the city's first gated enclave were an embarrassment to the Labor government. The semiautonomous Major Projects Unit had become a vehicle for the loosening of state control, the outcome demonstrated the slippery ground of public–private agreements. Faced with massive community opposition and a growing recession, the Sandridge City proposal collapsed in late 1992, just as the Labor government were thrown out of power.

BEACON COVE

The Major Projects Unit, which was largely responsible for the Sandridge fiasco, retained control of the site and engaged briefly in a far more open process. This included a community design workshop that explored many of the principles of 'new urbanism' – new housing typologies, permeable street networks, walkable neighbourhoods and public transport. One of the plans from this workshop appeared on the cover of an international compendium of good urban design.[10] It showed a concern to incorporate the heritage of the site into the design, particularly a small lighthouse built in 1924 to guide ships into the pier that remains in use. Some of these ideas percolated into a new development proposal known as Beacon Cove (Figure 12.2).[11] The project as constructed is a mix of high-density high-rise on the waterfront with a two-storey suburban hinterland. The south-facing waterfront is lined with a row of twelve-storey towers fronting a pedestrian promenade. A pre-existing light rail connection to the city is incorporated into the project. The suburban street plan laid out behind the high-density waterfront adopts many of the ideas from the 'new urbanist' movement and the earlier public workshop, but adapted to match the market. The alignment of the historic beacon with the shipping channel became the central organising axis for the new suburb. A street connection with Garden City was re-established, but set well back from the waterfront and aligned to deter through traffic. The street layout is highly impermeable, formed of a series of loops leading to small 'village greens' surrounded by two-storey suburban housing (Figure 12.3). While Beacon Cove is not a gated enclave, the design adopts the spatial structure of the enclave. Pre-existing street connections with the surrounding context have been systematically removed to generate a spatial structure that operates as an enclave at the large scale, coupled with a highly 'ringy' interior with roads and paths looping back to generate a 'village' effect. This is a form of urbanism where the production of urban character as a form of symbolic capital is strongly linked to the production of social capital – an exclusive 'place' where bonds of community trust can develop free from the contaminations of a social mix.

The most offensive aspect of the design is the manner in which it cuts off the public housing area in the north-east of the site. This is the public housing constructed as part of the strategy to generate a social mix in the area – the public part of the public–private partnership has been systematically walled off from the Beacon Cove development, visually and functionally. On this edge between social classes the private housing turns its back on the public housing with a visual effect known locally as the 'Berlin Wall'.

Work on Beacon Cove began in 1995 and the first phase of 900 houses and apartments, plus recreation club and child care centre, were complete and occupied in 2000. By 2002 Beacon Cove had over 2000 residents and was the main contributor to a rapidly polarising social demography – Port Melbourne has been largely

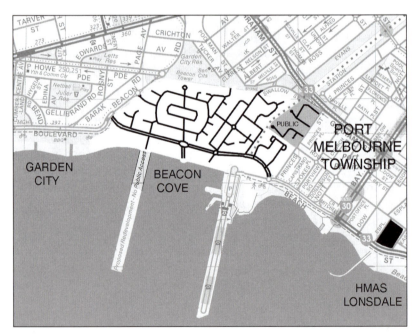

Figure 12.2
Beacon Cove development
(*Adapted from* Melways Street Directory, *Edition 30, 2003*;
Courtesy of Melway Publishing P/L)

deserted by middle-income groups.[12] The development is oriented towards the construction of new forms of social capital and community within the new development, yet insulated from and contrasting against the older Port Melbourne community. While the low-rise parts of the development are infused with nostalgic imagery this is a very new kind of 'community'. The new residents are primarily managers and professionals, highly mobile home owners who are reportedly too busy to join community organisations.[13] There is uncertainty over the future of local schools as most new children travel outside to private schools. There have also been impacts on the broader Port Melbourne community resulting in a new local politics enmeshed in the production of envy; one report suggests that: 'Some who might otherwise not consider themselves poor now measure their own situation against the perceived life in the wealthy estate across the road that boasts a health centre with gymnasium, tennis courts, food store, cafe, medical centre,

Figure 12.3
Beacon Cove's interior 'village'

solarium and physiotherapist's rooms'.[14] A proposal for a second stage of Beacon Cove, primarily waterfront towers and housing on the pier, remains under consideration.

While I am critical of the Beacon Cove project, it is far superior to Sandridge City. The retention of the historic beacon alignment brings a shaft of public history through the centre of the project with a public artwork on the foreshore. The mix of densities diminishing with distance from the water makes sense, although here one sees the all-too-common polarisation between the suburban house and the high-rise tower with little in between. The urban density changes from about 300 dwelling units/hectare on the waterfront to less than a tenth of that across the road. The towers lining the south-facing waterfront generate an unfortunately shady and therefore dull promenade during the middle of the day. The development is driven by proven formulae, rather than creative innovation in housing design – there is little mixing of housing types and little mixing of functions. Once one retreats into the interior of this secluded suburb by the bay, there is no functional mix, no real diversity of architecture and social differences are excluded. The new urbanist ideal of a highly consistent streetscape design has been adopted without the typological, social and functional mix. The developer's complete control over the architecture has produced some very anodyne streetscapes saturated with small variations on singular basic designs.

The most serious damage created by Beacon Cove lies in its lack of integration with its context. Sensible planning would demand a reintegration. This could include extending the main axis to link with local streets to the north; measures could also be taken to generate better access for public housing tenants to the adjacent pocket parks – this could be immediately achieved by the demolition of a single house in the 'Berlin Wall'. Any such measures would be fiercely opposed by Beacon Cove residents because they would puncture the carefully constructed sense of seclusion and control, and they certainly have the power to stop any such move. Beacon Cove now appears in an international compendium of model communities.[15] However, it is primarily a model of how the rhetoric of 'place', 'integration' and new urbanism can be used as a cover for urban segregation and a suffocating sense of urban identity. Beacon Cove is a mix of an overdeveloped and over-shaded waterfront with an underdeveloped and over-enclosed suburb. Thirty hectares of public land and a great opportunity to invent a new and genuinely public waterfront was squandered. This is not, however, a failure of private enterprise; the developers

(Mirvac) were simply pursuing profit and satisfying market desire. The enclave ideology of this project derives from a contradictory desire to be both urban and yet retreat from the city. This was apparent in the name – the 'cove' is not a hollow in the shoreline, but a metaphor for the protective social enclave that it constructs through urban design; Beacon Cove is a retreat, not from the sea, but from the city.

HMAS LONSDALE

About 500 metres east of Beacon Cove is a waterfront site with a peculiar history since it was at one time a small naval base (Figure 12.2). A small harbour at the mouth of a creek has long been filled in, but about a hectare of waterfront land had remained under federal government ownership. Its history of military use and federal ownership placed it in a rather fluid category with regard to planning law; not quite subject to the same kinds of local government control. Because of the creek, the site occupies a slight jog in the beach frontage and therefore terminates the view along Beaconsfield parade from the east. The busy waterfront boulevard is lined with palm trees and a pedestrian/bicycle/roller blade promenade on the beach side. From the beach a distinctive hook-shaped jetty projects into the bay and is a popular fishing site. The site is flanked by two-storey buildings on the east and a former starch factory to the west. The nineteenth-century factory, with a heritage listing, had become a local landmark that was converted into housing in the late 1980s and raised to a total of eleven storeys. The political context to this project is crucial to the forms of planning control exerted. From 1994 to 1996 the Kennett government abolished local government democracy and installed handpicked Commissioners to achieve certain reforms before local areas were amalgamated and elections were restored. One key agenda was to loosen community control over urban planning. The amalgamation of local government on the waterfront brought the entire area under discussion into one local government area (City of Port Phillip).

Until the early 1990s the local foreshore strategy stipulated a maximum height of four storeys for the Lonsdale site. In 1994, with the site coming up for sale, the Council commissioned an urban design study that proposed a maximum height of eight storeys at the rear of the site.[16] In early 1995 an extensive community consultation process resulted in a proposal to raise the height to eleven storeys or thirty-five metres to roughly match the

Figure 12.4
Lonsdale Project from Beaconsfield Parade
(*Architects: Nation Fender Katsalidis*)

heritage factory next door. Later that year the site was sold at a
price well in excess of valuations of the site based on the 35-metre
height limit. The development company was controlled by the
treasurer of the Liberal Party, which was in power at both state
and federal level.[17] Their proposal was for two 22-storey towers
at a height of seventy-nine metres, well in excess of anything in the
vicinity and setting a new precedent for the waterfront.

The extent of community opposition to this project was
astounding, about 850 submissions were received, including peti-
tions and formal submissions from institutional bodies such as the
Royal Australian Institute of Architects and the National Trust. In
some ways this outcry reflects the outrage at the loss of local
government democracy, but there was a widespread concern that
the character and amenity of the waterfront was about to be sacri-
ficed. There was broad community concern about corruption of
the planning system and the possibility that this site would be the
precedent that sets the pattern of developer expectation right

along the waterfront. Planning Minister Maclellan, frustrated by local resistance to planning reform, had long expressed his disdain for height limits and the belief had grown within the development industry that the way to achieve taller buildings was not through the planning scheme, but through a personal approach to the Minister.

In mid-1995 the Planning Minister appointed a Ministerial Panel to advise him on height limits for the site. The major issues were the effects on 'urban character' and overshadowing of the beach. The shadows of the towers at this height would remain on the beach and promenade all day for over three months during the winter, with partial shading for a further five months of the year.[18] Substantial areas of water, including the pier, would be in the shade during mid-winter. This was an interesting issue because it rested on a legal debate about the phenomenology of place. In the context of Melbourne's climate it is not difficult to establish that amenity will be damaged by overshading in winter – the desire to jog, cycle, sunbathe and fish in the sunshine is clear. However, all buildings cast long shadows early and late in the day, and it is exceedingly difficult to draw a line that establishes a public interest in this regard. What difference will one more floor make; and then another? Issues of 'place' and 'urban character' are dimensions of the fluid city that cannot be easily legislated. The task for urban regulation is to draw a line that is not arbitrary, but this is at times like drawing a line in the water. The experience of place is experiential rather than factual, to engage with it requires fluid rather than rigid thinking. To lock in the meaning of 'place' is to reduce, diminish and damage it. Yet to fail to contain these desires is to open the gates to place destruction. The beach is 'smooth' space, but it requires a robust form of 'striation' in order to keep it that way.

While the shading diagrams were matters of fact, the arguments against shading of the beach and promenade rest upon an understanding of the everyday experience. The primary experiences on this beach frontage are structured as a series of pathways: the waterfront boulevard; the pedestrians, cyclists and roller-bladers on the promenade; the beach strollers and swimmers along the water's edge; and the jetty that hooks out into the bay with a view back towards the city. The edge condition of the foreshore is crucial to its character. The primarily lineal structure of the fore-shore is reinforced and celebrated by the avenue of palm trees and by the clear edge of urban development along the boulevard. Each of the paths along the beach and all of the buildings participate in this 'edge effect' – the boundary between city and bay, sheltered by the land yet exposed to the elements. This effect is also aligned with the experience of the sublime – the aesthetic release in the encounter with a vast natural expanse. The beach experience here is that of escaping from the urban, on to the uninterrupted prospect and exposure to the elements of the beach and promenade. The sunshine is a highly significant aspect of the beach experience; indeed, it is most valuable precisely during the winter and equinox seasons when the sunshine is most enjoyable. The beach was of course the major attraction of this site – the shadows are the direct result of the desire to capture the views. This was a classic case of the market threatening the very amenity that creates urban value in the first place.

Another way of describing this is that the flows of desire which attract people to the waterfront intersect with the flows of capital and the desire to accumulate it. There is nothing wrong with these desires, but neither is satisfied in the long term by allowing the desire for wealth to damage the waterfront experience that generates the desire and the wealth in the first place. The value of a sunny beach is not difficult to establish, but since all buildings cast long shadows at dawn and dusk the issue becomes one of how much of the day and year one protects the beach from overshading.

The other issue that was debated at this time was the question of consistency with the 'urban character', another very fluid notion that mixes perceptions of urban form with those of community life. In formal terms urban character is linked to factors such as architectural style, building type, functional mix, materials, grain size, lot size, height, bulk, landscape, street setback and street layout. Community character stems from the social mix and from the patterns of events and experiences. In the vicinity of this site, Port Melbourne was a mix of single- and two-storey housing on small lots juxtaposed with larger industrial buildings. Urban character is not static; indeed, the most lively urban places change and develop in creative and dramatic ways. The issue here was one of fundamental disruption and violation to the urban character of Port Melbourne, rather than an incremental development of the character of the place.

At the Panel hearings, urban design consultants for the developers drew deep on their imagination, introducing a range of urban metaphors to justify the proposal. The urban waterfront from Port Melbourne to St Kilda was described as kind of 'bookshelf' that required a landmark building on this site as a 'bookend'. This metaphor had no basis in urban design theory and was supplemented with that of the 'gateway'. The historic role of the bay as an entrance to the city via the piers was to be celebrated by allowing tall buildings to frame the historic pathway as seen from the deck of a yacht in the bay. To this was added the idea of the bay as a sporting spectacle with the waterfront development as a 'grandstand'. This idea had some merit since the desire for the view of the bay and proximity to it was entirely responsible for the desire to develop the waterfront. However, it was an argument that can be turned against the proposal because the grandstand is a linear rather than a vertical landmark; it aims to generate a maximum density close to the field without overshading it. The Panel was astute and unconvinced:

> [The] proposal was described as a landmark, a bookend, part of the bayside grandstand and as a gateway ... What these concepts really mean and how they can be applied remains as much a mystery to the Committee as it does to most of the submitters. ... The site is not a gateway to anywhere ... The grandstand effect along Beaconsfield Parade has more to do with horizontal built form as a backdrop to the bay. Grandstands are more horizontal than vertical.[19]

The Panel advised that the proposal should not be approved on a range of grounds including heritage, urban character and over-shading of the beach. It recommended a performance-based principle to prohibit the overshading of the promenade between 10 a.m. and 4 p.m. on 21 June. This was consistent with the earlier community agreement and with the shadow precedent established by the heritage factory next door. The Minister, however, ignored the Panel and approved an eighty-metre height limit in June 1997. Within a few months of the Minister's decision to raise the height limit the site was sold at a substantial profit. The state Auditor-General later raised suspicions about the legality of this process:

> Shortly after approval of Amendment L51, which had the potential to substantially increase the value of the HMAS Lonsdale site, the undeveloped site was sold ... We were unable to determine whether due consideration had been given to the legislative requirements at all stages as documentation held by the Department of meetings, advice to the Minister and negotiations on the HMAS Lonsdale development was inadequate.[20]

The Minister justified his decision in part on the basis that the architectural design quality of the proposal justified the additional height. This was curious since the Panel had suggested that the design (by architect Bruce Henderson) was a major weakness. The new developers (Becton) employed architects (Nation Fender Katsalidis) of a far higher quality and the buildings were substantially redesigned within the approved envelopes while maintaining the same general typology – a podium base of five storeys with two 22-storey towers at the rear. The project, now known as 'HM@S Lonsdale' was largely completed in 2001 (Figure 12.4). The site frontage is marked by a series of glass enclosed spaces that cantilever out and upwards towards the beach, taking advantage of the high visibility of the site and adding architectural vitality to the urban frontage. The towers behind are shaped with elegant curves to take in the views. The overshading effects and serious disruption to the urban character do not prevent this building from being a fine piece of architecture, but neither does the latter justify the former. It would be an even finer work of architecture if it were more urbane, if it had a less damaging and intimidating effect on its neighbourhood, and especially if it did not shade the beach in winter. The failure in this case was urban rather than architectural, but architectural quality was used to legitimate urban damage.

ST KILDA

All good cities are centres of innovation, incubators of new ideas, cultures and identities. And there are parts of all great cities that excel in the production of diversity – places of difference, experimentation, creativity and transgression. St Kilda is the densest and most diverse residential area in Melbourne; it has a very distinctive creative 'buzz'. Beginning as both a port and a fashionable seaside resort, it has absorbed many generations of immigrants, bohemians and artists, moving somewhat down-market during the mid-twentieth century. Sustained gentrification has increased prices since the 1970s, but the place has also retained a good proportion of older and cheaper apartments. It is a thriving node of the music industry and arts community. St Kilda is a fine example of the kind of bohemian beach communities that emerge on the edge of mainstream culture and on the literal edge of the land. It is a place where rhizomatic transgressive practices such as prostitution and drug-use are camouflaged and proliferate within the density and diversity of street life. Dubbed by the tabloids as the 'suburb of sin' and 'seedy St Kilda', the seaside town has been continuously, but not thoroughly, cleaned up and gentrified for twenty years. It has more than its share of social problems and crime, but also a very distinctive and highly valued urban character with high levels of creativity. This is a city on the move in a very different sense to that suggested by the former state slogan.

The key issue for urban regulation in St Kilda lies in retaining this edgy, transgressive urban character. How does one regulate an urban area characterised by the creative transgression of regulation? To over-regulate the fluidity of the city is to stifle the creativity. The urban character has long benefited from both built forms and behaviours that push the boundaries of difference in the arts, architecture, music, food and public behaviour. Yet St Kilda's various sub-cultures find themselves increasingly squeezed by increasing property values and new residents who have become key urban actors in local government politics – attracted by the diversity and amenity of the area but determined to rid it of the people and practices they don't like. This is part of an older story known as gentrification: the displacement of the marginal and powerless from inner city neighbourhoods as the desire for 'diversity' strips it of its 'difference'. The St Kilda community has fought many struggles over urban development since the 1980s – projects for marinas, harbours, hotels, tall buildings, aquariums and baths. There are many stories one could tell here; for my purposes there are two.

The Esplanade is a heritage-listed three-storey hotel on high ground near the centre of St Kilda. The block on which it sits includes a development site to the rear with substantial opportunity for high-rise development. The bitter battle over this site was first fought from 1987–89 when an eighteen-storey proposal was whittled down to seven storeys before being rejected.[21] When the next major proposal came in the late 1990s it was for thirty-eight storeys, since the political context had changed. The developer (Becton) was the same as for the Lonsdale project. A limited design competition resulted in all participating architects vastly exceeding the established height limit of eighteen metres, generating the illusion that the bulk and height were autonomous artistic decisions. One of the architects was quoted: 'We got the impression that the Minister had already told Becton that the way to justify him approving a tower development would be to appoint a good architect and sell the design as something desirable. We certainly knew that they wanted high-rise.'[22] The production of aesthetic desire was hinged to the desire for profit; the architects were drawn into a Faustian pact where to win was to disregard planning law in the pursuit of symbolic capital. The winners were Nation Fender Katsalidis with a design that was to rise to a height of 125 metres: seven times the legal height limit.

A community group known as the 'Esplanade Alliance' fought the project on a mix of heritage and urban character grounds. However, the issue that caught the public imagination was the cultural significance of the building as a live music venue and an important incubator of local music. St Kilda's artistic production was portrayed as under threat; the counter-argument was that live-music venues are rhizomatic, moving from one building to another over time. The Espy, however, had become an anchor point for the music industry, a place where the symbolic capital of St Kilda's bohemian character had congealed over time. This symbolism was available for mobilisation as resistance to the new development, fuelled by support from famous musicians who had played there. While there remains dispute over the outcome, the Espy was substantially saved by community resistance. An eight-storey building was finally approved for the rear of the site – one storey higher, but a far better design, than that rejected over a decade earlier.[23]

The second story concerns a dispute that erupted around the design of a single house, which developed as part of a new small lot subdivision on a main street a few blocks back from the beach. The house, designed by architect Cassandra Fahey, was for well-known television sports commentator Sam Newman. The design was approved and built in 2000 before it became apparent that the entire three-storey street facade was etched glass with a seductive image of the face of Pamela Anderson, star of the television series Baywatch (Figure 12.5). There was no issue here with regard to building bulk or height; however, a public outcry emerged over the claim that the image of the house violated the urban character. The image was said to be offensive, like an advertising billboard in a suburban street. There was no unanimity on this since many people liked the image which was subtle, changing in different light and mixed with reflections of the sky and other buildings.

The site was one of a long row subdivided in the early 1990s and developed at a medium density with small lot-size and strict height controls. Stylistically, the row is bland and inconsistent, ranging from modern to mock-historic and known colloquially as the 'Gaza Strip'. The streetscape is highly visible from passing vehicles, but little used by pedestrians. A key question underlying this issue is: if architects are not permitted to innovate in a context such as this, then where? How is urban character to be created?

Figure 12.5
Baywatching – Newman House
(*Architect*: Cassandra Fahey)

The image comprises the face of a female television star and, while it exhibits a certain sexuality, it is not a sexual image and is in no way offensive to public decency in itself. This issue was muddied by the fact that the owner of the project is, to many people, an offensive character. Newman's public persona is brash and arrogant with an uncontained ego and sexual appetite. The identity and image of the house proved somewhat difficult to separate from that of the owner. However, as Newman quite reasonably argued at the time: 'I am hopeful that all views expressed in relation to the proposal are objectively based on proper planning and design considerations, rather than in my personality as a media commentator'.[24] While there may be people who would not choose Newman for a neighbour, the planning process cannot be used to effect such a choice and the urban character of St Kilda is one that holds the tolerance of difference close to its core. This building is consistent with that urban character, even though some citizens may indeed be offended.

It would seem that the image has been chosen in part because it shows the face peering across the rooftops of the reflected houses towards the bay – it is a playful reference to both 'baywatching' and the urban character of St Kilda as a baywatching community. It also engages with the way in which we watch the world through television and other media. Television personalities such as Newman or Anderson are images of desire that permeate the suburbs. The house juxtaposes the real with the reflected; the 'real' house virtually disappears beneath its represented and reflected images. This is an architecture of its time that engages with questions of image, myth and advertising. The image brings together issues of local urban character with global images of consumption and desire. It is a contentious house for a contentious television performer, located in a contemporary context and a diverse urban community characterised by creativity and difference. It pushes the boundaries between architecture and advertising. My point here is not so much to argue the aesthetic merit of the building, but what it does show is a sophisticated engagement with urban character and a significant contribution to the transgressive urban character of St Kilda. The facade design was eventually approved after several rounds of mass media exposure. The house became a virtual presence in the popular imagination; the highly visible location meant the house and its ownership became a tempting target for vandals. The glass frontage was soon pock-marked by rocks and Newman sold the house within two years of completion.

FUTURE FLOWS

In 2003 the florid Victorian-era pavilion that housed a kiosk at the end of St Kilda pier was burnt down. This was one of Melbourne's special places: an ice-cream kiosk and small restaurant well out into the bay with fantastic views of St Kilda, the bay and city. The news had hardly broken before the Mayor and the Premier were both on site, showing their dismay and vowing that the pavilion would be rebuilt in identical form. This decision was made as a knee-jerk reaction, in order to fill the sense of public loss. But there was also a deeper loss evident here; a loss of public debate, of imagination, of the spirit of creativity. There are many possible futures for this site and the desire to reconstruct the past would seem to violate St Kilda's urban character.

Also in 2003 a front-page headline on planning in St Kilda read: 'Walking into the jaws of conflict' as an architect and developer teamed up to take on the St Kilda community.[25] The proposal sounded interesting, opening up 'boulevards to the bay' with new public open space; the expected trouble was the proposed height of up to twelve storeys in a five-storey zone. The developer doesn't yet own the necessary property, but he's sure they will sell because land values will rise dramatically if the project is approved. For the developer, the architect (Ivan Rijavec) is the key: 'He's a brilliant artist. Without him this project would not go through'.[26] Rijavec is indeed a good architect, but the issue again is over the granting of a poetic licence to violate urban regulation.

The larger issue here is to open up the question of how the contradictions embodied in the creation and protection of urban character can be embodied in urban regulation. Urban development inevitably impacts upon urban character and flows of ideas and investment. To close off such flows is to paralyse the life and formation of urban character; to deregulate will kill it even faster. One approach is to draw the line of urban regulation 'just a little beyond where you think it should be'.[27] This suggests a strategy of incremental change, which engages with the paradox of how to regulate urban creativity. It incorporates a sense of openness to new flows of desire while excluding complete transformations of urban form produced by the projects outlined earlier from Sandridge City to the Espy. It does, however, produce further paradoxes. Such an approach translates in practice into a 'preferred' height limit for 'normal' projects and an 'absolute' height limit that may or may not be approved, based on an assessment of the public value of the design. Such public values include urban amenity (such as public open space or higher permeability), social value (affordable housing), high levels of environmental performance and aesthetic excellence. Flexible height controls, within limits, can be used as a lever to generate better quality outcomes. This is a tempting prospect for planners who are frustrated by a lack of control over design quality. The contradiction, however, is that the state is trading the damage wrought by excessive height against higher quality design; if the height is not excessive then why is the height limit not raised? If environmental performance is a public good then why is it not legislated? Since aesthetic judgements will vary we are surely drawn into state control of aesthetic value with height limits established by 'beauty contests'. Furthermore, if 'high-quality' projects are granted the privilege of unobstructed views, then surely equally worthy neighbouring projects must then be allowed to obscure them. Over time the privilege becomes a right; the exception becomes the rule; incremental changes produce a wholesale change to the urban character.

In some circumstances, however, such wholesale change may be desirable. The range of projects in both Port Melbourne and St Kilda show that this urban property market is and will remain strongly influenced by the desire to live close to the water with a view of the bay and city. It is also clear that such desires, if unregulated, would produce a continuous row of towers transforming not only Port Melbourne and St Kilda, but extending along the entire beachfront between them. The urban effect would be continuous overshadowing of the beachfront promenade. The creative destruction of an unregulated market kills the goose that lays the golden egg. In 1999 an urban design framework for the entire stretch of waterfront from Port Melbourne to St Kilda was proposed. Entitled 'Gateway to the Bay', it was typical of the planning documents of the time in producing a 'vision' rather than a plan.[28] The vision was that height controls were to be relaxed in the two cities yet enforced in the zone between them to create a 'gateway' effect with clusters of towers framing a gap between them. This was immediately recognised as a legitimation of projects like Lonsdale and Espy (there were 7000 objections) and it was not implemented. And of course there would never be any guarantee about the future of the gap between them. Having consumed Port Melbourne and St Kilda, the appetite for waterfront property will scarcely be sated.

The problem with urban design and planning in the 1990s was not that it lacked vision, but that the visions were entirely driven by market desires. Thus the 'gateway' was a crude urban design theory produced to legitimate market flows. But what happens if instead we begin with the immanent desire for the waterfront experience, with the everyday phenomenology of place outlined earlier in relation to the Lonsdale project? The long-term public interest here lies in ensuring that the maximum number of people can enjoy the amenity of the waterfront consistent with maintaining or enhancing the beach experience. The beachfront is a major asset for the city, but it is an urban beach and cannot be seen as the preserve of the few who currently live nearby. It follows that there is a public value in generating higher densities near the water so long as the amenity is protected. Flooding the market with waterfront housing will also reduce the average price of such housing, the waterfront becomes more available to Melburnians. In this context I want to return to one of the metaphors used unsuccessfully to justify the Lonsdale project – the 'grandstand'. The bay and beach is indeed a spectacle of yachts, cyclists, palms, roller-bladers, bathers, windsurfers, beach-walkers, birds and ships.

There is already a low-rise layer of continuous waterfront development from Port Melbourne to St Kilda, and it incorporates significant heritage and urban character. The issue here is one of how to balance the interests of higher density against those of heritage and existing urban character. The portion of the waterfront preserved under heritage overlay is primarily two-storey Victorian row houses and occasional freestanding buildings of the same vintage. However, the heritage value of this waterfront is not high by Melbourne's standards. There are many finer Victorian streetscapes throughout the city and while some individual buildings should be preserved the case is strong to allow a five- to ten-storey street wall to develop along much of the length of Beaconsfield Parade (Figure 12.6). To maintain the beach frontage as it is will ensure that the severe pressure for high-rise towers will continue. It is a matter of time before another anti-planning Minister decides to let the market decide the urban outcome. This will lead to a pockmarked waterfront studded with towers that shade the beach in winter and on summer mornings. To develop the waterfront at medium density is to defend it against overdevelopment. This stretch of waterfront does not have a secure future as a two-storey suburb; the attempts to preserve such a vision will leave it vulnerable to the worst excesses. Will this urban edge become increasingly pockmarked or properly urbanised?

There are many who have fought to defend the character of this beachfront over the years and who would strongly oppose such a view. I suggest it not only as a means of defence for the beach, but also because the city needs to engage in the creation of urban character, not merely the preservation of it. In the long term such a street wall would multiply the density many times and lower the price of waterfront housing. The traditional urban character would be largely transformed and the task would be to ensure that the new urban waterfront is even more highly valued. The best way to achieve this would be to maintain the current lot-size while raising the height limit. The small lot-size would ensure a diversity of architectural expression with scope for new flows of architectural imagination and a new transformation of Melbourne's image. The very architectural imagination that we have seen channelled into the legitimation of tall buildings can serve a far greater urban role in a context where height controls are coupled with highly innovative form-making and the invention of new housing types. And a real multiplicity of building form and type would enable some of the traditionally diverse urban character of both St Kilda and Port Melbourne to flow along the beachfront.

Figure 12.6
Beaconsfield Parade – existing (top, 2003)
and possible (bottom): pockmarked or urbanised?

A dense urbanity accentuates the edge between land and water, the edginess that has always characterised the best urban waterfronts. The bay and beachfront are good examples of a 'smooth' space where the strictures of urban life are escaped to some degree. One of the paradoxes is that a strongly striated (regulated) market protects the smooth and less-regulated space of the beach. This is not to suggest that the water, sand and promenade have no rules or boundaries, but that they are more fluid and that the desire for access is fundamentally linked to this experience of the beach as a place of freedom – the stripping of careers, cares and clothes. There are many possible futures for this bayscape; the main choice is whether to create one of them or to cling to an unsustainable heritage as it becomes pockmarked by periodic eruptions of lunacy or corruption. The desires to be near the water will continue to flow, but how will they become actualised in built form? While the riverscapes and dockscapes are now largely done deals, this bayscape remains in contention. The question remains as to what kind of deal will be done here; the task is to put in place a layer of development and an urban design framework that brings life and urbanity to the beachfront without killing the amenity. It is to create a waterfront with enough imagination and vision that the thought of destroying it again will disappear. The quest to defend urban character will ultimately fail unless we engage with the task of creating it.

CHAPTER THIRTEEN

LOOSE ENDS

A final chapter generally ties up loose ends, providing closure and resolution. Here I intend to unravel them. The transformation of the Melbourne waterfront offers a diversity of case studies and outcomes of varying value from the formularised and privatised waterfronts of the casino and docklands to the *avant garde* excursions of 'water world' and Federation Square; from the enclosure and conformity of Beacon Cove to the authentic resistances of St Kilda and Southbank; from the eruptions of height (Grollo, Eureka, Lonsdale and the Espy), to the dynamic forms of the Exhibition Centre and explosions of fire lining the Casino. These projects are all laced with the contradictions of the time. While I have been critical of many of them and of the lost opportunities, there is little doubt that the Melbourne waterfront is a more vibrant and interesting place as a result. Fluidity is a condition all cities must face up to: like its opposite of 'stability', fluidity in urban development is both good and bad. Fluidity is flexibility and change; it is flows of money and desire; it is the formation of new identities of both people and places. The flows of desire for a better future are the very basis of urban place-making, yet unregulated desires are also the source of urban destruction. In the passage quoted earlier from his remarkable book *Invisible Cities*, Calvino draws a distinction between cities that 'give their form to desire' and cities where 'desires either erase the city or are erased by it'.[1] This is the central issue for those who believe in gearing the urban development process to the creation of a better future; from it stem the two primary yet contradictory imperatives of urban development – to produce a city that is open to the flows of desire, yet protected from the ravages of them.

PUBLIC INTERESTS

One role of the state is to regulate the flows of desire. As its name suggests, the 'state' has a 'stabilising' function; its role is to rule, to regulate the fluid city. It is to stand against the creative destruction of the market as a mediator of public interests. However, the role of the state is also to stand up for the 'right to the city', to open and defend the flows of desire. As outlined earlier, the public interest is a multiplicity of interests that are marshalled, debated and manipulated into collective interests that are then often misrecognised as a singular 'public interest'. Yet because the public space of the city is shared, there lies beneath this multiplicity a shifting but common ground of interests in the future of the place. While this is common ground in the sense of shared space, it is uncommon ground in terms of urban planning and urban design. When one strips the 'public interest' of its ideological underpinnings, it turns out to be as fluid as the flows of capital. The 'public interest', like any interest, is a form of congealed desire, a stabilised flow.

Such a multiplicitous conception of public interests will be forever in contention and there can be no simple quest for democratic consensus. The significant transformation of public attitudes towards Federation Square suggest that the value of the project would have been significantly diminished if majority public support were required before the project was approved. Good urban design, like good art, often challenges current community expectations and always does more than simply meeting the expectations of the market based on precedent and formula. It constructs and unleashes new desires and identities through the design process. Yet the various transformations in public perceptions of the Melbourne Docklands reveal how easily such perceptions and desires are manipulated when the market replaces the state as the 'ground' of public legitimation. Urban design creates new values in terms of both new qualities of place and new subjects who inhabit them.

One of the threads that winds through these chapters is that of the ways in which certain opportunities for urban futures are perceived or imagined, taken or missed. It is a key task of the state to identify and exploit such opportunities. There is a crucial distinction, however, between public and private opportunity which parallels that between public and private interests. The word 'opportunity' derives from the Latin 'portus': literally the 'wind blowing into the harbour'; the 'opportunity' flows into the waterfront as a gateway for traffic in ideas and opportunities. Taking an opportunity often involves the breaking of rules; opportunity is a new flow that creates exceptions to urban regulations. In an urban context the exception does not prove the rule, rather it becomes a precedent for a new rule. In the fluid city this dialectic between exceptions and rules rarely stabilises. In terms of public opportunity, projects such as Federation Square must break the rules if they are to succeed in catching the public imagination. Yet the private desire to 'stand out', to produce the exception, so often produces the predictable; the 'ever the same' continuously returns in the guise of the 'ever new'. Opportunity folds into opportunism.

The public interest is far broader than the local community whose desires and ideas, while based in a legitimate fear of place destruction, are often also based on the desire to protect privilege: the NIMBY syndrome. Yet the presumed broader knowledge, skill and taste of the professional classes of planners, architects and landscape architects cannot stand in for broader public interests. One of the lessons of this study is that when the winds of power shift, the professionals often follow. We have seen many examples of new relationships between architecture and urban planning through the mediating ground of urban design, together with new forms of professional identity.

PROFESSIONS

The role of architects in this is crucial because of their role in the production of symbolic capital and the construction of desire. The work of DCM (Exhibition Centre, Grollo Tower), ARM (Docklands), NFK (Eureka Tower, New Quay, Lonsdale, Espy) and LAB (Federation Square) has led much of this waterfront transformation. While the formal and social outcomes differ they all share a situation in which architecture takes on a far more urban role, an infusion of architecture into the vacuum left by the retreat from comprehensive and rational urban planning.

Architecture intersects with politics in new and complex ways. These intersections can be construed as 'insinuations' in the sense that the architecture is wound up with the politics and the politics with the architecture. These insinuations of architecture with politics are forms of enfolding, the windings and turnings through which one becomes insinuated into the other. Public architecture becomes implicated in and complicated by politics; the politics becomes implicit as the architecture becomes complicit. This is not a problem for architecture, rather it is the condition of architecture as a public art. The flows of increasingly footloose capital in the deregulated market serve to 'deterritorialise' the city, bringing opportunities and dangers. Deregulation opens up spaces of design autonomy and for architects, constrained and frustrated by the controls of the state, this can be a highly seductive space. But the autonomy of this space is limited and illusory, subject to the imperative production of symbolic capital.

Architecture both benefits and suffers from its political connections. The ever-renewed market in symbolic capital opens up opportunities for innovative architecture that can scarcely be ignored, lest the city becomes filled with the mediocre and unimaginative. Many such projects engage in 'lines of flight' that, like all aestheticisations of politics, are at once exciting and dangerous. Yet they also tend to operate within and reinforce a much older myth about the autonomy of architecture from politics. If there is a problem here it is not that the architecture is political (it was always thus), it is the tendency for so many architects to cling to the myth of autonomous practice. The work of Nonda Katsalidis is exemplary in this regard; evident here in the architecture of the New Quay, Eureka, Lonsdale and Espy projects. Of Greek-Australian background, Katsalidis is a product of the mutliplicitous Melbourne society that has developed from postwar migration. He often negotiates an economic interest in the projects he undertakes, ensuring more control over the design and a share in the symbolic capital when it is cashed. The architecture is described by a journalist as '... a multitude of angles, contrasting materials and colours, sculptural concrete masses, curving steel and a brace of overlapping geometric planes'.[2] The work is finely geared to its market, as Katsalidis puts it: 'I don't have a particular idea of architecture or theory I'm pursuing ... We are trying to make buildings entertaining, apartment buildings should be entertaining. They should communicate to people, not to architects with a capital A'.[3] His early work, and his finest housing, is on tightly constrained sites where both the sculptural and urban qualities are widely recognised and promulgated as exemplary urban housing. Yet this sculptural quality is later deployed as the excuse to shatter height limits; exceptional quality becomes the excuse for exceptional quantity. Architecture becomes the 'Trojan horse' that penetrates the gates of urban regulation.

The state's role is a very difficult one to manage, regardless of the intentions of the particular planners involved. The flows of capital in urban development are so significant that there will always be those who believe that the public interest is served by deregulating urban development with the desire for a better urban future subsumed into the desire for a bigger urban cake. The state planning bureaucracy in Melbourne was led during the late 1990s by John Paterson, who has argued for the inevitable determinism of market forces: 'Use the force, Luke' – but for what ends?[4] Mees suggests that an ideology equating public interests with deregulated planning was institutionalised in the state planning apparatus in Melbourne in the 1990s to such an extent that it survives under a legitimating cover of community rhetoric.[5] With the retreat from comprehensive urban planning in full swing, a disturbing number of planners moved seamlessly into new professional identities, where the primary role was to serve political masters and legitimate the market. While I have been critical of this retreat from comprehensive planning there is no suggestion of a simple return to a rational comprehensive model of urban regulation. Nor can there be any simple ideal of community-based planning. On Southbank and the Melbourne Docklands there was no local community whose current interests were threatened; just opportunities taken or squandered. Insurgencies along the bay are generally directed at preventing change and have often been short-sighted. Public interests cannot be conflated with a simple collection of existing interests.

One of the characteristic shifts in planning practice over the period studied has been the proliferation of public–private partnerships. While such developments are certainly here to stay, the 'balance' of public and private interests needs a complete reassessment. While private interests can service public interests, the public–private partnership embodies a conflict of interest at its core. Planners need to get far better at understanding how flows of private capital can be channelled into public infrastructure. The tragedy of Melbourne Docklands was one of public capital channelled into private infrastructure; and the profession remained mute as public planning was largely replaced by advertising. Plans for docklands were hatched in private, Southbank plans were abandoned and local government planning became difficult; many public planners moved to the private sector. Yet ironically, by the late 1990s there was a surge of demand for planning expertise, particularly for those who understand what happens at the intersection of architecture with planning – urban design.

I define urban design as simply the 'shaping of public space' – it is more than planning because it is a form of design and it is more than architecture because it is public. It follows that there is no such thing as 'private urban design' – private space is not truly 'urban'. Urban design is not a discrete 'discipline' like architecture or planning, rather it is multi-disciplinary. It is the fluid practices that operate between architecture and planning. It is the glue that holds them together. Urban design cannot be stabilised with fixed boundaries because the ways in which urban design melts into other disciplines is fundamentally important. Urban design falls through the cracks between the disciplines. It is in one sense, at least, undisciplined. It is a fluid and muddy deterritorialised zone.

Architecture, planning and urban design are united as 'place-making' practices – everyday urban life is always grounded in a particular phenomenology of place. Yet the concept of 'place' can be seen as yet another example of a flow of desires that have become stabilised in urban form. And the desire for an idealised 'sense of place', devoid of dispute and difference, can be linked to the desire for a sense of purity, a closure of identity and community. Urban place-making can stimulate a certain anti-urban closure of meaning and form – whether enclosed with walls, regulations or guards – in ways that hold difference at bay.

Place-making practices are rarely as simple as they seem, riven with struggles over politics, profit, privilege and the public interest. They are the most contradictory of practices – torn between a radically optimistic belief in the creation of a 'better' world, and a certain complicity with the prevailing order. The place-making professions engage with a multiplicity of desires; with the imagination and realisation of dreams and interests. Yet they also embody a fundamental conservatism as the inertia of built form 'fixes', 'stabilises' and 'frames' the world and our identities within it. The ideologies of 'place' are deployed to hold back the fluidity of life.

MEDIATING DESIRES

The first task in changing cities lies in changing our ways of thinking about the city. This book has tried to plot a rather uneasy course between theory and practice. In chapter 1, I introduced a series of theoretical frameworks, each of which was construed as flows – flows of everyday life, events and actions; flows of meaning and narrative; flows of capital and flows of desire. These are frameworks for thinking, and while many may see them as mutually exclusive, for me the many dimensions of urban life demand a multiplicity of intellectual frameworks. These are tools for thinking through the city and its complexities; lenses that focus our vision in different ways. Like all tools, they are matched to particular purposes and the range of waterfront projects explored here has called for all of them. This range is not meant to exclude others; it is just the toolkit deployed on this occasion.

Good theory, if it is at the cutting edge, is always a challenge to current practices. The paradox is that the challenge is reduced in proportion to the depth of theory – pure theory is only of academic interest. The demand in practice is for a body of theory with contradictions excised and reduced to a set of principles for good urban waterfronts: mixed-use, authenticity, permeability, access, sustainability, integration, innovation, sense of place, identity, character, public space, public art, diversity, density, amenity and so on. Many of these are now well embedded in at least the rhetoric of practice. Yet the less one picks apart what these principles really mean and the practices they entail, the easier it is to get projects on the ground.

These principles are also based in flows of desire (for access, authenticity, place and identity) and they potentially enable the city to flourish as a rhizomatic socio-spatial network. Yet it remains a great struggle to implement them in an integrated manner. The waterfront projects described here are often conceived at a massive grain-size and lot size, with relatively low densities and a strong focus on controlled access to the water. Where such principles are deployed they are often then enclosed and commodified, both spatially and discursively. The result is often zones of controlled access with high levels of symbolic capital; sequestered zones of spectacle, consumption and a suffocating mythology of 'place'.

There has also been a focus here on the discursive dimensions of waterfront development. The image and iconography of the city is transformed as meanings and narratives are constructed (and at times overturned) through design, advertising and spatial practice – the billboard building, the state 'on the move', the explosions of fire; the Casino as fortress; the camouflage of federation; the deleting of shards; the watery world of fluid streets and shimmering facades; the heroic penetrations of height limits; the 'Melbourne Torch'; the 'decadent diversity' of a place '... for everyone'. There are many intersecting desires in the fluid city. Some of the deeper questions remain: of how everyday flows of desire become geared to flows of capital and how flows of capital construct new flows of desire.

How are cities to manage and develop their waterfronts (or any other places for that matter) under the conditions described here? I want to suggest two quite different imperatives without reconciling the contradictions between them. The first is that the city must be opened up to new flows of desire that enable the formation of new places and identities. This requires a reconception of ideas of place and space, a turn away from the static and closed conceptions incorporated into housing enclaves of both the vertical (Grollo Tower) and horizontal (Beacon Cove) variety. The pseudo-diversity of waterfront formulae, whether theme park, casino or 'eatertainment', all share this suffocating sense of enclosure and conformity. These are places complicit in the production and regulation of consumption; citizens become consumers who are lined up facing the water, consuming the view and a controlled sense of urban diversity while insulated from authentic flows of urban life.

The second imperative is to open the flows of communication in urban development, consistent with what is broadly known as communicative rationality. This is the Habermasian ideal of a society where values and interests are debated openly, transparently and democratically.[6] This ideal is widely dismissed because it is ideal rather than real; it sets up a model of how urban development 'should' happen rather than what actually happens. Such a model was utterly abandoned during the main phases of Docklands planning and appears to many to be an unnecessary brake on flows of desire that enable cities to re-invent themselves. This dismissal is too easy. Communicative rationality needs to be pursued not as a transcendent ideal but as a pursuit of the possible, grounded in immanent flows of communication.

One of the revelations of the fluid city is that oldest lesson of modernity where 'all that is solid melts into air'. We have seen plans, regulations, visions, building forms, identities and places all becoming fluid. Many of the stock words and phrases upon which urban values and decisions are based – the public interest, urban character, sense of place – all turn out to be fluid. 'Reason' is also in this category. One of the reasons for the collapse of the rational comprehensive model of urban planning is that it is not rational –

economically or socially – to exclude design imagination from urban development. One of the strengths of communicative rationality is that it has the capacity to remain open to the critique of its own rationality, debating the value of its values. One of its weaknesses is that it becomes a brake on new ideas, it sets limits to the Nietzschean idea of the will to power. Planning decisions become reactive rather than affirmative, controlled by 'priests' rather than 'prophets'. The first imperative is to unleash the 'poets' and 'prophets'; the second is to subject their visions to critical debate.

Urban innovation is always, to some degree, a 'line of flight', designed to address 'wicked problems' with unpredictable outcomes. The dilemma is to engage in a manner that incorporates prophets, insists on difference, and opens the flood of desires for a radically better urban future without permitting the place destruction and the predictable sameness of a deregulated market. The task is to enable the unthinkable to happen without causing harm. And there is nothing irrational in that.

NOTES

Introduction

1 Calvino, I. *Invisible Cities*, London: Picador, 1979, p.30.
2 Appadurai, A. *Modernity at Large*, University of Minnesota Press, Minneapolis, 1996.
3 Castells, M.*The Power of Identity*, Blackwell, Oxford, 1997.
4 Bauman, Z. *Liquid Modernity*, Cambridge University Press, Cambridge, 2000. See also: Hogan, T. 'The Spaces of Poverty', *Thesis Eleven*, 70, 2002, pp.72–87.
5 Colebrook, C. *Understanding Deleuze*, Allen & Unwin, Sydney, 2002.
6 Sandercock, L. *Towards Cosmopolis*, Wiley, Chichester, 1998. Deutsche, R. *Evictions: Art and Spatial Politics*, MIT Press, Cambridge, Mass. 1996.
7 Deutsche, *Evictions*.

Chapter 1: Flows

1 Hoyle, B. 'Development Dynamics at the Port-City Interface', in: Hoyle, B., Pinder, D. and Husain, M. (eds) *Revitalising the Waterfront*, Belhaven, London, 1988, pp.3–19.
2 Reich, R. *The Work of Nations*, Vintage Books, New York, 1992.
3 See: Breen, A. and Rigby, D. (eds) *Waterfronts*, McGraw Hill, New York, 1994; Malone, P. (ed.) *City, Capital and Water*, Routledge, London, 1996; Marshall, R. (ed.) *Waterfronts in Post-Industrial Cities*, Spon, London, 2001; Hoyle et al. *Revitalizing the Waterfront*; Gordon, D. *Battery Park City*, Gordon and Breach, Amsterdam, 1997; Brownill, S. *Developing London's Docklands*, Paul Chapman, London, 1990; Edwards, B. *London Docklands*, Butterworth, Oxford, 1992.
4 Hannigan, J. *Fantasy City*, Routledge, London, 1998.
5 Malone, P. *City, Capital and Water*; Fainstein, S.*The City Builder*s, Blackwell, Oxford, 1994.
6 In Dublin docklands a 40 per cent local tax was slashed to 10 per cent to attract investment; the effect was to siphon local investment with a net tax loss of 30 per cent. See: Malone, P. 'Dublin', In: Malone, P *City Capital and Water*, pp.65–89.
7 Philo, C. and Kearns, G. 'Culture, History, Capital', In: Kearns, G. and Philo, C. (eds) *Selling Places*, Pergamon, Oxford, 1993, pp.1–32.

8   Hubbard, P. and Hall, T. 'The Entrepreneurial City and the New Urban Politics', In: Hall, T. and Hubbard, P. (eds) *The Entrepreneurial City*, Wiley, Chichester, 1998, pp.1–23.

9   Harvey, D. *Spaces of Hope*, Edinburgh University Press, Edinburgh, 2000, p.141.

10   Lynch, K. *The Image of the City*, MIT Press, Cambridge, Ma., 1960.

11   Harvey, D.*The Art of Rent*, unpublished seminar paper, University of Melbourne, 2000.

12   Hubbard and Hall, 'The Entrepreneurial City'.

13   Crilley, D. 'Architecture as Metaphor', in: Kearns and Philo, *Selling Places*, pp.231–52.

14   Goodwin, M. 'The City as Commodity', in: Kearns and Philo, *Selling Places*, p.158.

15   Relph, E. *Place and Placelessness*, Pion, London, 1977; Sorkin, M. (ed.) *Variations on a Themepark*, Hill & Wang, New York, 1992; Hannigan, *Fantasy City*.

16   Goodwin, 'City as Commodity', pp.147–8.

17   Mitchell, W. *E-topia*, MIT Press, Cambridge, Mass. 1999, p.15.

18   Mitchell, *E-topia*, p.7.

19   Storper, M. and Venables, A. 'Buzz: The Economic Force of the City', DRUID Summer conference, Elsinore, 2002.

20   Dear, M. *The Postmodern Urban Condition*, Blackwell, Oxford, 2000, pp.158–9.

21   Graham, S. and Marvin, S. *Splintering Urbanism*, Routledge, London, 2001. See also: Castells, M. *The Rise of the Network Society*, Blackwell, Oxford, 1996.

22   Hannigan, *Fantasy City*.

23   Hannigan, *Fantasy City*, p.7.

24   Crilley, 'Architecture as Metaphor', p.232.

25   Jacobs, J. *The Death and Life of Great American Cities*, Penguin, Harmondsworth, 1965; Alexander, C. 'The City is not a Tree', in LeGates, R. and Stout, F. (eds) *The City Reader*, Routledge, London, 1996 (originally published 1965).

26   Hillier, B. *Space is the Machine*, Cambridge University Press, Cambridge, 1996; Hillier, B. and Hanson, J. *The Social Logic of Space*, Cambridge University Press, Cambridge, 1984.

27   Dovey, K. *Framing Places*, Routledge, London, 1999, Ch. 9.

28   Sennett, R. *The Uses of Disorder*, Penguin, Harmondsworth, 1973; Sennett, R. *Flesh and Stone*, Faber & Faber, London, 1996.

29   Canetti, E. *Crowds and Power*, Phoenix, London, 1962, p.18.

30   Allen, S. 'From Object to Field', *Architectural Design*, 127, 1997, pp.24–31.

31   Allen, 'Object to Field'.

32   Lefebvre, H. *The Production of Space*, Blackwell, Oxford, 1991; Lefebvre, H. *Writings on Cities*, Blackwell, Oxford, 1996; See also: Borden, I. *Skateboarding, Space and the City*, Berg, Oxford, 2002.

33   Lefebvre, *Production of Space*, pp.389–91.

34   de Certeau, M. 'Practices of Space', In: Blonsky, M. (ed.) *On Signs*, Johns Hopkins University Press, Baltimore, 1985, p.131.

35 For further discussion see: Dovey, *Framing Places*, Ch. 2.

36 Barthes, R. *Mythologies*, Paladin, Hertfordshire, 1973; Barthes, R. *The Semiotic Challenge*, Blackwell, Oxford, 1988. While Barthes' work is regarded by many to have been superceded by Derrida, Foucault and others, his early work remains the most useful for understanding the ways in which discourse works as depoliticised speech.

37 There is not space here to explore methodological issues, see: Fairclough, N. *Critical Discourse Analysis*, Longmans, London, 1995.

38 Sources on Bourdieu include: Bourdieu, P. *Outline of a Theory of Practice*, Cambridge, London, 1977; Bourdieu, P. *Distinction*, Routledge, London, 1984; Bourdieu, P. *In Other Words*, Polity, Cambridge, 1990; Bourdieu, P. *The Field of Cultural Production*, Columbia University Press, New York, 1993; Bourdieu, P. *Pascalian Meditations*, Columbia University Press, New York, 2000; Swartz, D. *Culture and Power: The Sociology of Pierre Bourdieu*, University of Chicago Press, London, 1997. For architectural interpretations see: Stevens, G. *The Favored Circle*, MIT Press, Cambridge, Mass. 1998; Dovey, K. 'The Silent Complicity of Architecture', in: Hillier, J. and Rooksby, E. (eds) *Habitus: A Sense of Place*, Ashgate, London, 2001, pp.267–80.

39 Portes, A. 'Social Capital', *Annual Review of Sociology*, 24, 1998, pp.1–24; Putnam, R. *Bowling Alone*, Simon & Schuster, New York, 2000.

40 Bourdieu, *Pascalian Meditations*, pp.240–3

41 Bourdieu, *Distinction*, p.172.

42 Sources for Deleuze include: Deleuze, G. *The Fold*, University of Minnesota Press, Minneapolis, 1993; Deleuze, G. *What is Philosophy?*, Columbia University Press, New York, 1994; Deleuze, G. and Guattari, F. *A Thousand Plateaus*, Athlone, London, 1987; Colebrook, C. *Understanding Deleuze*, Allen & Unwin, Sydney, 2002; Massumi, B. *A User's Guide to Capitalism and Schizophrenia*, MIT Press, Cambridge, Mass. 1992; Patton, P. *Deleuze and the Political*, Routledge, London, 2000; Rajchman, J. *The Deleuze Connections*, MIT Press, Cambridge, Mass. 2000; Doel, M. 'A Hundred Thousand Lines of Flight', *Environment and Planning D*, 14, 1996, pp.421–39.

43 Deleuze and Guattari, *A Thousand Plateaus*, Ch. 14.

44 Deleuze and Guattari, *A Thousand Plateaus*, p.486.

45 See: Dovey, K., Fitzgerald, J. and Choi, Y. 'Safety Becomes Danger', *Health and Place*, 7 (4), 2001, pp.319–31.

46 Deleuze, *The Fold*, p.3.

47 Deleuzian philosophy informs the work of architects and urbanists such as Koolhaas and Lynn. See: Koolhaas, R. and Mau, B. *Small, Medium, Large, Extra-Large*, 010 Publishers, Rotterdam, 1995; Lynn, G. *Folds, Bodies and Blobs*, La Lettre volée, Brussels, 1998. Some of this work has been criticised for its superficiality. See: Crysler, G. *Writing Spaces*, Routledge, London, 2003, pp.70–5; Dovey, K. 'Multiplicities and Complicities', *Urban Design International*, 3 (3), 1999, pp.89–9.

48 Colebrook, *Understanding Deleuze*, p.127.

49 Harvey, D. *Consciousness and the Urban Experience*, Blackwell, Oxford, 1985, p.25.
50 Cain, J. 'Keynote Address', in: *Docklands, The Olympics and Beyond*, conference proceedings, Building Owners and Managers Association, Melbourne, 1989, p.3.
51 Eliade, M. *Patterns in Comparative Religion*, Meridian, New York, 1958, Ch. 5.
52 Freud, S. *The Ego and the Id*, Norton, New York, 1962.
53 Eagleton, T. *The Ideology of the Aesthetic*, Blackwell, Oxford, 1990, p.263.
54 Deleuze, G. and Guattari, F. *A Thousand Plateaus*, pp.479–80.
55 Sadler, S. *The Situationist City*, MIT Press, Cambridge, Ma., 1998.
56 Jinnai, H. *Tokyo: A Spatial Anthropology*, University of California Press, Berkeley, 1995, p.93.

Chapter 2: Riverscapes I – Overview

1   Davison, G. *The Rise and Fall of Marvellous Melbourne*, Melbourne University Press, Melbourne, 1978.
2   Brown-May, A. *Melbourne Street Life*, Australian Scholarly Publishing, Melbourne, 1998; Lewis, M. *Melbourne: The City's History and Development*, Melbourne City Council, Melbourne, 1995.
3   On this changing relationship between Melbourne and Sydney see: Spearritt, P. *Sydney's Century*, Allen & Unwin, Sydney, 2000; Connell, J. (ed.) *Sydney: The Emergence of a World City*, Oxford UP, Melbourne, 2000; O'Connor, K. and Edgington, D. 'Producer Services and Metropolitan Development in Australia', in Daniels, P. (ed.) *Services and Metropolitan Development*, Routledge, London, 1991, pp.204–25.
4   Goad, P. *Melbourne Architecture*, Watermark Press, Sydney, 1999.
5   In the Australian context local government falls under the control of the state government. There has always been tension between the two, especially regarding 'capital city' functions.
6   Government of Victoria and City of Melbourne, *Creating Prosperity*, 1994, p.4–6.

Chapter 3: Riverscapes II – Precincts and projects

1   Architect Peter Carmichael, quoted in: Austin, G. 'Fantasy Across Yarra', *The Age*, 3 July 1987, p.15.
2   The developers were Costain, the initial urban design was by Daryl Jackson Associates, and the architecture was by Spowers.
3   Reed, D. 'Along the Yarra Development Should Flow', *The Age*, 20 September 1993, p.13.
4   The developers were Jennings and the architects were Buchan Partnership, together with US consultants.
5   Hills, B. 'What Happened to Southgate?' *Herald Sun*, 16 June 1988, p.16.
6   In 1989 Jennings were offered $29 million for land that had cost $11 million in 1987.
7   Day, N. 'Something Old, Something New, Something Bland, Something Blue', *The Sunday Age*, 4 October 1992, p.17.

8   Dovey, K. 'Southbank/SouthGate/Surrogate', *Architect*, January 1993, pp.6–7.

9   Hart, B. 'SouthGate gets Snappy', *Herald Sun*, 29 July 1998, p.17.

10 Letter to Esso from a senior government planner (Paul Jerome), November 1991.

11 Dovey, K. 'Should Southbank look like this ... or this?' *The Age*, 9 November, 1993, p.15.

12 Reed, D. 'A Case for a Museum Site Rethink', *The Age*, 8 September 1990, p.18.

13 The Zelman Cowan Award from the Royal Australian Institute of Architects.

14 *Passport to Melbourne*, Open House, 9 October 1995, p.3.

15 Etlin, R. *Modernism in Italian Architecture 1890–1940*, MIT Press, Cambridge, Mass. 1991.

16 Trioli. V. 'Project-ing Melbourne', *The Age*, 1 June 1995, p.7.

17 'The Melbourne Exhibition and Convention Centre', publicity brochure, undated.

18 The Pacific consortium included Sheraton Hotels and Leighton; Crown consortium was controlled by Hudson Conway.

19 These included a series of editorials in *The Age* including those on 19 May and 27 July 1993.

20 The Design Panel was chaired by Peter McIntyre, architect and Professor of Architecture at the University of Melbourne. It included Bill Corker, a director of Denton Corker Marshall. Some of the concerns about the secrecy stemmed from the perception of close relations and conflicts of interest between some of the parties. The Crown bid was controlled by Lloyd Williams and Ron Walker, both close confidants of the Premier. McIntyre was a confidant of Walker, who was also Treasurer of the Liberal Party.

21 Forbes, M. 'Casino secrets revealed', *The Age*, 9 October 1994, p.1.

22 The Casino architects were: Daryl Jackson Associates; Bates Smart; and Perrott, Lyon, Mathiesson.

23 Reed, D. 'Leaving Nothing to Chance', *The Age*, 7 September 1993, p.19.

24 The architects were Cox Sanderson Ness.

25 Joe Bergman from Las Vegas was brought out in 1994.

26 Much was later made of the fact that Williams had purchased property and commissioned a house from McIntyre after the February rejection and before the June and November approvals. See: Ewing, T. 'A Man of Influence', *The Age*, 9 September 1996, p.3.

27 Documented in: Costello, T. and Millar, R. *Wanna Bet? Winners and Losers in Gambling's Luck Myth*, Allen & Unwin, Sydney, 2000.

28 Lane, T. 'Temple of Mammon or House of Cards', *The Age*, 23 March 1997, p.18.

29 Elias, D. 'Vegas-on-Yarra', *The Age*, 8 March 1997, p.19.

30 Rollo, J. 'Crown to be Launched on a Sea of Acclaim and Scorn' *The Age*, 7 May 1997, pp. 1 and 7.

31 Collis, B. 'The Casino – A New Deal', *The Age*, 24 June 1994, p.15.

32 'And What Do the Architects Think' *The Age*, 14 April 1997, p.C5 (no author).
33 Jones, M. 'Crown Approach All New, Says Director' *The Age*, 31 March 1994, p.5.
34 Carroll, J. 'The Joker's Tour of Casino Culture', *The Age*, 15 May 1997, p.19.

Chapter 4: Appropriations

1   City of Melbourne, *Code of Conduct for Busking, Activities Local Law 1999*.
2   See the web site: <http://www.arts.monash.edu.au/visarts/globe/issue8/tbtitle.html>.
3   de Certeau, M. *The Practice of Everyday Life*, University of California Press, Berkeley, 1984.
4   Jacobs, J. *The Death and Life of Great American Cities*, Penguin, Harmondsworth, 1965.
5   Featherstone, M. *Consumer Culture and Postmodernism*, Sage, London, 1991.
6   Hannigan, J. *Fantasy City*, Routledge, London, 1998, p.7.
7   Bakhtin, M. *The Dialogic Imagination*, University of Texas Press, Austin, 1984.
8   Lefebvre, H. *Critique of Everyday Life*, Verso, London, 1991, p.202.
9   Deleuze, G. and Guattari, F. *A Thousand Plateaus*, Athlone, London, 1987, Ch. 15.
10 Pile, S. 'Introduction', in: Pile, S. and Keith, M. (eds) *Geographies of Resistance*, Routledge, London, 1997, pp.1–32.
11 Iveson, K. and Scalmer, S. 'Contesting the "Inevitable"', *Overland*, 161, 2000, p.4.
12 Iveson, K. and Scalmer, S. 2000, pp. 11–12.

Chapter 5: Urban living

1   Government of Victoria, Ministry for Planning and Development, *Southbank: A Development Strategy*,1986.
2   Government of Victoria, Department of Planning and Housing and City of South Melbourne, *Southbank Urban Design Guidelines*, 1992 (John Curtis P/L, consultants).
3   Quoted in: Stevens, J. 'Progress According to Plan', *The Age*, 18 March 1995, p.19.
4   This distance is commonly used in urban design literature as a measure of the limit to which people will generally choose to walk.
5   Government of Victoria, Department of Infrastructure and City of Melbourne, *Southbank Structure Plan*, 1998.
6   *Southbank Structure Plan*, p.43.
7   *Southbank Structure Plan*, p.76. The contradictions in this plan can be partially explained by the fact that it was co-authored by the Department of Infrastructure and the City of Melbourne. The senior planners and urbanists of the Department were firmly in the grip of a market-driven model, while those at the City had a broader view; the state clearly controlled the plan.

8   Government of Victoria, *New Format Planning Scheme*, March 4, 1999.
9   For a full listing of Southbank developments see: <http://www.skyscrapers.com> (accessed 18 August 2003).
10 Government of Victoria, *Victorian Planning Scheme*, Amendment C20, 19 December 2002.
11 Buying 'off the plan' avoids stamp duty tax; 'negative gearing' is the capacity to claim a loss on investment property against tax; one effect is that a failure to rent the property is converted to a tax benefit and subsidised through the public purse. Although it is widely regarded as a tax rort, negative gearing has remained legal primarily to prevent the consequent loss of housing investment and supply.
12 See: Findlay, S. 'Southbank's Last Piece About to Fall into Place', *The Age*, 29 August 2001, p.7.
13 McCamish, T. 'Where the Living is Not Easy', *The Age*, 27 August 2003, pp.A3–4.

Chapter 6: Federation

1   Government of Victoria, Ministry for Planning and Melbourne City Council, *Princes Plaza Design Study*, 1985 (consultants: Denton Corker Marshall).
2   *Princes Plaza Design Study*, p.33.
3   One proposal by developer George Herscu for private retail, commercial and hotel development was approved but lapsed for economic reasons.
4   The city and state made such a pledge in 1995, but it was three years later before the federal funding flowed, by which time the budget had blown out to $220 million. The final budget for Federation Square was $480 million.
5   'Flinders Gate' Project at 172–192 Flinders Street; it was not constructed.
6   Trioli, V. 'Fury Over Kennett's Museum Rebuff', *The Age*, 14 February 1996, p.3.
7   Government of Victoria, Federation Square Design Competition Brief.
8   The jury was Chaired by Neville Quarry (Professor of Architecture, University of Technology Sydney) and included Daniel Libeskind (Architect), plus Dick Roennfeldt (Victorian Government, Office of Major Projects), Catherin Bull (Landscape Architecture, Queensland University of Technology), Brett Randall (Victorian Arts Centre), Rob Adams (Architect and Head of Urban Design, City of Melbourne) and Peter Clemenger (Advertiser and National Gallery of Victoria).
9   There were two Melbourne firms (Ashton Raggat McDougall and Denton Corker Marshall), one from Sydney (Chris Elliott) and two international (Jenny Lowe and LAB)
10 The decision was reached by the jury on 13 June 1997 and announced on 28 July. LAB then worked in collaboration with Bates Smart for the duration of the project.
11 Barclay, A. 'Vision For a New Century', *Herald Sun*, 28 July, 1997, p.5.

12 Donald Bates was a principal associate on the Jewish Museum project in Berlin.

13 Lyon, K. 'Brilliant Losers Exhibit Designs', *The Age*, 3 August 1997, p.6.

14 Quoted in Styant-Browne, A. 'Federation Square', *Architecture Australia*, November–December 1997, pp.78–81.

15 LAB Architects, Federation Square, 2nd stage submission, June 1997.

16 LAB, 2nd stage submission

17 Rados, A. 'Future City', *Herald Sun*, 28 July 1997, pp.1 and 4.

18 Carroll, J. 'Is This the Best We Can Do?' *The Age*, 17 February 1998, p.13.

19 Humphries, B. Letter, *The Age*, 6 August 1997, p.18; Humphries, B., Letter, *Herald Sun*, 22 August 1997, p.20. See also: Bevan, R. 'Collage Education', *World Architecture*, 112, January, 2003, pp.32–40.

20 Coslovich, G. 'Popular New Landmark Already One in a Million', *The Age*, 9 January 2003, p.3.

21 The politics of this are linked to a current obsession with boundaries and 'border protection', and the effective use of the 'race' card in national politics. See: Hage, G. *White Nation: Fantasies of White Supremacy in a Multicultural Society*, Pluto Press, Sydney, 1998; Hage, G. *Against Paranoid Nationalism*, Pluto Press, Sydney, 2003.

22 Dovey, K. 'The Square Dilemma', *The Age*, 12 April 1996, p.15.

23 Hage, *White Nation*.

24 Rawls, J. *Political Liberalism*, Columbia University Press, New York, 1993, p.xviii.

25 'Nearamnew' was undertaken in collaboration with LAB. Carter is also an academic historian with a focus on postcolonial understandings of spatial history and public space. See: Carter, P. *The Road to Botany Bay*, Faber & Faber, London, 1987; Carter, P. *The Lie of the Land*, Faber & Faber, London, 1996; Carter, P. *Repressed Spaces*, Reaktion Books, London, 2002.

26 Bourdieu, P. *Distinction*, Routledge, London, 1984.

27 Mitchell, W. 'Fair Dinkum Aussie', *RIBA Journal*, 110 (3), 2003, p.18.

28 A good overview of the facade and atrium design is provided in Day, N. 'Federation Square', in Day, N. and Brown-May, A. (eds) *Federation Square*, Hardie Grant, Melbourne, 2003, pp.74–89; See also: <www.federationsquare.com.au>.

29 Hartoonian, G. 'The Tectonic of Camouflage', *Architecture Australia*, 92 (2), 2003, pp.60–5.

30 Bevan, 'Collage Education'; Day, 'Federation Square'.

31 Interestingly, during 2003 SBS was heavily criticised in the federal parliament and the broadsheet dailies for becoming too mainstream in its programming.

32 Deleuze and Guattari describe the facial 'tic' as: '... the continually re-fought battle between a faciality trait that tries to escape the sovereign organization of the face and the face itself, which clamps back down on the trait, takes hold of it again, blocks its line of flight, and reimposes its organization upon it.' Deleuze, G. and Guattari, F.

A Thousand Plateaus, Athlone, London, 1987, p.188. Thanks to Stephen Wood for drawing attention to this reference.

33 The ARM-designed Storey Hall (at the other end of Swanston Street) is also promoted by Jencks in this manner.

34 Jencks, C. *The New Paradigm in Architecture*, Yale University Press, New Haven, 2002.

35 Jencks, 'The New Paradigm in Architecture', *Architectural Review*, 1272, February, 2003, p.75.

36 Davey, P. 'Lab Experiments', *Architectural Review*, 1275, May 2003, pp.54–63, p.62.

37 Davey, 'Lab Experiments', pp.56 and 62.

38 Macarthur, J. 'The Aesthetics of Public Space', *Architecture Australia*, 92 (2), 2003, pp.48–9.

39 Hage, *White Nation*, pp.117–40. Here Hage discusses the narrative in the Australian children's story of 'the stew which grew' as an exemplification of the 'magical' role often portrayed by mainstream Australians in getting the multicultural 'mix' just right.

40 Most ticketed events were held in the BMW Edge auditorium, and in terms of accessibility this has operated as the main exclusionary space in the development, with 90 per cent of events there being either private or ticketed.

41 Dean, A. 'Picky About Picketers', *The Melbourne Times*, 14 May 2002, pp.8–9.

42 Johnstone, B. 'Are You Concerned About Access at Federation Square?', Newsletter of the Western Region Disability Network, Vol. 37, October 2003.

43 Millar, R. 'Square Squatters Say They are Staying', *The Age*, 19 August 2003, p.6.

44 Peter Seamer, CEO of Federation Square Management, quoted in: Simpson, N. 'Melbourne's Federation Square Revamp Means Displacing the Homeless', ABC PM program, 21 August 2003: <www.abc.net.au/pm/content/2003/s929533.htm>.

45 Birnbauer, B. and Munro, I. 'Shard' *The Age*, 23 September 2001, pp.21–2; Trioli, V. 'Aussie Rules', *Metropolis*, February 2001, p.5.

46 Sparrow, J. and Sparrow, J. *Radical Melbourne*, Vulgar Press, Melbourne, 2001, pp.83–7.

47 The overall scheme was designed and conceived by the City of Melbourne (landscape architect Ron Jones); the pedestrian bridge and bell plaza is by architects Swaney Draper; the bells are by Neil McLachlan (composer) and Anton Hasell (sculptor). See: Selenitsch, A. 'Field of Bells', *Artichoke*, 2 (1), pp.99–103.

Chapter 7: Dockscapes 1 – overview

1 Melbourne had been host of a highly successful Olympics in 1956 and with a good deal of the sporting infrastructure already in place was considered by many a good prospect for another turn.

2 Cain, J. 'Keynote address', In: *Docklands, the Olympics and Beyond*, Conference proceedings, Building Owners and Managers Association, Melbourne, 1989, p.2.

3   See: Gillman, J. 'Melbourne–Sydney Games Bid Conflict', *Sunday Herald*, 16 December 1990, p.10; Attwood, A. 'Sydney 2000 – Melbourne 1996', *The Age*, 28 August 1993, p.E1. Sydney's primary competitor for the 2000 games was Beijing, which shared the time-zone problem.

4   Government of Victoria, Ministry for Planning & Environment, *Melbourne's Docklands: Strategic Planning Framework*, Melbourne: Victorian Government publication, 1989.

5   Docklands Task Force, *Melbourne Docklands: Strategic Options*, Victorian Government publication, Melbourne, 1990; Docklands Task Force, *Melbourne Docklands: Draft Strategy for Redevelopment*, Victorian Government publication, Melbourne, 1991; Docklands Task Force, *Docklands Strategy*, Victorian Government publication, Melbourne, (2 vols), 1992.

6   In December 1990 the Task Force published a list of seventeen consultant's reports completed during that year with a further seven in process. See: Docklands Task Force, *Melbourne Docklands: Strategic Options*.

7   The findings of this consultation process were reported at length in *Melbourne Docklands: Draft Strategy for Redevelopment* and *Docklands Strategy* (vol.2).

8   Ogilvy, E. Mahar, A. and Higgs, P. (eds) *Picking Winners: Melbourne's Urban Development Game*, Social Justice Coalition, Melbourne, 1991.

9   The Committee for Melbourne was led at the time by John Elliott, the then highly successful CEO of Fosters brewery.

10   Anderson Consulting, *Multifunction Polis Final Report: Feasibility Study Consultancy*, Committee for Melbourne, 1990, p.11.

11   See: Kiely, J. 'The Road to Supercity', *The Age*, 28 September 1988, p.6; Davidson, K. 'MFP Documents Show it is a Glorified Resort Development', *The Age*, 23 June 1990, p.19.

12   Committee for Melbourne, *Melbourne Docklands: A Discussion Paper*, 1990; Committee for Melbourne, *Melbourne Docklands*, 1990.

13   The MFP was initially awarded to Queensland, then Adelaide before the Japanese withdrew the offer; in retrospect it appears to have been driven by the desire for a Japanese enclave.

14   Kyne T. 'Council Slams Docklands Bill', *Herald Sun*, 17 April 1991, p.76.

15   Quoted in: Gome, A. 'The New Boy on the Dock', *Herald Sun*, 13 March 1992, p.34. Annells was a former public service manager.

16   Chris Marks from Jones Lang Wootton (JLW), quoted in: Rados, A. 'Docklands Plan a Disaster', *Herald Sun*, 17 June 1992, p.27.

17   Taylor, T. 'Black Museum for Docklands', *The Age*, 20 May 1993, p.8.

18   Docklands Authority, *Docklands Plan*, Victorian Government publication, Melbourne, 1993.

19   Docklands Authority, *Annual Report, 1994*, Victorian Government publication, Melbourne, 1994.

20   Chris Marks from JLW, quoted in 'Bid to Weigh Private Docklands Demand' *The Age*, 18 May 1994, p.31 (no author).

21 Docklands Authority, *Melbourne Docklands: Towards the 21st Century*, Victorian Government publication, Melbourne, August 1995 (pamphlet, updated in December 1995).

22 Docklands Authority, *Melbourne Docklands Area: Melbourne Planning Scheme Amendment L202*, Victorian Government publication, Melbourne, 1995 (2 vols).

23 Docklands Authority, *Melbourne Docklands: Urban Design Guidelines*, Victorian Government publication, Melbourne, 1995.

24 Quotes are from the author's field notes; see also: Dovey, K. 'Trouble on the Waterfront', *The Age*, 18 September 1996, p.18.

25 Chris Marks, from JLW. The suggestion was made in the press that prices for waterfront land could be as low as $50 per square metre—less than 10 per cent of the price of suburban land. See: Hurley, J. 'Low Price the Key to Docklands', *The Age*, 13 March 1996, p.7.

26 Quoted in: Hurley, J. 'Plan Places Park in Centre of Docklands', *The Age*, 22 May 1996, p.8.

27 Docklands Authority and JLW, *Melbourne Docklands: Hard Copy of Interactive Presentation*, Victorian Government publication, Melbourne, November 1995.

28 This was a major consultancy worth half a million dollars in design fees; see: Docklands Authority, *Annual Report 1997*, Victorian Government publication, Melbourne, 1997.

29 Ashton Raggatt Macdougall and Docklands Authority, *Mebourne Docklands: Conceptual Planning and Design Framework and Visions*, Victorian Government publication, Melbourne, November 1996, p.1.

30 Berman, M. *All that is Solid Melts into Air*, Verso, London, 1983.

31 On the 'space of flows' see: Castells, M. *The Power of Identity*, Blackwell, Oxford, 1997; on 'flexible accumulation' see: Harvey, D. *The Condition of Postmodernity*, Blackwell, Oxford, 1989; on 'smooth space' and 'folding' see: Deleuze, G. and Guattari, F. *A Thousand Plateaus*, Athlone, London, 1987; for popular architectural adaptations, see: Lynn, G. (ed.) 'Folding in Architecture', *Architectural Design*, Profile No. 102, 1993.

32 Ashton Raggatt Macdougall and Docklands Authority, *Mebourne Docklands: Conceptual Planning and Design Framework and Visions*, Victorian Government Publication, Melbourne, 1996, p.37.

33 'This is the Place for a Vision', Editorial, *The Age*, 2 November 1996, p.33.

34 On London Docklands see: Malone, P. (ed.) *City, Capital and Water*, Routledge, London, 1996; Brownill, S. *Developing London's Docklands*, Paul Chapman, London, 1990; Edwards, B. *London Docklands*, Butterworth, Oxford, 1992.

35 Quoted in: Birnbauer, B. 'What's Up Dock?' *The Age*, 31 March 1997, p.11.

36 Proceedings were taped, transcribed and published: Long, C. (ed.) *Private Planning ... Private Cities*, People's Committee for Melbourne, Melbourne, 1997.

37 Long, *Private Planning*, p.56.

38 Hurley, J. 'Chill Wind Blows at the Docks as Tenders Close', *The Age*, 9 April 1997, p.B5.

39 Rados, A. 'Giants Team up for Docklands', *Herald Sun*, 14 February 1997, p.2.

40 Quoted in: Docklands Authority, *Five Precincts Launch*, Victorian Government publication, Melbourne, 8 September 1997. Eric Mayer has Chaired the Authority since its inception.

41 Docklands Authority, *Annual Report 1998*, Victorian Government publication, Melbourne, 1998.

42 *Towards the 21st Century*.

43 Discussed in: Dovey, K. *Framing Places*, London: Routledge, 1999, Ch. 11.

44 Munro, I. 'Why isn't this Man Smiling?' *The Age*, 26 February 2000, p.7.

45 Watkins, S. 'Bypass Plan May Breach Law', *The Age*, 10 February 1999, p.5. Rob Adams, Director of City Projects at the City of Melbourne, who was also on the Design and Planning panel of the Authority, argued for constraining rather than diverting the traffic. He resigned from the Panel over this issue.

46 Hansen, K. 'City Faces a Bright Future', *Herald Sun*, 9 February 1999, p.8; also: Hansen, K. 'High Praise for Bridge', *Herald Sun*, 9 February 1999, p.8.

47 MacArthur, R. 'New Peril in Yellow Arch', Letter, *Herald Sun*, 15 February 1999, p.20.

48 Hopkins, P. 'Lack of Port Rail Link Slated', *The Age*, 15 November 1999, p.5.

49 Hopkins, P. 'Our Port Must Now Face the Future', *The Age*, 10 April 2000, p.B1.

50 Rados, A. 'Great Moment in History', *Herald Sun*, 25 February 1997, p.11; Rados, A. 'Blossoming of a Wasteland', *Herald Sun*, 23 August 1997, p.25; Hansen, K. '20 Million to Visit Docklands', *Herald Sun*, 25 August 1998, p.4.

51 'Hands off Docklands', *Herald Sun*, Editorial, 10 October 1998, p.24.

52 Dunlevy, M. 'Developers to Dump Docklands', *The Australian*, 25 June 1999, p.3; Booth, D. 'Docklands Vision Unfolds', *Herald Sun*, 22 May 1999, p.3; Lally, G. 'Pieces Fitting into Waterfront Jigsaw', *Herald Sun*, 5 June 1999, p.26.

53 Docklands Authority, *Integration and Design Excellence*, Victorian Government publication, Melbourne, July 2000, p.2.

54 Employing architects ARM and landscape architects EDAW.

55 Dockland Authority website: <www. docklands.vic.gov.au> accessed December 2001.

56 Tschumi, B. *Event-Cities: Praxis*, MIT Press, Cambridge, Mass. 1994; Tschumi, B. *Event-Cities 2*, MIT Press, Cambridge, Mass. 2000.

57 Finlay, S. 'Social Structures Focus of Latest Docklands Plan', *The Age*, 1 February 2001, p.6. The Bracks government gained power unexpectedly, most of its Ministers were inexperienced, and the Major Projects Ministry that incorporated the Docklands Authority was given a low priority.

58 In early 2000 Leonie Sandercock and I were offered access to all of the design and planning files of the Docklands Authority by the new Planning Minister (John Thwaites) under Freedom of Information rules. Despite the Minister's support, we were soundly defeated by a team of expert bureaucrats within both the Docklands Authority and the Department of Infrastructure. We eventually abandoned the quest.

Chapter 8: Dockscapes II – Precincts and projects

1 The key media interests were those controlled by Rupert Murdoch, Kerry Packer and Kerry Stokes. The winning consortium was Stokes (7 Network) with KPMG, Balderstone Hornibrook, Westpak, Merrill Lynch, Citipower and Honeywell.

2 Docklands Authority, *Annual Report 1998*, Victorian Government Publication, Melbourne, 1998.

3 Canetti, E. *Crowds and Power*, Phoenix, London, 1962, p.28.

4 Millar, R. 'Wild Colonial Boys', *The Age*, 3 September 2001, p.16.

5 Biggs, B. 'Wise Head for a Deal', *Herald Sun*, 14 September 1997, p.57.

6 Davidson, K. 'Docklands Wool over AFL Eyes', *The Age*, 29 March 1997, p.2; Millar, 'Wild Colonial Boys'.

7 Millar, 'Wild Colonial Boys'.

8 The consortium comprised MAB corporation and YarraCity Ltd (Australian–Malaysian partnership); the architects and urban designers were Nation Fender Katsalidis (NFK), Synman Justin Bialek (SJB) and Tract. The scheme included 1350 dwelling units, plus restaurants and marina.

9 The consortium comprised Davies Corporation, Paramount (Viacom), Macquarie Bank, Thornley Holdings (Visy), WIN Television and Crawford productions.

10 The idea of a film and television studios as part of intercity competition had been fuelled in 1995 when Rupert Murdoch threatened to take his Fox studios from Sydney to Melbourne if he couldn't get the deal he wanted in Sydney.

11 The $350 million theme park was to be completed by 2000. The Yarranova section on the waterfront was to involve $600 million of investment over ten years with 1500 apartments in multi-storey waterfront buildings with 100 000 square metres of offices to the north.

12 YarraCity Ltd was no longer part of this deal; it comprised 1800 apartments, 300 marina berths, 100,000 square metres of office, an art gallery and a 360-room hotel. See: Lally, G. '$900m Docklands Plan', *Herald Sun*, 4 May 1999, p.22.

13 Each tower was named after an architect or artist: the 'Palladio', 'Boyd', 'Arkley' and 'Conder', each with a distinctive image and identity.

14 This is a variation on the self-destruction syndrome identified long ago by Jacobs.

15 See: MacKenzie, A. 'Public Liability?', *Architectural Review Australia*, 2002, pp.42–7.

16 'Rules no Barrier for Planning Minister', *The Age*, 28 May 1997, p.7 (no author). His example was the Republic Tower in the central city.

17   Coslovich, G. 'A Development of Paramount Importance', *The Age*, 25 August 1998, p.B5; '$350m of Fun', *Herald Sun*, 5 November 1998, p.1.
18   The developers are ING Real Estate and Lewis Land Group; the architects are Hassell and BDP.
19   The Universities were Deakin, Monash, RMIT and VUT. The developers were BZW and Multiplex.
20   The Vice-Chancellor of Monash University, Mal Logan, was a member of the Docklands Authority Board from 1992–1996. He was later also a consultant to the YarraCity consortium on the Batman's Hill precinct.
21   Thompson, S. 'Rome by the Docks', *Herald Sun*, 11 August 1998, p.1; Thompson, S. and Lawson, A. 'Little Italy, Big Doubts', *Herald Sun*, 12 August 1998, p.8.
22   Digital harbour initially included the University of Melbourne, La Trobe University, Microsoft, KPMG, Baulderstone Hornibrook, Jones Lang LaSalle (JLW), Telstra, Cisco, Edgate and JGL. Both KPMG and Jones Lang LaSalle (JLW) had a long association as consultants to the Docklands Authority.
23   See: <www.digitalharbour.com.au>, the architects are Bates Smart and ARM.
24   Brain, P. 'How Australia an Survive the 21st Century', *The Age*, 19 April 1999, p.B1.
25   Winner, L. 'Silicon Valley Mystery House' in Sorkin, M (ed.) *Variations on a Theme Park*, Hill & Wang, New York, 1992, pp.31–60.
26   <melbournedocklands.com> accessed September 2003
27   The Melbourne Docklands Consortium comprised Mirvac, Lend Lease & Hudson Conway. Architects and urban designers were Bates Smart, Peddle Thorpe & Lend Lease Design Group. The YarraNova consortium was almost identical to that for the Business Park: MAB Corporation and YarraCity. Architects and urban designers were Nation Fender Katsalidis; Synman Justin Bialek, and Tract.
28   The urban vision was also transformed with the density more than doubled to 1932 units and total investment projected at $650 million.
29   Docklands Authority, Media Release, December 1997; only $14 million had been paid by 2000. See: Millar, R. 'Docklands: The Hidden Costs', *The Sunday Age*, 28 October 2001, p.15.
30   The consortium comprised YarraCity, Riverside Properties, Berhad, Goldengate Properties, MAB and Thiess Contractors. Architects and urban designers were Cox Sanderson Ness.
31   This consortium was identical to that for Batman's Hill.
32   The consortium comprised Brierley Investments, Walker Corporation; GBM group. Architects and urban designers were Spoerry and ER Ashton Architects.
33   Ferguson, J. 'Battle at the Docks', *Herald Sun*, 16 October 1999, p.10.
34   The Lend Lease proposal was for 2100 apartments, 160 000 square metres of commercial space, plus retail and community facilities. Given the secrecy surrounding such decisions, the current and former connections of several key decision-makers with Lend Lease were cause for concern. Authority CEO John Tabart was formerly

employed by Lend Lease for fifteen years. Peter Droege at that time held the Lend Lease Chair of Urban Design at the University of Sydney and Ross Bonythorn was formerly employed by the Lend Lease Design Group; both were members of the Planning, Amenity and Design Panel of the Authority.

35 <victoriaharbour.com> accessed September 2003.

36 Lend Lease, sales brochure, October 2002.

Chapter 9: Grollo Tower

1   The investigations were on allegations of unpaid tax on $59 million linked to the earlier construction of the Rialto building. See: 'Police Raid Grollos – Documents and Computer Seized', *The Age*, 14 August 1993, p.1.

2   McManus, G. 'Bruno's Reaching for the Sky', *Herald Sun*, 9 October 1994, p.7.

3   Farrant, D. 'Plans for Tower Aspire to Heavenly Touch', *The Age*, 2 January 1995, p.5.

4   Heinrichs, P. '2001 – An Office Space Odyssey', *The Age*, 27 April 1995, p.1.

5   'Give a Name to Bruno's Vision', *Herald Sun*, 1 April 1995, p.4 (no author).

6   Quoted in: 'Faulty Towers', Editorial, *The Age*, 4 May 1995, p.17.

7   Gettler, L. 'Architects Bring Tower Plan Back to Earth', *The Age*, 4 May 1995, p.5. Architecture critics who publicly opposed the tower included Neil Clerehan, Dimity Reed, Leon van Schaik, Haig Beck, Ian MacDougall, Norman Day and myself.

8   Beck, H. 'Giantism is Old Hat', *Herald Sun*, 4 May 1995, p.13.

9   See: 'Grollo Brushes Aside Poor Polls', *Herald Sun*, 10 May 1995, p.35; Gettler, L. 'Poll Finds Few Friends for Grollo Mega-Tower', *The Age*, 8 May 1995, p.1.

10 See: King, A. 'Worlds in the City', *Planning Perspectives*, 11, 1996, pp.97–114.

11 Seidler had a history of disputes with urban planners, most notably with Rob Adams from the City of Melbourne who sat on the Design, Amenity and Planning Panel of the Authority.

12 Quoted in: Rollo, J. 'Etiquette and the Giant Obelisk', *The Age*, 12 December 1998, p.5.

13 See: Dovey, K. *Framing Places*, Routledge, London, Ch. 8.

14 McKay, S. 'Third Runway Needed Sooner', *The Age*, 8 December 1998, p.2; Hansen, K. 'Air Traffic Hurdle', *The Age*, 12 November 1998, p.16.

15 Quoted in: 'Is Bigger Better? What the Architects Think', *The Age*, 20 January 1998, p.7. Beck's support was used by Grollo to support the bid and published on the Grollo web site. See: Grollo, B. 'My Tower is Just What Melbourne Needs', *The Age*, 26 November 1998, p.9.

16 *Herald Sun*, Editorial, 4 May 1995, p.12.

17 Grollo, B. 'My Week – Bruno Grollo', *The Age*, 12 December 1998, p.8.

18 See: Beck, H. 'Will the Grollo Tower Enhance our City? Yes' *The Age*,

9 December 1998, p.15; Lewis, M. 'A Lost Opportunity or a Narrow Escape', *The Age*, 18 April 1999, p.22.

19 Lefebvre, H. *The Production of Space*, Oxford: Blackwell, p.287.

20 The Grollo identity remained fragile during this period; the brothers were acquitted in mid-1997 on the criminal conspiracy charges, but were still defending tax fraud charges in 1998. Bruno Grollo's wife had a disabling stroke during his conspiracy trial; he partially retired and handed control of the project to his son Daniel. See: Cant, S. 'Grollos Hid profit, Court Told', *The Age*, 2 June 1998, p.2.

21 Robinson, P. 'New Grollo Vision', *The Age*, 11 October 1998, p.3.

22 This was separately confirmed by two members of that Committee.

23 There was an offer to pay $20 million with the rest to follow during construction, but the government and Docklands Authority would not agree.

24 Munro, I. 'Grollo's Tower Bites the Dust', *The Age*, 14 April 1999, p.1.

25 Robinson, P. 'Grollo Tower to go Ahead in Dubai', *The Age*, 27 February 2003, p.7.

Chapter 10: Hype and hope

1 Parking at New Quay costs $12 and reduces to $7 if one exceeds a threshold of expenditure.

2 Millar, R. 'Docklands: The Hidden Costs', *The Sunday Age*, 28 October 2001, p.15. These costs include operating costs ($136 million), infrastructure ($246 million), decontamination ($52 million) and Commonwealth grants ($22 million).

3 Millar, 'The Hidden Costs'.

4 Shield, H. 'Docklands Could Cause City Property Glut, Access Warns', *The Age*, 9 July 1998; Catalano, A. 'Study Clears Docks', *The Age*, 22 July 1998, p.9.

5 Quoted in: Munro, I. 'Why Isn't This Man Smiling?' *The Age*, 26 February 2000, p.7.

6 Developer, quoted in: Millar, 'The Hidden Costs'.

7 Developer, quoted in: Munro, 'Why Isn't This Man Smiling?'.

Chapter 11: Constructing desires

1 This chapter is an edited and rewritten version of the final chapter from: Wood, S., Desiring Docklands, unpublished PhD dissertation, Faculty of Architecture, Building and Planning, University of Melbourne, 2003.

2 Committee for Melbourne, *Melbourne Docklands: A Discussion Paper*, 1990, pp. 4 and 12.

3 Friedmann, J. *Planning in the Public Domain*, Princeton University Press, Princeton, 1987.

4 Colebrook, C. *Understanding Deleuze*, Allen & Unwin, Sydney, 2002; Colebrook, C. *Gilles Deleuze*, Routledge, London, 2002.

5 Massumi, B. *A User's Guide to Capitalism and Schizophrenia*, MIT Press, Cambridge, Mass. 1992, p.201.

6 Deleuze, G. and Guattari, F. *Anti-Oedipus*, University of Minnesota Press, Minneapolis, 1983, p.28.

7   Goodchild, P. *Deleuze and Guattari*, Sage, London, 1996, p.99.
8   Habermas, J. *The Structural Transformation of the Public Sphere*, MIT Press, Cambridge, Ma., 1989.
9   Flyvberg argues persuasively that while Habermasian theories of power may constitute an ideal, Foucaultian notions of power as micropractices offer a better explanation of how urban planning is practiced. See: Flyvberg, B. 'Empowering Civil Society' in Douglas, M. and Friedmann J. (eds) *Cities for Citizens*, Wiley, Chichester, 1998, pp.185–211.
10   Foucault, M. *Power/Knowledge*, Pantheon, New York, 1980.
11   Hardt, M. 'The Withering of Civil Society', in: Kaufman, E. and Heller, K. (eds) *Deleuze & Guattari*, University of Minnesota Press, Minneapolis, 1998, p.32.
12   Massumi, B. 'Requiem for Our Prospective Dead (Toward a Participatory Critique of Capitalist Power)', in: Kaufman and Heller, *Deleuze & Guattari*. pp. 54–5.
13   Massumi, 'Requiem...', pp.58–9.
14   Colebrook, *Understanding Deleuze*, p.129.
15   Approaches that focus on the 'forces' embodied in a discourse draw on the lessons of speech-act theory, and are most readily associated with Peircean and/or Hjelmslevian semiotic frameworks.
16   Deleuze, G. *Foucault*, University of Minnesota Press, Minneapolis, 1988, p.71.
17   Colebrook, *Gilles Deleuze*, p.46.
18   Hardt, M. and Negri, A. *Empire*, Harvard University Press, Cambridge, Mass. 2000.
19   Massumi, 'Requiem...', p.59.
20   Colebrook, *Gilles Deleuze*, p.132.

Chapter 12: Creating and defending urban character

1   Victorian Government, Major Projects Unit, Sandridge Site Development Brief, 1985.
2   Sandridge City Development Corporation, led by local architect Robert Peck.
3   Sandridge City Development Corp, *Environmental Effects Statement*, 1987.
4   *Landscape Australia*, 4, 1987.
5   Shaw, K. (ed.) *Bayside Views: A Collection of Critical Views on the Bayside Development*, Melbourne, 1988.
6   Shaw, *Bayside Views*.
7   Bartley, M. and Davies, V. 'The Bayside Legislation', in: Shaw, *Bayside Views*, pp.63–72.
8   Sandridge City advertisement, *The Age*, 20 November 1990, p.8.
9   Sandridge City, proposed by-laws, 1990.
10   Haywood, R. and McGlynn, S. (eds) *Making Better Places*, Butterworth, Oxford, 1993.
11   The developers were Mirvac.
12   City of Port Phillip, 'Beacon Cove Population Bulge', Media Release, 25 February 2002.

13 Schwartz, L. 'Division Street', *The Age*, 1 April 2001, p.6.
14 Schwartz, 'Division Street'.
15 Gause, J. (ed.) *Great Planned Communities*, Urban Land Institute, Washington D.C., 2002, pp.32–40.
16 Williams and Boag, Architects, Urban Design Report on the Lonsdale Site, 1994.
17 Hudson Conway, headed by Ron Walker.
18 This analysis was first undertaken when I appeared as an expert witness appearing before the Panel.
19 Advisory Panel, HMAS Lonsdale Site, Report to the Minister for Planning and Local Government, November 1996.
20 Victorian Auditor-General, 'Land Use and Development in Victoria: The State's Planning System', Victorian Government publication, 2000, Para 4.97.
21 See: Innes, P. 'St Kilda Wins Rehearing of Hotel Case', *The Age*, 4 November 1989, p17; Svendsen, I. 'Residents Continue Battle Over Hotel Changes', *The Age*, 3 July 1989, p.5.
22 Quoted in: Jackson, D. 'Urbanity', *Architecture Australia*, November/December, 1998, pp.20–1.
23 See: Shaw, K. 'Planning for the Espy', *Planning News*, 29 (10), 2003, pp.28–9.
24 Newman's submission to the planning application, City of Port Philip, 2000.
25 Millar, R. and Coslovich, G.*The Age*, 1 November 2003, pp.1 and 8.
26 Quoted in: Millar and Coslovich.
27 This line comes from City of Port Philip's astute Urban Design Manager, Jim Holdsworth.
28 Government of Victoria, Department of Infrastructure, *Gateway to the Bay*, Victorian Government publication, 1999.

Chapter 13: Loose ends
1   Calvino, I. *Invisible Cities*, Picador, London, 1979, p.30.
2   Munro, I. 'Nouveau Nonda: The Man Who Gave Us the High Life', *The Sunday Age*, 22 April 2002, p.16.
3   Munro, 'Nouveau Nonda'.
4   Paterson, J. 'Choice and Necessity in Metropolitan Planning', *Urban Policy and Research*, 18 (3), 2000, pp.377–86.
5   Mees, P. 'Paterson's Curse', *Urban Policy and Research*, 21 (3), 2003, pp.287–99.
6   Habermas, J. *Theory of Communicative Action*, Beacon, Boston, 1984; Calhoun, C. *Habermas and the Public Sphere*, MIT Press, Cambridge, Ma., 1992; Forester, J. (ed.) *Critical Theory and Public Life*, MIT Press, Cambridge, Mass. 1985.

SELECTED BIBLIOGRAPHY

Alexander, C. (1996) 'The City is not a Tree', in LeGates, R. and Stout, F. (eds) *The City Reader*, Routledge, London (originally published 1965).

Appadurai, A. (1996) *Modernity at Large*, University of Minnesota Press, Minneapolis.

Barthes, R. (1973) *Mythologies*, Paladin, Hertfordshire.

——(1988) *The Semiotic Challenge*, Blackwell, Oxford.

Bauman, Z. (2000) *Liquid Modernity*, Cambridge University Press, Cambridge.

Bentley, I. et al. (1985) *Responsive Environments*, Architectural Press, London.

Berman, M. (1983) *All that is Solid Melts into Air*, Verso, London.

Bourdieu, P. (1977) *Outline of a Theory of Practice*, London: Cambridge.

—— (1984) *Distinction*, Routledge, London.

—— (1990) *In Other Words*, Polity, Cambridge.

—— (1993) *The Field of Cultural Production*, Columbia University Press, New York.

—— (2000) *Pascalian Meditations*, Columbia University Press, New York.

Breen, A. and Rigby, D. (eds)(1994) *Waterfronts,* McGraw Hill, New York.

Brownill, S. (1990) *Developing London's Docklands*, Paul Chapman, London.

Calhoun, C. (1992) *Habermas and the Public Sphere*, MIT Press, Cambridge, Mass.

Calvino, I. (1979) *Invisible Cities*, Picador, London.

Castells, M. (1997) *The Power of Identity*, Blackwell, Oxford.

Colebrook, C. (2002) *Understanding Deleuze*, Allen & Unwin, Sydney.

Dear, M. (2000) *The Postmodern Urban Condition*, Blackwell, Oxford.

de Certeau, M. (1984) *The Practice of Everyday Life*, University of California Press, Berkeley.

Deleuze, G. (1993) *The Fold*, Trans. T. Conley, University of Minnesota Press, Minneapolis.

—— (1994) *What is Philosophy?* Columbia University Press, New York.

—— and Guattari, F. (1987) *A Thousand Plateaus: Capitalism and Schizophrenia*, Athlone, London.

Deutsche, R. (1996) *Evictions: Art and Spatial Politics*, MIT Press, Cambridge, Mass.

Doel, M. (1996) 'A Hundred Thousand Lines of Flight', *Environment and Planning D: Society & Space* 14, pp.421–39.

Dovey, K. (1999) *Framing Places: Mediating Power in Built Form*, Routledge, London.

Edwards, B. (1992) *London Docklands*, Butterworth, Oxford.

Fainstein, S. (1994) *The City Builders*, Blackwell, Oxford.

Fairclough, N. (1995) *Critical Discourse Analysis*, Longmans, London.

Featherstone, M. (1991) *Consumer Culture and Postmodernism*, Sage, London.

Forester, J. (ed.) *Critical Theory and Public Life*, MIT Press, Cambridge, Mass.

Gold, J. and Ward, S. (eds) *Place Promotion*, Wiley, Chichester.

Goodchild, P. (1996) *Deleuze and Guattari: An Introduction to the Politics of Desire*, Sage, London.

Habermas, J. (1984) *Theory of Communicative Action*, Beacon, Boston.

—— (1989) *The Structural Transformation of the Public Sphere*, MIT Press, Cambridge, Mass.

Hall, T. and Hubbard, P. (eds) (1998) *The Entrepreneurial City*, Wiley, Chichester.

Hannigan, J. (1998) *Fantasy City*, Routledge, London.

Hardt, M. and Negri, A. (2000) *Empire*, Harvard University Press, Cambridge, Mass.

Harvey, D. (1989) *The Condition of Postmodernity*, Blackwell, Oxford.

—— (2000) *Spaces of Hope*, Edinburgh University Press, Edinburgh.

Hillier, B. (1996) *Space is the Machine*, Cambridge University Press, Cambridge.

Hoyle, B., Pinder, D. and Husain, M. (eds) (1988) *Revitalizing the Waterfront*, Bellhaven, London.

Jacobs, J. (1965) *The Death and Life of Great American Cities*, Penguin, Harmondsworth.

Kearns, G. and Philo, C. (eds) (1993) *Selling Places*, Pergamon, Oxford.

Lefebvre, H. (1991) *The Production of Space*, Blackwell, Oxford.

—— (1996) *Writings on Cities*, Blackwell, Oxford.

Lynch, K. (1960) *The Image of the City*, MIT Press, Cambridge, Mass.

Malone, P. (ed.) (1996) *City, Capital and Water*, Routledge, London.

Marshall, R. (ed.) (2001) *Waterfronts in Post-Industrial Cities*, Spon, London.

Massumi, B. (1992) *A User's Guide to Capitalism and Schizophrenia*, MIT Press, Cambridge, Mass.

Relph, E. (1977) *Place and Placelessness*, Pion, London.

Sandercock, L. (1998) *Towards Cosmopolis*, Wiley, Chichester.

Sennett, R. (1996) *Flesh and Stone*, Faber & Faber, London.

Sorkin, M (ed.) (1992) *Variations on a Themepark*, Hill & Wang, New York.

INDEX